Seven Miracles
That Saved America

Seven Miracles
That Saved America

WHY THEY MATTER AND WHY WE SHOULD HAVE HOPE

Chris Stewart
and
Ted Stewart

SHADOW
MOUNTAIN

In memory of Jim Snarr,
one of the world's greatest teachers.
—C. S.

To Lora and our posterity.
—T. S.

First printing in hardbound 2009
First printing in paperbound 2014

Visit us at ShadowMountain.com

Library of Congress Cataloging-in-Publication Data

Stewart, Chris, 1960–
    Seven miracles that saved America / Chris Stewart and Ted Stewart.
        p. cm.
    Includes bibliographical references and index.
    ISBN 978-1-60641-144-5 (hardbound : alk. paper)
    ISBN 978-1-60907-926-0 (paperbound)
    1. United States—History—Religious aspects—Christianity.
    2. America—Discovery and exploration.   3. Miracles.   I. Stewart, Ted.   II. Title.
    E179.S845 2009
    973—dc22   2009027679

Printed in the United States of America
Lake Book Manufacturing, Inc., Melrose Park, IL

10   9   8   7   6   5   4   3   2   1

Contents

Introduction

Casablanca, Morocco
January 2007

THE AMERICAN FELT ISOLATED and alone. He knew he had too much money in his pockets, and the American passport he carried wouldn't help him here. The neighborhood around him was as filthy, desperately poor, and anti-American as any in the world. Al-Qaeda was strong and growing in Northern Africa, with fourteen of the eighteen terrorists responsible for the latest bombings in Spain having come from the neighborhood in which he stood.

He hunched on the worn cement stairs below one of the rock turrets that guarded the ancient walls around the old town, his head low, his eyes taking in the unfamiliar surroundings. The walled section of the city had changed very little over the past seven hundred years. Everything was old: the great wall, the stone streets, the buildings, the wooden guard shacks that used to house the Arab armies. The rock paths that ran through the old quarter were smooth as glass, and the sky, silver from the reflected ocean less than two kilometers away, could barely be seen above the unbroken line of two- and three-story buildings. A thousand strands of patchwork telephone and electrical wires were stretched across the street.

The crowd pushed noisily around him. Most of the men avoided walking too close, and all of the women, many of their faces covered, refused to even make eye contact with him. The streets were an overkill of color, movement, and smells, some of them wonderful, some of them foul, the air hot and humid with human perspiration and salty air. All of the rock-and-mortar buildings towering above the alley were open to the street. The spice shops smelled of mint and olives from Meknes, oranges and lemons from Fez. An old man beside a wooden cart sold peppered soup and dates.

A beggar approached him, gesturing to take his picture for a few centimes. The American indicated that he didn't have a camera—he wasn't a tourist—but the beggar still moved closer, his smell tart. The American produced a couple of twenty-centime coins. The beggar bowed and thanked him, smiling through missing teeth. The American checked his watch, then stood and started walking.

Half a dozen buildings down, he stopped. Something had caught his eye. He stood before an open storefront, its metal bars folded back against the cement walls. The shop owner stooped against the back wall, protecting a metal money box. Behind him, an old and tattered poster, written in English, had been tacked to the ancient framing. The American pulled off his dark glasses and leaned toward it. The words were instantly familiar.

Four score and seven years ago our fathers brought forth on this continent a new nation, conceived in Liberty, and dedicated to the proposition that all men are created equal.

Abraham Lincoln. The Gettysburg Address.

The shop owner, an old man with a wispy beard and careful eyes, stared at the American. The two men studied each other for a long moment, then broke into understanding smiles.

2

American Exceptionalism

Millions of people in our country honestly believe there is something special, something *exceptional,* about the United States. And the idea of American exceptionalism is not confined to within our borders. Millions of people scattered across the world believe the same thing, *wish* the same thing, *want* the same thing to be true.

They look to us for an example.

They look to us for hope.

Belief in a nation's exceptionalism seems to be almost entirely an American trait. For example, as documented in a recent survey, nearly three-quarters of U.S. citizens say they are proud to be Americans. Fewer than a third of the people in France, Italy, Germany, or Japan feel the same about their country.[1] Two-thirds of Americans believe they can achieve success within their nation by individual effort, while only a third of Europeans put their faith in such a concept.[2] There isn't a more optimistic or confident group of citizens than can be found within the United States, this at a time when many parts of the world are awash in hopelessness and despair. As just one example, substantial majorities in most North African and Middle Eastern countries express dissatisfaction in their nation's ability to produce the meaningful employment opportunities that are necessary to better their lives.[3]

And while it is true that, on some level, many people from other nations are proud of their countries—and we believe people *should* feel a sense of pride and duty to the lands in which they were born—as the above statistics show, there is something tangibly extraordinary about the country in which we live.

Many people hate us for this difference. Some rail against the influence we have had upon the world. Some are jealous. Too many of our own countrymen reject the idea that we are different, seeing us as no better, and maybe worse, than India or England or Malaysia or anywhere else.

But we *are* demonstrably different.

And that's been apparent from the very start.

The idea of American exceptionalism is nothing new. The concept was first explored in detail by the French political writer and statesman Alexis de Tocqueville,[4] but the idea dates back much earlier and may have been first expressed in 1630 by the governor of the Massachusetts Bay Company, John Winthrop, when he described his colony as the "city on the hill."[5] President Ronald Reagan reintroduced the phrase and enlivened it just a little by adding, "*shining* city on the hill."[6]

Though difficult to define precisely, the idea of American exceptionalism encompasses at least these general principles:

- Americans' long-held belief that all of God's children are created equal. Because of this, Americans accept and adhere to the principle that all are equal *before* the law and all should have equal access to the *protection* of the law. Holding to this principle has led generation after generation of Americans to walk the long and difficult path that leads to a destination where equality is a reality and not just a goal.

- America's Constitution—the fact that the "highest law of the land" emphasizes individual rights and decentralization of power, thus assuring protection for liberty and freedom. Further, the nature of the United State's Constitution and wholesale acceptance by our citizenry that it is "supreme" results in a stability that is a distinct and significant advantage over other forms of government.

- The American belief that personal liberty and freedom is the highest priority—a higher priority even than a risk- or want-free life. From our very inception, "give me a chance and I can do it!" has been a much more common sentiment than a "someone's got to help me" attitude.

- A belief in a meritocracy—that we should be judged by what we accomplish and what we can do, not by our family lineage. Indeed, from the very beginning, Americans have specifically (and quite happily) rejected any form of royalty or aristocracy.

- Adherence to private morality—a belief that there can be no public virtue without private morality, and that public virtue is essential to the success of our government and the preservation of individual liberty and freedom.

• Cultural makeup—Americans are inherently more patriotic, religious, independent, and inventive. As an outgrowth of these traits, we are uniquely committed to competition and entrepreneurship, an attitude that allows our decentralized and market-driven economy to provide opportunity for extraordinary individual success.[7]

• Social integration—a commitment to the social integration of individuals from various racial, religious, and ethnic groups, making it possible for them to find themselves part of the American landscape.

• Geographical—recognition that our geography, climate, and abundant natural resources provide us an enormous opportunity for material well-being.

By these measuring sticks, it is difficult not to acknowledge that the United States is exceptional as compared with other nations. Indeed, it seems clear that the United States stands alone, being much more different from other nations than they are from each other.

But there is another criterion of American exceptionalism that has come to be accepted in the common definition: a *supernaturalist* explanation, or the idea that *God intended* for our nation to be a beacon on the hill.

Is it possible that God considers the United States an exceptional place? A country with a mission? A special nation with a specific purpose in His plan? Is it possible that He has blessed us and so expects more of us than of other nations?

Is it possible that God has ordained, created, sustained, and defended the United States? At critical points in our history, when the odds were stacked against us—and there have been many times when the great experiment we call America could have and should have failed—did God intervene to save us?

Did He intend then, and does He still intend, for us to survive as an example of democracy and freedom (as well as other virtues) to the rest of the world?

What Does History Say?

The evidence of God's interest in America is overwhelming.

In the following chapters, we hope to show that the United States of America is a divinely appointed nation with a special place and purpose in this world. At critical junctions in our history, God *has* provided miracles to assure this nation's survival in a world where despotism and tyranny are the rule. Specifically, we're going to explore these seven events in history:

1. Christopher Columbus's discovery of the New World and the undeniable hand of God that led him here.
2. The miracle at Jamestown and the English colonists' survival of the "starving time," which assured that America would be settled by a religiously oriented and religiously tolerant people.
3. The Battle of New York during the Revolutionary War, in which an unexplainable fog shrouded the East River on an August morning, allowing General George Washington and his army to escape annihilation at the hands of the British troops.
4. The miraculous creation of the United States Constitution, forever setting the United States up as the "shining city on the hill."
5. The miracle of Abraham Lincoln and Gettysburg, in which God answered the president's desperate prayer—an event that literally changed the future of the world.
6. The incredibly unlikely scenario that played out in the Battle of Midway during World War II, paving the way for the Allies to win the war.
7. The miracle that saved the life of President Ronald Reagan, allowing him to go on to play a major role in defeating communism, smashing the Iron Curtain, and "tear[ing] down this wall."

Parts of these stories will be told in a historically accurate context portrayed fictionally through the eyes of certain participants. Parts of the stories will be told through pure historical narrative. Taken together, these stories will clearly demonstrate that miraculous events *have* taken place at critical junctions in our nation's history. And though such an idea may be denied, ignored, and ridiculed, that doesn't make it untrue.

That leads us to a second important question:

Even if it's true, does it really matter anymore?

What Have We Forgotten?

There was a time in this country when it was accepted that America was a blessed land—that its rise, protection, and preeminence were the result of God's active will. It was simply understood to be a fact.

Such understanding came very early in our history. Thomas Jefferson, Benjamin Franklin, George Washington, and other Founders shared the tenets of what some have called our "public religion": a belief that there is a God who created all human beings to be equal and endowed with the rights of life, liberty, and the pursuit of happiness, and that God holds not only individuals but nations accountable for their conduct. Most relevant, the Founders, and many great men and women since, unquestionably believed that this God cares deeply about what happens in this world as a whole and, in particular, what happens to America, because America is a special product of this God.[8]

It was commonly accepted that Providence ruled the fate of this nation—and that certain of our leaders were placed here by God to lead us through times of crisis. For example, Benjamin Franklin, in the summer of 1787, had something to say about American exceptionalism during the convention called to create our Constitution. While the delegates were struggling to the point that it seemed exceedingly unlikely they would ever reach an accord, Franklin made the following suggestion: "In the beginning of the contest with G. Britain, when we were sensible of danger, we had daily prayer in this room for Divine protection—Our prayers, Sir, were heard, & they were graciously answered . . . I have lived, sir, a long time; and the longer I live, the more convincing proofs I see of this truth, that God governs the affairs of men!"[9]

And in 1865, Ralph Waldo Emerson paid this tribute to the recently assassinated Abraham Lincoln: "There is a serene Providence which rules the fate of nations. . . . It makes its own instruments, creates the man for the time, trains him in poverty, inspires his genius, and arms him for the task."[10]

A Hotly Disputed Perspective

Today, such views are shunned by many. Indeed, millions of Americans reject the contention of American exceptionalism with intense fervor. The things they say, the things they write, the demonstrations they organize, the petitions they sponsor, the ideas they promote, and the institutions they seek to weaken, make it evident that this is true.

It should be noted that dim views of America are nothing new. Indeed, men have risen in opposition to America since its inception. In the mid-eighteenth century a group of European intellectuals laid the seeds for anti-Americanism when they developed the *degeneracy theory,* the idea that natural and atmospheric elements in the Americas physically weakened men and animals. American-born people were considered physically weak and mentally inferior. In 1768 the Dutch philosopher Cornelius de Pauw described America as "degenerate or monstrous."[11]

French intellectual and writer Abbe Raynal said in 1770, "America has not yet produced a good poet, an able mathematician, one man of genius in a single art or a single science."[12] (Raynal conveniently forgot one of his contemporaries, an American named Benjamin Franklin, who was one of the most accomplished scientists and inventors in history. In fact, Franklin's fame was such that he was considered a hero throughout all of Europe, including in Raynal's own France, as well as in the United States.)

Contemporary arguments against American exceptionalism can be found in the writings of historian Howard Zinn. Huge numbers of his book *A People's History of the United States* have been sold over the last several decades. In fact, his book has been required reading in many high schools and colleges throughout the nation and has become deeply ingrained into our culture. The major theme of Mr. Zinn's work is that America's only exceptional quality is her greed. Columbus, the Founders, the Civil War, even World War II were, according to Zinn, driven by nothing more than selfish financial interests and a rapacious lust for profit.

For example, of our Founding Fathers, Zinn has written: "The Founding Fathers did lead the war for independence from Britain. But they did not do it for the equal right of all to life, liberty and equality. Their intention was to set up a new government that would protect the property of slave owners, land speculators, merchants, and bondholders."[13]

These men, who Zinn so contemptuously asserts were consumed by selfishness and greed, are the same ones who risked their lives, their fortunes, and their sacred honor by throwing down a gauntlet before the most powerful nation on earth in the form of the Declaration of Independence. This remarkable document states that "all men . . . are endowed by their Creator with certain unalienable Rights"—one of four direct references to God within that document. The Declaration became the equivalent of a modern-day "mission statement" for America, and its principles and ideals are among the most cogent and beautiful ever penned by a human being, allowing generations from around the world to raise it as an example they seek to follow. To dismiss it as nothing more than a grab for profit and power, as well as to dismiss the sacrifices of those who acted to make it the inspiration for a new nation, seems not bold but simply ignorant.

Among the many noblemen who, according to Zinn, set up a government to enhance their own status and wealth was George Washington. This man, an "unquestioned superior" among the men of his age, sacrificed much in service to his country, freed his slaves upon his death, and rejected the opportunity to become the "king" of America following the war for independence. Was he motivated by power? A lust for profit?

History tells us this isn't true.

Upon concluding his recitation of the presidential oath the first time, Washington improvised by adding the words "So help me God," then kissed the Bible on which he had just placed his hand.[14] In the inaugural address that followed, he proclaimed:

> It would be peculiarly improper to omit in this first official act my fervent supplications to that Almighty Being who rules over the universe, who presides in the councils of nations. . . .
>
> No people can be bound to acknowledge and adore the Invisible Hand which conducts the affairs of men more than the people of the United States. Every step by which they have advanced to the character of independent nation seems to have been distinguished by some token of providential agency.[15]

Simply stated, George Washington was one of the Founders who believed that he was fulfilling God's plan. (It might be noted as an interesting aside that in referring to God in his first inaugural address, he initiated a tradition that has been kept by every president in every inauguration since.)

Yet Mr. Zinn, who is considered by so many to be an authority on America, still considers the idea of American exceptionalism a myth, declaring, "The true heroes of our history are those Americans who refused to accept that we have a special claim to morality."[16]

Zinn thus firmly rejects the beliefs of Thomas Jefferson, the Founder who is most often held up by modern secularists as a man who did not believe. Yet Jefferson's own words make it clear that he believed that Americans are a chosen people. In his second inaugural address he said: "I . . . shall need, too, the favor of the Being in whose hands we are . . . and to whose goodness I ask you to join with me in supplications, that he will so enlighten the minds of your servants, guide their councils, and prosper their measures."[17]

Inscribed on the walls of the Jefferson Memorial in Washington, D.C., are his words: "And can the liberties of a nation be thought secure when we have removed their only firm basis, a conviction in the minds of the people that these liberties are a gift from God."[18]

When considering whether we are an exceptional and divinely appointed nation, whom do we choose to believe, Howard Zinn or George Washington and Thomas Jefferson?

Noam Chomsky is a world-famous linguist at the Massachusetts Institute of Technology. He is also an author, lecturer, and political activist extraordinaire who has been called one of the twentieth century's most important figures. And he certainly hates America. As an example, he has said, "I have often thought that if a rational Fascist dictatorship were to exist, then it would choose the American system."[19]

It is acknowledged by most historians and constitutional scholars that James Madison is the man who can take the most credit for proposing the broad themes of the Constitution and working to assure that the Constitutional Convention was a success. Chomsky would find laughable Madison's belief that the Constitution of the United States is a remarkable document. However, Madison clearly gave credit to a divine source: "It is impossible for the man of pious reflection not to perceive in it a finger of that Almighty hand which has been so frequently and signally extended to our relief in the critical stages of the revolution."[20]

Chomsky's view of the founding of America mirrors that of his friend Zinn, "The country was founded on the principle that the primary role of government is to protect property from the majority, and so it remains."[21]

Both Zinn and Chomsky would also mock the deeply held beliefs of another American president:

On the evening of June 6, 1944, President Franklin D. Roosevelt addressed the people of the United States, announcing the invasion of mainland Europe. He knew how critical this moment in the history of the world really was. Had the invasion force on D-Day been repulsed, it would have given Germany the time necessary to perfect a number of its advanced weapons, fighters, bombers, and perhaps even an atom bomb. Given a little more time, the outcome of the war might have been very different. Failure on D-Day would have, at the least, led to tens of thousands more deaths in the Nazi concentration camps.

In announcing the D-Day invasion, Roosevelt composed a prayer that was published in newspapers all over the country, along with his appeal that it be recited by the citizens of the United States as he read it over the airwaves.

In that prayer, Roosevelt implored:

> Almighty God: our sons, pride of our nation, this day have set upon a mighty endeavor, a struggle to preserve our Republic, our religion and our civilization, and to set free a suffering humanity. . . . They will need Thy blessings . . . and we know that by Thy grace, and by the righteousness of our cause, our sons will triumph. . . . With Thy blessing, we shall prevail over the unholy forces of our enemy. . . . Thy will be done, Almighty God.[22]

Roosevelt knew that the people of the United States believed in the public religion. As *Newsweek* reported, "America turned to prayer."[23] Throughout America, churches and synagogues were filled with worshippers. People knelt in the streets, on their porches, and in their private places.

Despite such history, Zinn and Chomsky have enormous followings and have become wealthy espousing their anti-American views. And they are just two of many historians and political activists who have found fame and fortune appealing to Americans (as well as to millions of people outside of America) who despise this nation.

But there is no doubt that the greatest leaders in our history believed God would move His hand to protect this country.

But do we, as a people, believe this anymore?

Today, our popular culture is ripe with anti-Americanism. Our celebrity icons, many of whom have little education or practical experience, have declared their disdain for this country. Actor Viggo Mortensen put his feelings most simply when he stated, "We [the

United States] are not the good guys."[24] Comedian Janeane Garofalo scoffed, "The dumb and the mean love patriotism."[25] Michael Moore, a perennial favorite among the anti-American crowd, has declared Americans as being "possibly the dumbest people on the planet" as well as "culpable in committing so many acts of terror and bloodshed that we'd better get a clue about the culture of violence in which we have been active participants."[26] Such feelings were perhaps best summed up by the renowned thinker Sigmund Freud when he simply declared, "America is a great mistake."[27]

The brilliance and emotionalism of American's detractors aside, we still believe this fact is demonstrably true: *The United States of America is a blessed and promised land!*

In today's suffocating politically correct environment, many are shocked by such a nationalistic and simple-minded sentiment. But their unwillingness to believe the evidence doesn't make it untrue.

Why It Matters

Facing the challenges we do today, it's understandable that many of us feel some discouragement. The trials we face as a people and a nation, the discord that has grown up between us, the never-ending news of discouragement, the financial crises, the pain of war and the threats of war to come, the erosion of our institutions, the slow poison of ridicule and cynicism, the erosion of the faith in one another that has bound us in the past, all of these things make the future seem somewhat less than bright.

But are the challenges we face now *really* greater than any we've ever faced before?

Is our country facing a more dire circumstance than in the middle of the Civil War? Than Jamestown, when almost ninety percent of the occupants died from starvation or disease? Than during the summer of 1776, when Washington faced certain destruction at the hands of the British army? Than during the early days of World War II, when defeat at the hands of fascism seemed almost inevitable?

Do the challenges we face now measure up to the challenges our fathers were called on to endure and overcome?

And if God provided miracles to ensure our survival in the past, would He choose to desert us now?

Has the character of our nation so changed that we are no longer worthy of His hand?

Does America matter any longer?

Or has our time passed?

This much we hope to demonstrate in this book: At critical times in our nation's history, God provided miracles to save us. And there are miracles yet to come. Why? Because America *still* represents something important to Him. Because there is still much good around us. Because there are still enough patriotic citizens seeking for the good of, praying for the blessings of, and sacrificing for the benefit of this nation, as to ensure our continued existence as the "shining city on the hill."

This is God's chosen nation, His magnificent cause.

And because this is true, we still have reason to hope.

Notes

1. Schuck and Wilson, *Understanding America: The Anatomy of an Exceptional Nation.* We relied on this source for many of our points about America as an exceptional nation.
2. Ibid.
3. Ibid. See also "The Muslim West Facts Project," June 2008, www.muslimwest-facts.com/mwf/108028/Young-Arabs-Poised-Maximize-Their-Potential.aspx
4. See de Tocqueville, *Democracy in America.*
5. The phrase was used by Winthrop in his discourse "A Model of Christian Charity," written while on his way to Massachusetts in 1630. See Bartleby.com, "Respectfully Quoted," June 30, 2009, http://www.bartleby.com/73/1611.html. A more complete copy of the discourse can be found at http://www.mtholyoke.edu/acad/intrel/winthrop.htm.
6. Ronald Reagan used the phrase often throughout his political career. He explained what he intended by its use in his "Farewell Address to the Nation" on January 11, 1989, to be found at http://www.ronaldreagan.com/sp_21.html.
7. This is explored in detail in Schuck and Wilson, *Understanding America.* See also Gordon, *An Empire of Wealth,* xiv, where the author points out that although the

United States makes up only 6 percent of the world's land mass, we produce 30 percent of the world's gross domestic product; further that by every economic measure as well as number of books published, number of Nobel Prizes won, and so on, we lead the world.

8. An excellent discussion of this "public religion" can be found in Meacham, *American Gospel.* See also Gelernter, *Americanism—The Fourth Great Western Religion.*

9. Meacham, *American Gospel,* 89.

10. Speech delivered by Ralph Waldo Emerson, April 19, 1865, four days after Lincoln's assassination, at the Unitarian Church, Concord, Massachusetts, to be found at http://xroads.virginia.edu/~cap/LINCOLN/emerson1.html.

11. Larraín, *Identity and Modernity,* 56.

12. Raynal, "Histoire philosophique et politique."

13. Zinn, "Greatest Generation."

14. Meacham, *American Gospel,* 14.

15. See George Washington's "First Inaugural Address in the City of New York," delivered April 30, 1789, to be found at http://www.bartleby.com/124/pres13.html.

16. Zinn, "The Power and the Glory."

17. See Thomas Jefferson's "Second Inaugural Address," delivered March 4, 1805, to be found at http://etext.lib.virginia.edu/etcbin/toccer-new2?id=JefAddr.sgm&ima.

18. Originally from Jefferson's *Notes on the State of Virginia,* "Manners."

19. June 30, 2009, http://www.brainyquote.com/quotes/authors/n/noam_ chomsky.html.

20. Hamilton, Jay, and Madison, *The Federalist,* 193.

21. June 30, 2009, http://en.thinkexist.com/quotes/Avram_Noam_Chomsky/.

22. The text of the prayer can be found online from the Franklin D. Roosevelt Presidential Library and Museum at http://www.fdrlibrary.marist.edu/odddayp .html.

23. See Meacham, *American Gospel,* 168–72.

24. *Charlie Rose Show,* February 11, 2003, http://www.rumormillnews.com/cgi-bin/ archive.cgi/noframes/read/28554

25. http://rightvoices.com/2003/06/23/.

26. As quoted by David Brooks in *New York Times,* Saturday, June 26, 2004.

27. Bowman, "Understanding American Exceptionalism."

Chapter 1

The Miracle of
Christopher Columbus
and the Discovery of
the New World

To fully appreciate the miracle of Christopher Columbus and his unlikely discovery of the New World, we have to start a century earlier and on the other side of the world. We have to start in China and consider the extraordinarily advanced civilization the Middle Kingdom had then become.

While the European continent lay in squalor and decay, the Dark Ages full and ripe, with Western culture still retarded in almost every intellectual area, China had become the most powerful nation on earth. While the kingdoms of Europe squabbled with each other, fighting brutal skirmishes that made up a series of meaningless wars, the Middle Kingdom had been united into the world's largest empire. While the capitals of Europe built a few modest castles and called them masterpieces of architecture, China built the Forbidden City, still one of the wonders of the world. While the royalty of Europe gathered a few hundred books and a couple of dozen scholars and called it a university, scientists in China were discovering and advancing scientific theories beyond anything the West had yet imagined, including sunspots, equatorial astronomical instruments, solar winds, novas, solar and lunar eclipses, Halley's Comet, a calendar year to within 26 seconds and sea navigation using terrestrial navigation tools and techniques. While monks throughout the Western kingdoms were copying scripture by hand, China had already put to use paper and movable type; at a time when the total library of King Henry V of England (1387–1422) consisted of six handwritten books, the emperor of China commissioned 2,000 scholars to produce an encyclopedia with 4,000 volumes. When most of Europe was burning whale oil, China was searching for, discovering, and exploiting natural gas. While millions died in Europe from smallpox, China had developed and deployed a method to inoculate against the disease. Engineering, medicine, mathematics, transportation, warfare—China excelled in them all.[1]

Perhaps there was no area of expertise more important to the future of the world than oceanic exploration, and in this, as in almost everything, China excelled. Their ability to navigate and explore the oceans was unparalleled. At a time when Europe hardly dared wander beyond the Straits of Gibraltar, China was building fleets capable of circumnavigating the world.

That raises a very important question.

Why didn't China discover the New World? Why didn't they settle the Americas? Being so much more advanced than the Europeans, why didn't they colonize the Western hemisphere, spreading Chinese people, language, and culture, including Oriental religions and philosophy, to this sphere of the world?

Every piece of evidence indicates that they should have.

The Forbidden City, China
Summer 1421

THE EMPEROR STOOD IN THE magnificent hall built in the middle of the Forbidden City, capital of the most powerful nation in the world. A thick wall surrounded the inner court, with a second wall around the outer, wrapping him in a cocoon of garrisons and swords and guards. The splendid Hall of Supreme Harmony rose almost a hundred feet over his head. The Forbidden City lay before him, the fruit of a million workers and fifteen years of construction. With eighty-foot logs of the rare nanmu wood found only in the most remote jungles of southern China, enormous blocks of marble quarried at the cost of human blood, intricate wooden carvings depicting dragons spewing balls of metal, multiple thrones rising over various halls, with palaces for his wives and concubines, the pathways between them literally paved with gold, the emperor was surrounded by more wealth and power than anyone outside the kingdom had ever seen.

Standing atop the inlaid bricks, he lifted his hands and slowly turned, taking in the glory of the city. Five hundred thousand servants stood before him. The sky was clean and pure. He was standing at the center of the universe. He couldn't help but smile.

Fat, strong, black-haired, long-bearded, ambitious, steely-eyed, cunning, quick to smile, kindly to his sons, uncaring to his daughters, Emperor Zhu Di was the most powerful man on earth. And this great city around him was the crowning jewel of it all.

For more than a month, they had been celebrating the dedication of the Forbidden City. Ambassadors from twenty-eight different countries had gathered for the festivities, some from as far away as the east coast of Africa: dignitaries, kings, queens, military commanders, princesses, religious leaders, merchants, warriors, scholars—the most powerful leaders in the East. Having invited thousands of dignitaries to the celebration of China's new capital, the emperor had also accepted the responsibility of seeing them home. The Treasure Fleet—the largest and most powerful fleet ever built—was getting ready to depart. The fleet commander, Zheng He, planned on sailing south along the Chinese and Indonesian coast, then west around Malaysia, along the Indian coast, across the Arabian Sea, up and down the Persian Gulf, then finally south along the eastern coast of Africa. The expedition would take more than two years to complete while covering more than ten thousand miles.

Turning, Emperor Zhu Di walked toward the naval commander,

who was waiting at the foot of his throne. Commander Zheng He stood erect, his shoulders taut, his eyes down. The two men knew and loved each other dearly, their companionship dating to their childhood, but the naval officer never presumed the casualness of friendship, even when they were alone.

"This will be the sixth of the Treasure Fleet's great voyages," the emperor observed.

Commander He's eyes lit up and he took a step forward, the emotion on his face impossible to contain. "It will be the greatest voyage of them all! Three hundred and fifty ships. Nearly twenty-eight thousand men. We will sail farther than we ever have. We will . . ." He turned his head and looked southeast, toward the ocean. "If you let me, Emperor, I will complete the task we talked about before."

Zhu Di frowned. "I am told it can't be done," he answered doubtfully.

"It is not impossible, my master. I know some of your advisors tell you that, but . . ."

"Not *some* of my advisors. All."

The naval officer waited, saying nothing.

"It is far too dangerous," the emperor went on. "And even if you were successful, what are we to gain?"

"What are we to gain? What are we to gain!" The commander's voice was incredulous. "We gain access to the world! We prove our supremacy to every kingdom that lies between us and whatever else is out there! We grab hold of trade routes, cultures, and kingdoms we don't even know about. We would solidify the power of the kingdom for a thousand years to come."

The emperor watched his commander's face and listened before he said, "It is a great risk to my fleet, Commander He."

"But we have been so close already. By my evaluation, we have already been halfway around the world. In truth, once we are near the end of our planned voyage, it might be the shorter route to keep on going rather than to turn around to come home. We have enough men, enough courage, enough ships, enough cargo and provisions. The risk of going forward is no greater than the risk of coming back.

"We have the chance to strike now. No other people are as prepared as we are. I beg you, master, let me go sail around the world. Let me find the New Lands and plant our people there, scattering your seed and power! Let me spread the blood of China in every land throughout the world!"

Emperor Zhu Di stood silent, deep in thought. His soul was extremely troubled. He didn't know what to do. He considered for a long time, then turned west, his dark eyes looking out upon his kingdom.

The naval commander waited, hardly breathing, his head low.

"All right," the emperor finally answered, "for the glory of my kingdom, I grant you license to explore. But if you fail, Commander He, remember, the shame you will bring will not be easily borne by either a monarch or a warrior. Succeed, and you bring me glory; fail, and we both will be destroyed."

• • •

So it was that, at a time when the monarchies and kingdoms of Europe were struggling just to survive, a courageous and brilliant military leader from China set out to sail around the world, intent on discovering new lands beyond the borders of Eastern Africa, about which he already knew.[2]

The Treasure Fleet

Shortly after the end of the celebration dedicating the Forbidden City, Zhu Di, the Yongle Emperor of China and the third of the Ming Dynasty emperors, held court overlooking the Yangzi River near ancient Nanjing. His view included the docks of Longjian, the largest shipbuilding yards in the world. Here, communities of twenty to thirty thousand workers—carpenters, ironsmiths, caulkers, and sail and rope makers—were constructing, upgrading, and maintaining an immense imperial fleet.

The jewels of this fleet were the "treasure ships." These monster boats were 400 feet long and 160 feet wide. Designed for traversing the deep seas, each had nine staggered masts and twelve square sails made of red silk. Most important, each treasure ship was constructed with sophisticated systems for surviving ocean storms: a V-shaped hull, heavy ballast, watertight compartments, and a balanced rudder that was thirty-six feet long.

Although each of these massive ships was equipped with twenty-four bronze cannons, they were not designed for warfare but to extend the power and influence of the Chinese emperor through trade and diplomacy. One look at them made this obvious. Each ship had grand chambers for the emperor's envoys, with windowed halls and carved balconies and railings. The prows were adorned with carved animal heads and dragon eyes, and the sides were painted with bright colors.

Deep inside the ships' holds were valuable goods collected from throughout the emperor's vast kingdom: silks, porcelains, cotton cloth, iron, salt, hemp, tea, wine, oil, and candles, all of it demanded by the emperor from his various provinces.

Magnificent as they were, the treasure ships were only a part of the massive fleet assembled by the Yongle Emperor. There were also eight-mast horse ships, only slightly smaller than the treasure ships, which carried horses for trading as well as for equipping the Chinese military. Other ships transported all the tools and materials needed to repair the fleet's ships, as well as additional trade goods. The fleet also contained troop transports, five-masted warships, and fast patrol boats to keep pirates at bay. Tucked in the middle of the convoy were supply ships that carried food and drinking water, allowing the fleet to stay at sea for three months and travel 4,500 miles without making landfall. Considering that the fleet had crews and soldiers numbering 28,000 men, and that the voyage about to be undertaken might be more than two years in duration, with the ability to restock in question, these ships were heavy laden.

The crews included the eunuch commander-in-chief, Zheng He, and various directors. Each ship had a military commander, secretaries for preparing official documents and for keeping track of supplies used;

protocol officials, astrologers and geomancers, translators, and one medical officer for every 150 crew members, as well as workmen for making whatever repairs were called for at sea. Communication among the ships was conducted by flags, signal bells, banners, drums, gongs, and lanterns. Carrier pigeons were also brought along for long-range communications.

Emperor Zhu Di commanded the largest navy in the history of the world: 3,500 vessels, of which 250 were the giant treasure ships. In contrast, the next-largest navy at that time was the Venetian, which consisted of 300 small galleys good only for traversing the Mediterranean Sea.

After he had come to power in 1403, one of Emperor Zhu Di's first commands had been to order the construction of the magnificent Treasure Fleet. Departing in 1405, the first of the famed Treasure Fleet voyages lasted two years. Commanded by Zheng He, the fleet had set out for Calicut, an influential city-state on the west coast of India, the purpose of their voyage to announce the ascension of Emperor Di to the throne while throwing the doors open to foreign traders.

Over the course of nearly twenty years, Emperor Zhu Di sent out half a dozen Treasure Fleets, sending emissaries to Japan, Thailand, Indonesia, Malaysia, and the Indian state of Cochin, even to Africa's eastern coast. Commander Zheng He traversed the China Sea and the Indian Ocean, docking at ports in Sumatra, Ceylon, India, and Africa. He visited the Persian Gulf, the Arabian Peninsula, and the east coast of Africa, going as far south along that coast as Kenya, at least. Perhaps Mozambique. The ships returned with exotic animals such as zebras, elephants, and giraffes for the pleasure of the emperor. Their trading would secure them ivory, spices, precious stones and metals, and medicines.

The early voyages of the Treasure Fleets were intended to bring more foreign rulers within China's tribute system—a system whereby such rulers would pay a regular tribute to China in return for special trading rights as well as protection with the Chinese fleet. Being granted by the richest and most powerful nation on earth, such rights were of considerable worth. But the Treasure Fleets had another purpose beyond trade—they were sent out to explore, map, and expand China's power, allowing China to become creator of kings and power throughout the world it traversed. Zhu Di gave and revoked the right to rule various cities and nations according to what he thought would assure peace.[3]

During his reign, the power, wealth, and prestige of the Middle Kingdom continued to grow until there was no question that Emperor Zhu Di presided over a nation far more advanced than any other in the world. So it was that, on that summer day in 1421, the emperor watched with tremendous pride as his fleet organized itself on the Yangzi and set off.

The Treasure Fleet sailed away.

Two and a half years would pass before it returned.

The Forbidden City, China
Summer 1423

THE EMPEROR HAD NOT SLEPT in three days. He paced, pulled at his garments, and stared east. He moved constantly, sometimes lying upon various beds in various palaces, but he'd never found a moment's rest. Reports of the approaching Treasure Fleet had made it impossible to sleep, impossible to relax, impossible to sit still. He hadn't eaten. He barely talked.

For the past day, he'd hovered in a private room on the top floor of the East Glorious Gate, staring across the city to the rolling plains and low hills that separated him from the ocean. Every time he thought of it, his heart skipped a beat, his chest tightening into a ball of nerves. Commander He had been gone so long. The entire Treasure Fleet—the kingdom's greatest asset—had sailed off and disappeared far beyond the lines of communication. There was nothing the emperor could do but hope and wait, knowing that much of his future relied on the outcome of the Treasure Fleet's voyage.

He'd taken a huge risk. Like any emperor, Zhu Di was surrounded by ambitious men—some of them his sons—who valued power more than family, and many of the kingdom's most powerful leaders were snapping at his heels. They claimed that he had thrown it all away, that he'd wasted the Treasure Fleet, sending it on such a dangerous mission. For months, and then years, the emperor had put them off while waiting for the return of the fleet.

Pacing, the emperor walked to an open window and looked out, the evening breeze blowing at his flowing beard.

Was it true, what his scouts had reported? Were ships approaching from the north?

Had Commander He been successful? Had he really sailed around the world?

The outer reaches of the kingdom had been the first to report the sighting of the ships, their unmistakable huge sails billowing off the coast of Shanghai. The local commanders had dispatched military carriers toward the capital with the information. The emperor hadn't slept or relaxed ever since.

Standing at the open window, Emperor Zhu Di heard the light brush of flowing robes behind him and slowly turned around. His son, Zhu Gaozhi, was there, staring at him. How long had he been watching? Why hadn't he said anything? Something in the look on his son's face made the emperor's skin crawl.

"I've been looking for you," Gaozhi said.

The emperor didn't answer.

The son nodded toward the open window. "You've heard the rumors?"

Zhu Di nodded. "The Treasure Fleet has returned."

Zhu Gaozhi pressed his lips together. "Maybe. We will see."

His father turned back to the window. Gaozhi walked toward him. "I hope, for all of us, my dear emperor, that Commander He has been successful. If not, what a waste it will have been."

The emperor squinted against the sun and hunched his shoulders. He was old now and getting older, the aging process seeming to have accelerated over the past two or three months. A body that had been so quick and vibrant was suddenly winding down, and he would soon be walking the pathway to his ancestors, he was sure.

Gaozhi watched his father. "Have you considered my proposition?" he asked.

Zhu Di shook his head. "I will never do it. You'll have to wait until I die."

Based on the ghostly pallor of his father's cheeks, that wouldn't be too long, Gaozhi thought as he stared at his father.

The emperor glanced over Gaozhi's shoulders, looking for the younger man's various aides and advisors, knowing they would be close. His son was never alone now, having surrounded himself with mystery men spouting smoke and chants and foolish words of wisdom the emperor knew were nonsense of the most dangerous sort. The influence of extreme Confucian philosophy had nearly consumed his son. The words his son repeated often rolled around inside the emperor's head:

"With coarse rice to eat, with water to drink, and my crooked arm for a pillow—is not joy to be found therein?"

"Riches and honors acquired through unrighteousness are to me as the floating clouds."

The ancient philosophies had been around for generations, but they were finding growing power among the rising generation of the kingdom's leaders.

The emperor pulled on his beard and wondered. Was it evil to send out the Treasure Fleet? Was it evil to expand his power? Was it contrary to the will of nature or the deities to seek the interest of his kingdom?

Four days later, Commander He stood underneath the magnificent Gate of the Divine Might. He looked older now, but quicker, his eyes bright and alive. Without waiting, he moved toward the mighty emperor, taking the stairs two at a time, then bowed and kissed the ground below him. Zhu Di reached to lift him. The two men stared at each other; then the emperor drew the commander close. "Tell me!" he whispered into his ear.

Commander He pulled back, smiled, then reached down to a leather satchel at his side. Opening it, he pulled out a series of parchment maps. "Look at this, my emperor. Look at what we've done!"

He spread the maps out on the golden bricks at their feet.

The emperor knelt beside the commander, then started laughing with pure joy and relief.

Zhu Gaozhi, soon to be the emperor of the Middle Kingdom, watched from behind a silver curtain. Seeing the excitement in his father's eyes, he didn't smile.

How Far Did the Commander Go?

Some historians have speculated that Commander He's sixth voyage was special, that it ended up in a two-and-a-half-year expedition that traversed the world.[4] Chinese map segments that show details of the west coast of Africa are part of the evidence supporters use to contend that this voyage went well beyond any others. Further, a few Europeans seemed to be in possession of maps that show details of the Atlantic they had not yet explored. Before he explored it, Magellan knew of the strait on the southern tip of South America that would bear his name. Bartolomeu Dias, who discovered the Cape of Good Hope on the southern tip of Africa in 1488, had some information about the Cape before he set sail. Columbus had a map with Caribbean islands marked on it. It is assumed that such maps made it to Europe through Arab trade routes during the 1400s.[5]

The truth is, whether or not China did in fact make it to the Americas in 1421 does not matter. With its capabilities, it would have happened eventually. The *crucial* question is: Why didn't China continue to expand its discoveries and influence? With the wealth, the technology, the experience, and the vision of its rulers, China should have, by all rights, been the nation that colonized the Americas.

Yet it wasn't.

Why?

Zhu Di died soon after the return of the sixth Treasure Fleet. The *very first* edict issued by his son, Zhu Gaozhi, the new emperor, called for the end of the treasure ships. All foreign emissaries of China were to return home. The construction and repair of treasure ships was to cease. Though Zhu Gaozhi's reign was brief, the die had been cast.

By 1440, the emperor's fleet was reduced by half. By 1500, it was a capital offense to build boats of more than two masts. In 1525, an official edict called for the destruction of all oceangoing ships and the arrest of the merchants who might have sailed them. By 1551, it was a crime to go to sea in a multimasted ship, even for trade. The prejudice against seafaring was so intense that the logs and charts of Zheng He's voyages were purposely destroyed.[6]

The rise of the Middle Kingdom had reached its crest. Soon it would subside, and the empire would lose much of the power and knowledge it had already attained. China turned completely inward, leaving the New World to the Christian Europeans, who would soon discover their own way across the ocean on a mission to colonize the Americas in the name of their God.

The first miracle in the colonization of the Americas is, then, that the Chinese didn't do it.

The second is how Christopher Columbus did.

Who Was This Man?

Few men in history generate such diverse views as does Christopher Columbus. On the one hand, he is afforded a national holiday. On the other, he is viewed as the raper and destroyer of a paradise. The passion with which his detractors assault Columbus often clouds an honest examination of the man. Setting aside for the moment the debate over the consequences of his vision and bravery, the facts reveal a man who was extraordinary in the confidence with which he pursued his belief that a great discovery awaited the determined voyager to the west. He was persistent in lobbying for the necessary patronage to undertake his voyage. He was tenacious in preparing himself to undertake such a voyage. Further, his own writings reveal that his motivations were noble. He truly believed his success was the result of heavenly guidance prompted by that noble motivation.

The Europe into which Columbus was born (in Genoa, probably

in 1451) was a land of great pessimism. It was a time when little seemed to be going right for the Christians of the Western world.

Among its most distinct failures was Christian Europe's inability to wrest control of Jerusalem and the Holy Land from the Muslims. For centuries, pope after pope had called for a crusade to regain control of the Holy Sepulcher, but such calls fell upon deaf or impotent ears.

Despite the success of the Christian royalty in driving the Moors from the Iberian Peninsula, Christianity was losing ground to the armies of Islam. Constantinople fell to the Ottoman Turks two years after the birth of Columbus, thus ending the Byzantine Empire. During the ensuing decades, the Turkish Ottoman Empire would add Greece, Bulgaria, Serbia, Bosnia, Albania, Romania, and Hungary to its dominated states. Its expansion into Europe was not to be halted until 1529, when Turkish armies were finally defeated in their first attempt to take Vienna. Such defeats had to be repeated in 1566 and 1683 before a Christian Europe was secure.

In the mid- to late-fifteenth century, the Catholic church was in turmoil. Some scholars contend that it reached its lowest point when, in 1492, Rodrigo de Borgia bribed, blackmailed, and coerced his way to election as the newest pope, Alexander VI. Wealthy and robust, the father of numerous illegitimate children, Borgia was to propound policies that generated continual war and dissension throughout the Italian peninsula. Among his vices was the selling of ecclesiastical office to the highest bidder until his excesses triggered the Reformation that began in 1517.

In the land that was to become known as Spain, King Ferdinand and Queen Isabella initiated the Inquisition in 1478. Originally, the Inquisition focused on assuring purity and orthodoxy within the Catholic faith, but it soon evolved to include the banishment of all Jews from Spain. This was accomplished in 1492. A few decades later, the target became Protestants.

In the secular world, there were few nations but rather innumerable kingdoms and fiefdoms that were at constant war with one another.

With no powerful governments to curb it, violence was everywhere. With no authority to offer protection, crime was pervasive.

Disease and plague were common. The Black Plague had done most of its death-work earlier, but it still erupted from time to time in various regions. Europe's crowded and squalid cities and towns were also home to smallpox, measles, diphtheria, typhus, influenza, and leprosy, to name but a few of the prevalent sources of high death rates.

Famine visited Europe frequently. Although sometimes the famine would be local, often it was general in nature. Grains were the primary source of food. If there was inadequate moisture, the land did not produce. Seemingly all of Europe was but one or two bad crop seasons away from mass starvation.

Progress in science, education, and medicine was stalled.

These dire conditions led the people of Europe to believe that the Millennium had to be near. It was, in fact, the only hope for the future in the minds of many.[7]

But Christopher Columbus would not succumb to this pessimism. From the time that he was young, he felt driven by a cause. Ultimately that drive would do much toward leading Europe into a more enlightened age.

Genoa, Italy
1462

THE WALLS THAT ROSE AROUND HIM were ancient and almost crumbling now. Genoa, like most of the primeval cities throughout Europe, had been built and destroyed and rebuilt again, layer upon layer of old bricks falling in ruins under new. Black Death had taken most of the occupants of Genoa a couple of hundred years before, but the city struggled on, its natural port too valuable to allow it to fade away completely.

The boy stood on the main dock, a large wooden structure that ran parallel to the rocky beach. Hemp rope held wooden barrels against the ocean waves, providing a buffer to the half dozen two-masted galleys that were tied up at the dock. It was nearly sunset, and the boy was waiting to shoot a mariner's quadrant and astrolabe—a quarter-circle made of brass—at one of the early evening stars. His instructor waited impatiently beside him, his breath foul, his clothing filthy, his shirt crusted with salt from the sea and sweat.

As the skies darkened over their heads, the star they'd been waiting for was one of the first to appear—the red planet the brightest object in the northeast sky, a scarlet twinkle directly above the moon. Ursa Major and the North Star also came into view. Kneeling, the boy lit a single candle, studied the sky a few moments, then set to work, moving quickly, his tutor watching intently without saying anything. Twenty minutes later he had the bearings. The large man with the slovenly beard and broken teeth leaned toward the candle. He checked the boy's equations—it should have taken much longer—said nothing for a moment. Finally he nodded. "It is right," he said in a disbelieving tone.

Christopher Columbus smiled lightly but didn't dare reply.

The instructor, captain of the nearest galley tied up at the port, one that had seen far too many trips across the Mediterranean, shook his head again. "How did you get the equations for the bearings?" His voice was low now, skeptical and accusing. "You were out here last night. Someone helped you. They must have."

Columbus shook his head. "No, sir. I only did what you instructed."

The captain growled. "You did more than that," he sneered.

It had to be a trick, some kind of hoax from his drunken friends. He raised his head and looked around, thinking a couple of his mates might be hiding and laughing at him now. But the docks were empty, the wind blowing lightly from the Mediterranean Sea, salty and cool. He looked back at the boy, his anger rising. Did the lad think he was a fool! There simply wasn't any way he could have gotten the right quadrants and angles, not without significant help. Many a ship captain wouldn't have been able to figure out the problem by himself, yet the young boy had come up with the answer—and done it very quickly.

And it made the captain angry. Something wasn't right.

Columbus stood before him. The captain scowled at the boy and turned around. "That is all I'm going to teach you, boy!" he sneered. He started walking, the sound of his leather boots atop the heavy planks swallowed up in the lapping of the gentle waves against the dock.

Columbus followed after him. He was not afraid. "Sir, I paid you for instruction. It was my hard-earned money. I could have bought cabbage for a week for what I paid you . . ."

The captain swung around, his eyes burning in the dark. "Something's wrong with you, boy!" He spat the words. "No man without ten years of sailing could have figured that problem out. This is a joke. At my expense!" He lifted his head and looked around again.

"Sir," Columbus pleaded, "I don't know what you mean . . ."

The captain tapped the boy's chest and glared. "Stay away from me," he muttered.

The captain pushed him back, then turned and walked away, fingering the coins the boy had paid him to teach him navigational skills he obviously already understood.

Columbus watched the sailor walk away, leaving him alone on the rocking dock, then looked down and swallowed. He'd been scraping coins together for months, rummaging through garbage, working as a slop boy in the filthy animal pens behind the dock, doing anything he could to earn a few denaris in order to pay for his instruction. His father would be furious if he knew he'd lost it for an hour or two of celestial navigation instruction that should have taken a week.

He'd lost the money. Worse, he'd been humiliated. He stared down at the ground, shaking with shame and anger, knowing that if he had to do it all again, he would.

The ambition burned inside him, the familiar drive that forced him to move forward in his learning, no matter what the cost. His father thought he was crazy. His mother didn't know. Even he couldn't explain it sometimes. It was like there was a light inside him that drove him to explore. And it wasn't something new. He'd felt it now for years.

"You have a mission," the voice inside him seemed to say. He looked toward the sea, which drew him like a moth toward a flame.

"You have a mighty purpose. Believe that and continue. The path will be long and dangerous, but I will lead you," the whisper seemed to say.

Divine Appointment

Columbus was the son of a weaver named Domenico. Little is known of his youth except that he came from a poor family and was motivated by a desire to escape poverty. That, and the fact that he knew that he had a destiny.[8]

Columbus was self-taught. He was described as being a man of great intellect but little education. Later in his life he explained the sources of his education and preparation:

> I have had commerce and conversation with knowledge-able people of the clergy and the laity, Latins and Greeks, Jews and Moors, and with many others of different religions. Our Lord has favored my occupation and has given me an intelligent mind. He has endowed me with a great talent for seamanship; sufficient ability in astrology, geometry, and arithmetic; and the mental and physical dexterity required to draw spherical maps . . . with everything in its proper place.
>
> During this time I have studied all kinds of texts: cosmography, histories, chronicles, philosophy, and other disciplines. Through these writings, the hand of Our Lord opened my mind to the possibility of sailing to the Indies and gave me the will to attempt the voyage. . . . Who could doubt that this flash of understanding was the work of the Holy Spirit . . . ? The Holy Spirit illuminated his holy and sacred Scripture, encouraging me in a very strong and clear voice . . . urging me to proceed. Continually, without ceasing a moment, they insisted that I go on.[9]

Columbus acknowledged that he obtained his knowledge and understanding not from formal education, for he had little of that, but from his own intense efforts to learn and to become skilled in those areas that would permit a successful adventure to the West. He also freely acknowledged that God provided him with not only the inspiration but also the natural abilities and opportunities to learn what he needed to in order to undertake the voyage that changed the world.

He went to sea at a very young age, perhaps fourteen. His voyages through the mid-1480s took him throughout the Mediterranean, north to Iceland, to the west as far as the Azores, and to the south as far as the Gulf of Guinea. These journeys, most of them trading missions, exposed Columbus to the most remote points of then-established navigation.

Then, in 1476, Columbus nearly lost his life.

And the effect of this experience was certain to change the world.

Off the Coast of Portugal
1476

THE CANNONBALL IMPACTED THE HULL of the small trading ship just a foot below the waterline, a nearly perfect shot. Any higher, and the damage would have not allowed the sea into the breach; lower, and the water would have protected the ship's hull from the impact of the ball. As it was, the cannonball exploded through the four-inch hull, shattering a bushel-barrel-sized hole through the port side of the ship while sending a violent explosion up and down the mast.

The young mate, Christopher Columbus, knew immediately that the ship was going to falter. He could tell by the way it decelerated, the hole digging through the frothing sea like a huge brake. He could tell by the way the ship leaned into the water, by the screams that cried out from down below. The captain was already dead, along with half the mates around him. Attacking ships were on both sides, the enemy firing at the broken vessel and its crew. Chaos and blood and burning black powder surrounded him. There was no option of a parley, not with his captain dead. The ship's going down might be the best chance he could hope for. Better to face the sea than more swords or flying balls.

The attackers were going to win. He didn't know yet who they were—the entire region was at war, every state against the other, with more shattered agreements and broken treaties than he could possibly keep track of. The small convoy of trading ships never had a chance. With gunships having accelerated up both sides of the convoy, trapping the cargo ships between them, the battle had been short and one-sided.

Another crashing explosion sounded through the smoke. Cold seawater rained on his head. The ship lurched. Cracking wood. The main braces split with the sound of thunder as the timbers broke. Vibration against the waves now. Smoke and cries from the galley vents below. The setting sun turned the smoke into a rosy haze, the clouds on the horizon turning the sky bloodred.

The ship leaned further and he had to catch his footing against the wet and slippery boards. He ran to the port side, grabbed a torn rope that was hanging from the mainsail, wrapped it around his chest, held it with one hand, and leaned out, hanging over the frothing water. Looking toward the sound of the gushing water, he surveyed the damage. Half of the hole was below the waterline, allowing a steady stream into the ship. Every wave that splashed against the ship covered the hole completely, causing a deep and sickly gurgling sound. Even through the chaos he could hear the shouts from below as some of the surviving crew members struggled to repair the hole at least enough to slow the deluge. An eight-inch patch was thrown across the tattered hole but was immediately washed back. He held his breath and counted, still suspended over the green sea. The board appeared again, unseen hands trying desperately to hold it in place, but another wave crashed against the ship and pushed it back. The ship creaked and leaned forward, the bow dipping further into the sea. The hole was completely underwater now. Footsteps and the rattle of metal chains sounded behind him as crew members started scrambling up the ladder from below. The ship rolled and tilted starboard, rocking with the waves. He had been hanging out almost perpendicular to the water before, but he was angled upward now, 45 degrees against the horizon because of the ship's tilt.

The ship was going down. He knew that, and there was nothing he could do.

He bent his knees, fell toward the railing, stepped over, and dropped back onto the deck. The attacking ships were starting to move away. No more ropes were thrown between them. The attackers could see that his ship was sinking, leaving them no time to loot or salvage. Their captain wouldn't be very happy with this result.

Columbus slid across the deck, almost falling down as he slipped toward the port side, where he held onto the rail. The sea was safer on this side, the attackers having sailed farther away. He couldn't see the shoreline any longer—it was too dark and the smoke burned his eyes—but he knew the rocky shore of Portugal was out there, five or six miles to the east.

A white-hot ball of metal exploded through the main mast, tearing it from its moorings deep inside the bowels of the ship. Shattered wood exploded all around him, sending sharp pieces of shrapnel bursting through the air. Jagged splinters pierced his arm and side and leg, blood oozing from the open wounds. Pain ran up and down his side and he bit his lip to keep from screaming. He suddenly felt nauseated, his vision swooning, his forehead clammy, his armpits dripping in cold sweat.

He took a final look at the horizon to get his bearings—once he was in the water and it grew dark it would be difficult to hold his direction—then grabbed a half-full barrel of drinking water and tossed it overboard. Every motion sent chills of pain all through him, and his clothes were soaked in sweat and blood. Checking his coat pockets for his maps and navigational tools, the two things he valued as much as his life, he took a deep breath, braced for the cold water, leaned across the tilted railing, and jumped over the side of the ship.

Concealing himself behind the floating barrel, he watched his ship list and turn, the back lifting into the darkening sky and then bubbling through the waves, the top of the rudder finally disappearing below the murky surface. Farther to his right, a second ship went down, sucked into the cold sea with a froth of white. To his left, the flagship of his convoy was bathed in red smoke from a fire across its deck, its white sails illuminated from the final hint of sunlight and the fire. Dozens of sailors were in the water now. Some of them were wounded. Many couldn't swim. Calls of terror and desperation sounded from the growing darkness, sending an angry chill down his side.

Looking up, he tried to take his bearings, but the sky was still obscured by low clouds and smoke. Taking his direction from the position of the attacking ships, he started swimming. It would take him most the night, and he was already very cold.

Just before morning, he flopped upon the shore, one of the few who survived the bloody attack.

• • •

Columbus washed ashore, literally, in Portugal at a time when most of the nations and city-states of the Mediterranean were at war, his small Genoan convoy having been attacked by a Franco-Portuguese war fleet. Eventually, he found his way to Lisbon. And although his entry into Portugal was not auspicious, his taking up residence there proved to be very important.

The century into which Columbus was born was one in which the Atlantic Ocean dominated explorers' attention, and Portugal was at the center of this enterprise. During Christopher Columbus's early life, ocean exploration resulted in the discoveries of the two most remote islands of the Azores (1452). The Cape Verde archipelago was explored in about the same time frame. In the 1470s, the islands of the Gulf of Guinea were added to maps. The west coast of Africa was accurately mapped in the 1480s. Almost all of these daring explorations were undertaken by Portuguese seamen. Portugal was also the home of the most progressive mapmakers.

So it was that Columbus's unfortunate sea disaster resulted in his making a home in the one place where he could learn and train himself in all of the arts necessary to undertake his great adventure into the unknown regions of the western oceans.

In the decade before his voyage, Columbus spent less time at sea and more time learning the art of mapmaking and delving into those books then available to provide him insight as to what he might find in a westward voyage. He studied Ptolemy, a second-century Greek Alexandrian, whose book *Geography* was a collection of the ancient Greek and Roman knowledge of the geography of the charted world. He was familiar with *The Book of Marco Polo* and relied upon Polo for his understanding that there were many islands to the east of China and that any approach to China from the west would pass by those islands. He also relied upon Polo for the names of various places in Asia, in particular the island of Cipangu, today known as Japan. Polo said that Cipangu was outrageously wealthy, with the king's "mighty palace all roofed with finest gold, just as our churches are roofed with lead. The windows of that palace are all decorated with gold; the floors of the halls and of many chambers are paved with golden plates, each plate a good two fingers thick. There are pearls in the greatest abundance."[10]

By 1492, Columbus had equipped himself with the skills of a navigator and mapmaker and had an understanding of geography.

He spent this time learning and preparing, for it's clear from his own writings that he believed he was appointed to a task. Persistent, undoubting, physically strong and courageous, he was simply hard to break, his persistence always bolstered by his belief that he was directed by a heavenly cause. One biographer, Samuel Eliot Morison, said of him:

> Men may doubt this, but there can be no doubt that the faith of Columbus was genuine and sincere, and that his frequent communion with forces unseen was a vital element in his achievement. It gave him confidence in his destiny, assurance that his performance would be equal to the promise of his name. This conviction that God destined him to be an instrument for spreading the faith was far more potent than

the desire to win glory, wealth and worldly honors, to which he was certainly far from indifferent.[11]

When exactly Christopher Columbus decided upon a plan to cross the empty and unexplored Atlantic, it is not known. Perhaps it was something that he had considered for years before he made his intentions public. Morison has speculated whether he might have received inspiration as a youth, "at a season of fasting and prayer."[12] The fact is, Columbus never said exactly when he decided to undertake his expedition into the far reaches of the unknown. However, it is certain that at some point while in Portugal, Columbus made the decision to go where no European explorer had ever gone before.

He started sharing his idea.

Almost without exception, all he met was scorn. No one believed that it was possible. The most learned men of the time would call him foolish, sometimes insane. It would be a bitter and exhausting battle, lasting many years, for him to get the chance to prove if he was right.

Lisbon, Portugal
1484

CHRISTOPHER COLUMBUS STARED at the map of the western coast of Africa. A series of small islands were scratched into the parchment. La Palma. Las Palmas. Santa Cruz. The map indicated that the nearest of the islands was a little less than ninety miles off the coast, but he'd been around long enough to be skeptical of the charted distance.

His visitor, a wealthy Naples merchant, his fur and leather coat drooping below his wrists, tapped the hand-copied letter beside the map. Columbus turned around to face the setting sun and thought, then looked down at the letter once again.

Toscanelli, a famous Italian physician and one of Europe's best mathematicians and astronomers, had sent a letter to the court of Lisbon in which he provided his best estimate of how far it was from the Canary Islands across the Atlantic to Japan, or what the

Europeans called Cipangu. According to the letter, a copy of which the merchant had kindly brought to show Columbus, Toscanelli estimated the distance as 3,000 miles to Japan, 5,000 miles to China.

Most of the scholars throughout Europe thought the estimate was ridiculous. Columbus was certain Toscanelli was close to being right.

Leaning over, he studied the map again, his finger tracing the tiny island of Santa Cruz. "This is the key," he muttered. "But islands are not what I'm interested in. Islands don't have the capacity of changing the world. Islands, no matter their position or significance, will not change the fate of men, the fate of Europe, the fate of Christianity in the world. Only the unknown world is capable of doing that."

The Italian nodded. "Antipodes?" he asked.

Columbus smiled. "Antipodes. Yes. The great landmass. Some maps call it Hesperides. I call it the New World."

"So that is what you're after?"

"Not necessarily, my friend. A clear sea route to the Indies is just as important, for it would bridge our two worlds."

"The earth is too small." The wealthy merchant waved the copy of the Italian mathematician's letter. "There is no more room for another great land mass like Europe or Asia. The eastern shore of China is all you'll find out there. That, or the edge of the world." The Italian smiled at the thought of Columbus sailing to the edge of the earth and falling into a cold, black hole.

Columbus saw the sarcastic turn of the visitor's lips. "There is no edge of the world, Cornelius. Only fools still believe the world is flat. Aristotle understood that the world is a great globe. The Greek geographer Strabo, who lived during the time of Christ our Savior, understood this too. Most reasonable men agree the earth is round. The one thing we can't agree on is how large it really is."

Cornelius leaned back in his old chair, hearing the wood joints strain against his ample weight. The fire popped behind him, and Columbus turned to poke at the blackened pit. The merchant took a look around. The home was a small wooden shack overlooking the ocean. Scantily furnished. A stone fireplace. A single bed. A pair of wood tables, both of them covered with maps, papers, and parchments. How did Columbus provide for himself? Not very well, it seemed. But there was something about the sailor, something compelling that drew the merchant in.

Columbus kicked at an ember that had popped out of the fire, moving it back into the hearth, then turned back to face his visitor. "Around 200 B.C., a Greek, Eratosthenes, estimated the earth's circumference to be close to 24,900 miles. I think that is too large. The Moslem geographer Alfragan has calculated the circumference to be much less than that and I am convinced that he is right. Basing my thinking upon his calculations, I conclude that the distance between the Canary Islands and Japan is no more than 2,400 miles, and 3,550 miles to China. If that is all it is, then such a voyage is certainly possible."

The Italian was silent a very long time before he finally shook his head. He'd made up his mind. Christopher Columbus was a fool. He didn't care if the sailor was convinced that his life was guided by God. Columbus was a *sailor*, not a mathematician or a geographer. He wasn't trained in the higher thoughts. He had no education. No influence. No money. If God truly was so disposed to support him, why hadn't he been born into a royal family? If God intended for him to be successful, why hadn't He provided him with the proper background? Good information? A family patron? Any of the tools that were necessary to be successful in this world? God graced those He loved, and this man was anything but graced.

The sailor was a good man, but many good men were fools.

Columbus watched the Italian, then looked away. He'd seen the expression on his face, the sullen look that had suddenly clouded his eyes. He was familiar with such expressions. He'd seen them many times before.

Leaning from the fire, he lifted a finger at the man. "Hear me, Cornelius, and mark my words. Thousands of men have wondered at the possibility of crossing the great Atlantic. Thousands have talked about it. Planned it. Considered such an undertaking and how it might be done. But I'm not here to talk about it! I'm not here to ponder or pontificate. No, I'm going to do it! I am certain that I will. And it isn't me that guides me there, it is so much more than that." He tapped the map resting on the table, pointing to the Canary Islands. "This place, these islands, they are the key to how I'll do it. No one understands that yet, but I know that it is true!"

• • •

It's worth noting that Columbus's estimate of the earth's circumference was much smaller than what it actually is. In reality, it is 10,600 miles from Europe to Japan, and 11,766 miles to China. And it's ironic that his belief in his own miscalculations was one of the things that gave him the confidence and courage to proceed.

In Search of a Patron

Once he had decided on a course of action, Columbus needed funding and support.

A patron was required fare for any explorer of that era. The patron was first and foremost necessary to help fund the enterprise, to assemble the ships, and to aid in convincing a crew to sign on. Further, a discovery of new lands permitted a claim of ownership, but such claim had to be made in the name of the sovereign or ruler of a nation.

It's interesting to note that Columbus was not asking for much. Besides official sponsorship, which was at that time somewhat freely given, the sum of money he sought was relatively small: approximately two million maravedis, or the equivalent of $78,000 today, about the same as the annual income of a mid-level Spanish aristocrat in his day. In addition, Columbus sought certain titles and positions, a tenth of the wealth he might discover for the crown, as well as the possibility of other compensations.

Beginning in 1484, Columbus actively began searching for such a sponsor. For the next eight years, he traveled throughout Europe, penniless and alone, seeking after his goal. He worked doggedly, enduring the scoffs and scorns of those around him. Seven times he would provide formal proposals to various parties. Seven times he would be denied.

1. He first approached the King of Portugal, João II, a logical choice, for the Portuguese were the most successful explorers of the Atlantic. A committee of experts was assigned to consider Columbus's proposal, which called for several ships to sail for Japan.

The proposal was rejected—apparently because the experts did not believe in Columbus's calculations of distance and were uncertain about his geography. It was also possible that the king believed that Columbus was driving too hard a bargain, demanding too many honors and concessions should he be successful.

2. Disappointed but undaunted, Columbus moved on to Castile. The marriage in 1469 of the Castilian queen, Isabella, and the king of Aragon, Ferdinand II, had created a nation that would become known as Spain in 1516. Columbus and his son, Diego, sailed there in the middle of 1485. At the time, Columbus had no money—in fact, he left substantial debts behind him in Lisbon—and upon arriving in Spain at the port of Palos, he abandoned Diego at a monastery at La Rabida, a practice not uncommon at the time for parents unable to care for their offspring.

For the next six and a half years, he undertook a determined effort to convince King Ferdinand and Queen Isabella of the wisdom of his voyage. There was much to be gained by patronage from Castile. Perhaps most important, they had recently conquered the Canary Islands, which meant that the westernmost harbor at San Sebastian would be available for Columbus's use. His plan had been to sail southwest to the Canary Islands and then straight west. (This decision was perhaps the most important, although unpredictable, decision that Columbus was to make.)

Another appealing aspect of Castile was that the king and queen shared Columbus's belief that it was destiny that the wealth from the success of his mission would be used to liberate Jerusalem from the Muslims. Ferdinand and Isabella had inherited the title "King and Queen of Jerusalem." This was symbolic of the popular view, the result of prophetic writings by Abbot Joachim of Fiore and others, that a king of Aragon would be responsible for the liberation of Jerusalem as a precursor to the ushering in of the Millennium. Columbus was familiar with the writings of Joachim, and he firmly believed that the inspiration upon which he depended for success was a gift from God for the purpose of helping him fulfill the prophecy regarding Jerusalem.

Spain was also an appealing target for patronage because it was then engaged in a fierce competition with Portugal for dominance of trade routes and acquisition of new lands and possessions.

In May 1486, Columbus was given an audience by Queen Isabella in which he presented his vision of a westward voyage with great enthusiasm and confidence. After the meeting, his hopes were lifted, but unjustifiably so.

In late 1486 and early 1487, a panel of "wise men, learned officials and mariners" was commissioned by the king and queen to evaluate Columbus's proposal.[13] The proposal was not rejected outright, but taken under consideration. However, it was the consensus of the panel that Columbus's estimated distance to Indies couldn't possibly be accurate. (In this, of course, they were correct.)

While the panel considered the proposal, Columbus was put on a small retainer to help him survive, which ended in June of 1488. At that point he still had not heard from the commission.

3. Discouraged, Columbus turned his attention back to Portugal. Unfortunately for him, since he had left the country, Bartolomeu Dias had sailed around the southern tip of Africa under the flag of Portugal. King João II had found his route to the Indies, and he no longer had any interest in Columbus's dream.

4. Undaunted, Columbus sent his brother Bartholomew to England, where he was rejected by counselors to King Henry VII, who characterized Columbus's proposal as being vain. Bartholomew then turned to France, where he was still living when Columbus sailed in 1492.

5. In 1489, Columbus traveled back to Castile to await a decision from the royal commission. These were hard times for Columbus, and it is not known how he provided for himself. Though he remained absolutely convinced that his proposed expedition would be successful, his critics were nearly unanimous in their rejection of his geography and estimates of distances. He wrote of how so many had considered his

proposal and "unanimously treated it with contempt," forcing him to face "fatiguing opposition."[14] (Indeed, the way he was treated during his six-and-a-half-year effort stayed with him, and he mentioned it often in later years.)

Finally, in 1490, the commission spurned Columbus's proposal, determining it would take a voyage of three years to reach Asia. They further concluded that, even if he did encounter Antipodes, he would not be able to return.

At the time, Ferdinand and Isabella were engaged in the siege of Granada and were too preoccupied to pay much attention to the Columbus proposal. Though they did not accept their commission's outright rejection, they told Columbus to come back later.

6. Columbus delayed for another nine months before deciding he couldn't wait any longer. Turning his back on Castile, he set out for France to pursue a new patron in King Charles VIII. Completely dejected, he returned to Palos to retrieve Diego, where he met the head of the monastery, Fray Juan Perez, a man who had at one time been the confessor to Queen Isabella. Dismayed that Columbus would be giving up on Castile, he promised him another audience with the queen. Columbus reluctantly agreed. Fray Juan sent a letter to the queen, and she soon responded with an invitation for Columbus to proceed to court, including enough money for him to purchase suitable clothing and a mule.

7. Sometime in the later part of 1491, Columbus appeared before the queen. He was again told to subject his proposal to a commission of astronomers, mariners, and philosophers who would investigate the technical aspects of the proposal. Upon completion of their investigation, the matter was to be referred to the Royal Council of Castile, which was made up of royalty and ecclesiastical authorities. It appears as if the technical commission approved the plan but the Royal Council rejected it. Columbus was told that his enterprise was absolutely and finally rejected. King Ferdinand and Queen Isabella informed Columbus of this decision personally, after which he was ushered from the court.

Seven and a half years wasted! Seven and a half years of personal and financial hardship. Seven and a half years of being forced to defend himself from fools and kings.

With no other option, Columbus put his meager belongings into his saddlebag, mounted his mule, and, in the company of his loyal friend Fray Juan, began the long journey for France.

A day into their journey, they were overtaken by a royal messenger. Columbus was to return immediately! Without explanation, he was ushered into the presence of the queen and miraculously informed that his proposal had been accepted.

What caused the queen to change her mind? Some speculate that Luis de Santangel, keeper of the king's private purse, had gone to the queen and begged for her support. Others mention the queen's personal confidence in Columbus, despite the objections and condemnations of the most educated and powerful men within the kingdom. Maybe it was the queen's own intuition. We don't have enough evidence to really know.

Columbus believed it was simply the will of God.

But, as we shall see, it was *critically* important that he have the support of Spain. Had his patron been from England or Portugal or any other country, Columbus would have failed.[15]

Setting Sail

On the third day of August, 1492, a small fleet made its way from the southern tip of the Iberian Peninsula. Sixty-five feet long and twenty-three feet across, the *Nina* and *Pinta* were three-masted caravels typical of the ships that plied the Mediterranean Sea at that time. The third ship, the *Santa Maria,* was slightly larger, perhaps seventy feet long, and also had three masts. The *Santa Maria,* by virtue of its larger size, was the flagship of the small expedition. The three vessels were manned by a combined crew of eighty-eight men.

The course selected by Columbus was of immense importance to the success of the expedition. Sailors who depend on the wind, as did Columbus, need the wind behind them in order to propel them forward.

Most of the explorers who attempted Atlantic voyages before Columbus had set out from either the Azores or Bristol, where they found themselves tacking against a constant west wind. Making minimal progress, it wasn't long before they surrendered to the inevitable. Just seven years before, Fernao Dulmo and Joao Estreito had been commissioned by their king to sail west for forty days. They departed from the Azores, but the voyage came to nothing, for they couldn't overcome the constant headwinds, which forced them to join the ranks of many others who had attempted to sail across the Atlantic but failed.

Columbus chose to begin his transatlantic voyage by sailing 700 miles to the south, to the Canary Islands. By so doing, he picked up the northeast trade winds, which could propel him all the way to the Americas. When he returned, he first sailed to the north, where he picked up the westerlies that drove him home.

Some historians have speculated that such a critical decision must have been the result of knowledge Columbus had acquired on one of his previous sailing experiences. Some have said that he may have had this information imparted by an "unknown" pilot. How he became aware of such an important secret is never fully explained.[16]

But this simple fact remains: The Canary Islands were controlled by Spain and, in fact, were Spain's only major possession in the Atlantic. If Columbus had been sponsored by England, France, or Portugal, he would have likely chosen—or been forced—to leave from either the Azores or Bristol. In that event, he would have failed, and we would not remember his name.

Catching an easterly wind on September 6, the three ships left the harbor at San Sebastian on the Canary Island of Gomera and headed due west.

It is interesting to imagine what might have been on the minds of the men aboard those three small ships. The spirit of adventure and the promise of shared wealth will sustain a great adventurer only so far. As these men headed into the complete unknown, aboard ships of dubious worthiness on the high seas, captained by a man who was a complete stranger to them and a foreigner to boot, fear and doubt would have to have been constant companions. As they sailed to the west, day after day, with the winds generally behind them, they must have asked themselves whether there would ever be winds from the west to take them home.

In order to convince the Castilian king and queen, as well as his own crew, Columbus had said that the voyage from the Canaries to the Indies would be a "few days," a term subject to interpretation. That representation, important for getting the crew on board, began to be a problem once they were at sea. The crew's expectations of a brief voyage required constant attention by Columbus after just a short time. The most pressing problem for Columbus was this: At what point would his crew simply give up?

Hoping to keep the crew's concerns to a minimum, Columbus purposely reported the length of each day's voyage as shorter in distance than it actually was. By this means, he led his crew to believe that they were not all that far from land.

As they sailed west, where, to their understanding, no men had ever sailed before, the explorers were beset by two recurring problems. First, there was a series of false sightings of land. Each false sighting caused morale to suffer. Second, the farther west they sailed, the more fearful the men became that they might not find a favorable wind to take them home.

By the last week in September, it appeared the crew would mutiny. The men weren't stupid. They could go below and see that their supplies were diminishing. They could count the barrels and estimate how many days of water they had left. There was talk of the greedy Genoese leading them to their death so that he could become a wealthy master. Why not just heave him over and return home and tell the king and queen that he had fallen overboard? Columbus sensed their treason by the gloomy looks, the silence when he passed by, the gatherings of small groups of men looking furtively in his direction. His reaction was to speak softly and to act with even more confidence, which momentarily bolstered the crew's morale.

On the seventh of October, Columbus made a slight adjustment in his course that proved critical. Observing a large flock of birds flying southwest, and remembering that the Portuguese had discovered the

Azores by following a flock of birds, he set a course in the direction they had flown. It is clear this slight adjustment determined the entire outcome of the voyage.

First, had he continued due west, the fleet might well have headed beyond the islands of the Caribbean and been caught up in the Gulf Stream. They would then have been carried by that powerful current and made shore in Florida, then been carried past Georgia and the Carolinas. Had this occurred, no gold would have been encountered, the voyage would have been considered unprofitable, and the sponsorship of a second voyage might never have occurred.

Second, had their course not changed, it might have taken a full day more to sight land. The events of the next few days reveal how critical that single day may have been.

On October 9, the captains of the *Nina* and *Pinta* demanded a meeting with Columbus. The wind was light, which made it possible for them to assemble on the *Santa Maria,* where the other captains demanded that the search for land be abandoned and that finding a way home become the priority. Columbus agreed that if land was not found in three days, he would follow their desire.

By October 10, the men could endure no more. The false sightings of land, the lack of flotsam or weeds that would have indicated that land was near, more than thirty days out of sight of land (far more than recorded man had ever endured), the fact that they had long passed the point where their leader had predicted land would be found—all these disappointments simply proved too much.

A confrontation between the crew of the *Santa Maria* and Columbus resulted in open mutiny. Columbus "cheered them up in the best way he could," reminding them of the advantages that success would bring. But he also made it clear that notwithstanding their fears, " . . . he had to go to the Indies, and that he would go on until he found them, with the help of our Lord."[17] Still, despite his strong intent, he also promised that if land was not sighted within two or three days, he would turn back.

As evening fell on day one, he knew his time was very short.

Aboard the *Santa Maria,*
Somewhere in the Western Atlantic
1492

IT WAS BAD AND HE KNEW IT.

The men were angry and losing confidence and, worst of all, consumed by growing fear. How much farther could they go? Their supplies were growing short. The sun beat mercilessly upon them. They could picture it—their faces dead and rotting, their skin tanned from the sun to blackened leather, their bodies hollowed cores, three dead ships full of dead men that continued sailing west.

Columbus sensed their fear. He sensed their rebellion. He had asked his men to trust him, but they didn't trust him anymore. He had pushed too far.

One way or another, the next twenty-four hours would change their course. That was all the time he had now. They would either find land or they would kill him. They would either find land or they would abandon their mission and set sail to turn back, a disastrous decision that would lead to all of their deaths, for they couldn't tack against the trade winds that had been blowing them on this course.

After all these years, after all the sacrifices, all the pleadings, all that he had risked and given up, all that he and his men had suffered through, it all came down to this.

One day to find land, or it was over.

Columbus rolled over on his tiny bed. He listened to the water slap against the hull, estimating their speed from the force of the rushing sound. Twelve knots. Maybe a little slower.

His tiny stateroom was dark, though there was a hint of moonlight bleeding through the crack underneath the door. There was a full moon outside, and before retiring for the evening he had stood on the starboard side of the ship, watching the moonrise, the huge yellow orb a welcome face upon the far horizon, its dim light casting shadows across the whitecaps that glistened on the sea.

Lying on his bed, he listened to the night crew. All was quiet on the ship.

One day. Maybe two. That was all the time he had to live. And in that moment, alone against his crew, alone against the open ocean, alone against the winds and the vastness of the sea, alone against the realities of every waking moment, he finally had to wonder . . .

Sometime after midnight, a sudden knock sounded at his cabin door.

He hesitated, sucking in a quick breath.

Had they finally come to take him and throw him overboard? Would they come for him in the darkness? It would be easier, wouldn't it? If he had any allies—and he didn't think he did—they would be asleep.

The knock sounded again, this time more urgent.

He took another breath and stood to face them.

The night lookout was standing at the door. "Look at this, sir!" he whispered urgently, shoving a patch of greenery in his face.

Columbus took the sprig of green and stepped into the narrow hallway, then a few paces out onto the main deck. A lantern was burning at the helm, and he moved toward its light.

Holding the broken branch to his eyes, he examined it more closely. Green leaves. A tiny white flower. A freshly broken limb. He touched the leaves, feeling their freshness.

A fresh branch broken from an unseen patch of land during the storm the night before.

They were close.

They had to be close.

He closed his eyes and prayed.

• • •

The first true signs of land settled the men. On October 11, they found a piece of board, then a little stick that appeared to have been fashioned into a shape by a man.

Anticipation of sighting land grew to a nearly unbearable level. The men were anxious and fidgety and always searching, their eyes hardly leaving the horizon.

At 2:00 A.M. on the twelfth, under a moon slightly past full, the call went out. *LAND! LAND ON THE HORIZON!* The lookout on the *Pinta* had sighted a mound of darkness against the moonlight. A mighty cry rose up from the crew, though it was tempered—the men had been disappointed with false sightings of land before. But as dawn broke, what they had been watching in the moonlight became clear.

It is not known with certainty which of the islands of the Caribbean Columbus had discovered. Most likely it was Watling Island. Columbus promptly named it "San Salvador"—Saint Savior.[18]

Columbus returned to Spain with the *Nina* and *Pinta* in March of 1493, having visited a number of islands, including the Bahamas, Cuba, and Hispaniola, where he left behind a small colony. (The *Santa Maria* had foundered on Christmas Day, 1492, at Navidad on the island of Hispaniola.) He was greeted with great acclaim. He was to make three more voyages to the Americas, exploring more of the islands of the Caribbean and sailing along the coast of Central America before he died in 1506.

What If?

What would have happened if, about the time Columbus was born, China had not experienced such a dramatic inward turn? How would our world be different if China had continued to explore or even had colonized the New World? What would have been the fate of Europe if Columbus had not discovered the New World when he did? What if that discovery, which raised the wealth, the vision, the imagination, and the focus of the European nations, had not occurred until many years in the future? Would Europe have continued to suffer decline? Would it have had the means or the will to withstand the armies of Islam?

The impact on Europe of Christopher Columbus's discovery was immense. The weak and struggling Europe of 1492 was soon left behind. The New World became the source of unimaginable wealth in gold, silver, and other minerals for the European nations that followed Columbus to the West. New foods were imported that would become staples for the people of Europe, including corn, potatoes, and tomatoes. The New World would become the source of life-saving drugs. Most important, it became the place for the people of Europe to spread to, escape to, become free in, the geographical area encompassing the Christian world more than doubling instantly.

The morale of Europe changed dramatically in just a few years. Strong monarchs brought a new level of security to the continent. The Church was challenged by the Reformation and began to purify itself. The discovery of a New World triggered new thoughts, ideas, and inventions. Human thought now knew no bounds, as the earth itself seemed unbounded. The tenuous seeds of freedom and liberty found a place to take root, to grow slowly, eventually to ripen and spread.

That is what Columbus did for Europe.

What did he do for the rest of the world?

What if Columbus had not developed the faith that his mission was ordained of God, a faith that sustained him through rejections, ridicule, and mutiny?

What if Columbus had not been shipwrecked in Portugal, where he acquired the knowledge and skills to carry out his voyage?

What if he had not made the geographical miscalculations that gave him the courage to undertake the voyage of a "few days"?

What if Castile had not agreed to become his sponsor and Portugal, France, or England had? In that event, he would have sailed into the wind and, like all the others, he would have failed.

At what point in history would someone else have come forth with Columbus's combination of grit, stubbornness, knowledge, experiences at sea, ability to sell his concepts, navigation skills, and qualities to captain a ship? Some say it surely would have happened sooner or later. But with Europe in malaise and Islam on the rise, it might have occurred much later. Meanwhile, would Europe have fallen to militant Muslim armies first? Might the New World have become another conquered land ruled by the Koran?

What if Columbus had not made the changes in course on October 7? If he had returned home with no gold, would the Spanish crown, or any other sovereign, have been willing to sponsor another voyage?

A Different America

What would have happened to the Americas without the Judeo-Christian influence that the Europeans brought?

To answer that question, it makes sense to ask what the Americas were like before Columbus's discovery. There are those who contend that it was inhabited by noble people who lived peacefully and trod very lightly on the land—living in harmony with their fellowmen and with all of nature. But such was simply not the case.

The Americas were largely populated by warlike people with little regard for human life. The likelihood that they would have evolved into a society that would espouse the protection of life, liberty, and the pursuit of happiness seems impossibly remote.

Consider, for example, the Mexica, called by the Europeans the Aztecs. Rising from a captive state from about 1428 to 1440, they slowly increased their power and influence until they conquered all of the valley of Mexico and surrounding areas. The primary focus of their military prowess was the acquisition of human slaves for sacrifice. Aztec history reports the sacrifice of 80,000 people after one successful military campaign, just decades before the Aztecs were conquered by the Spaniards under Cortez in 1522.

The Aztecs had a highly advanced society in many respects. They had mastered the construction of large structures and certain aspects of agriculture, and craftsmen were treasured. All males were expected to go to school until they were sixteen years old. However, they were easily conquered by a small army under Cortez because their neighbors hated them for their bloodthirsty appetites and willingly joined the Spaniards in a war to destroy them.[19]

Another example of a civilization much advanced in agriculture, the arts, and even the sciences was the Inca culture of South America. By 1491, the Incas had used their military and economic power to gain control over one of the largest empires in history. They built 25,000 miles of roads, mastered the art of terrace-based agriculture, made advances in metallurgy, and employed a form of writing using knots in strings. The kings of the Incas minimized the likelihood of revolt by up-rooting conquered populations and moving them to where they could be used to operate farms or construct massive public-works projects. But the Incas were also fierce warriors who followed the practice of skin-ning the leaders of their conquered foes. Their religion was sophisticated and complex, but it also involved human sacrifice, usually of children who were perfect in their physical beauty.[20]

What little is known about the pre-Columbian history of the Americas—whether of the tribes of the southwestern United States, the mound builders of the southeastern United States, the Plains Indians, or any of the other known inhabitants of North or South America—reveals that they were constantly at war, and had either been recently conquered or were conquering others. They may have been advanced in many ways and had sophisticated societies by many measures, but they were almost uniformly warlike people with little respect for indi-vidual rights.[21]

A Barren Field to Sow the Seeds of Freedom

The Americas, populated by such peoples, would never have been the place where freedom and liberty could have found a home. A soci-ety based on respect for the individual, and the creation of governments to protect the rights of the individual, were critical to the forming of this nation. Such ideas were far from reality in the existing cultures of the land.

It is worth noting that the argument can be made that the Europe of the fifteenth century was not much different from the Americas at that time. It is true that Europe in that age was made up of warring city-states and kingdoms, dominated by absolute monarchs, subject to immense cruelty, as displayed in the Spanish Inquisition, but to com-pare it with the brutality of pre-Columbian America would be falla-cious. Most of Europe had come to recognize at least basic human rights, rights of private property, various religious institutions, and so forth. They had already written the Magna Carta, also called Magna

Carta Libertatum (Great Charter of Freedoms), which required the king of England to proclaim certain rights, respect certain legal procedures, and agree that the will of the king was bound by the law. Though limited, the influence of the Magna Carta reached throughout most of Europe and was held as a model for many of the European kingdoms around it. It certainly became one of the foundational premises upon which the American political system would develop, and its influence can be seen throughout our history, in the development of the common law and within the Constitution itself.

Such was the foundation for the ideas of individual freedom and liberty throughout Europe. With a foundation based on Judeo-Christian values, the United States was able to evolve into a place where respect for human life became a priority, where the power of monarchs was restrained, and where personal liberty and freedom could be espoused. Considering the pagan beliefs of the inhabitants of the land, no rational argument could be made that a similar evolution would have occurred throughout the Americas on its own. [22]

As It Happened

Through the centuries that followed Christopher Columbus's discovery of the Americas, there came an influx of peoples who created a positive influence on the founders of this nation, eventually culminating in a miraculous mix that resulted in the creation of the United States of America. That wonderful mix of beliefs, people, influences, opportunities, and circumstances resulted in a nation that has survived with a written Constitution intact for over 220 years. That nation has been the source of great economic power and influence, has saved the world from the tyranny of fascism and communism, and has served as a force for stability and a beacon of hope for liberty-loving people for two centuries.

America, as it evolved after the discovery by Christopher Columbus in 1492, became the one place on earth where constitutional government, dedicated to a commitment to universal human rights and liberty, could have happened.

Christopher Columbus died, likely from a heart attack, in 1506. During his fourth and final voyage to the New World, when alone and frustrated, he told of hearing a "compassionate voice" that addressed him, saying, "O fool, and slow to believe and to serve thy God . . . what did He do more for Moses, or for David his servant, than He has done for thee?"[23]

Notes

1. See www.china.org.cn/e-gudai/6.htm; Needham, *Science and Civilisation in China,* 64; Marrin, *Dr. Jenner and the Speckled Monster, The Search for the Smallpox Vaccine,* 32–33; "Smallpox Vaccine Revisited; The Smallpox Vaccine," *Medscape Today,* to be found at www.medscape.com/viewarticle/447730_4; Clayre, *Heart of the Dragon,* 218–20; Stewart, *Mysteries of History,* 88–90.

2. For evidence that Zheng He knew the borders of eastern Africa, see Freedman, *Who Was First,* 25; Stewart, *Mysteries of History,* 90–91.

3. Information on the Chinese navy and its "Treasure Fleets" comes from Freedman, *Who Was First,* 20–38; Levathes, *When China Ruled the Seas;* Menzies, *1421: The Year China Discovered America;* Stewart, *Mysteries of History,* 86–93.

4. See ibid.

5. Freedman, *Who Was First,* 27–30; Menzies, *1421: The Year China Discovered America;* Stewart; *Mysteries of History,* 92.

6. Freedman, *Who Was First,* 33–34; Levathes, *When China Ruled the Seas,* 179–80; Menzies, *1421: The Year China Discovered America,* 55–56; Stewart, *Mysteries of History,* 93.

7. For information about the condition of Europe and the Western world at the time of Columbus, see Morison, *Admiral of the Ocean Sea,* 3–6; Sale, *Conquest of Paradise,* 3–46.

8. See Morison, *Admiral of the Ocean Sea,* 11.

9. Columbus, *Book of Prophecies,* 67 and 69.

10. Morison, *Admiral of the Ocean Sea,* 237.

11. Ibid., 47.

12. Ibid., 56.

13. Fernandez-Armesto, *Columbus,* 53.

14. Columbus, *Select Letters,* 105–6.

15. For accounts of Columbus's efforts to obtain patronage, see Fernandez-Armesto, *Columbus,* 45–65; Morison, *Admiral of the Ocean Sea,* 69–108.

16. See Fernandez-Armesto, *Columbus,* 73.

17. Columbus, *Journal of Christopher Columbus,* 34–35.

18. For accounts of the voyage, see Columbus, *Journal of Christopher Columbus;* Fernandez-Armesto, *Columbus,* 67–81; Horwitz, *Voyage Long and Strange,* 93–103; Morison, *Admiral of the Ocean Sea,* 153–228; Sale, *Conquest of Paradise,* 56–64.

19. See Mann, *1491,* 115–32; Schweikart and Allen, *Patriot's History,* 5–6.

20. See Mann, *1491,* 64–92; July 7, 2009, http://philtar.ucsm.ac.uk/encyclopedia/latam/inca.html.

21. See Mann, *1491;* Horwitz, *Voyage Long and Strange.*

22. For a complete discussion of the impact of Christianity on progress in the West, see Stark, *Victory of Reason.*

23. Columbus, *Select Letters,* 184.

Chapter 2

The Miracle at Jamestown

Jamestown
March 1610

SHE WAS ALMOST TWELVE, though that was impossible to tell from looking at her. Her face was pale and sunken and her body was draped in a rough cotton dress that hung across her shoulders, heavy from the rain and mud. Her hair, dull and dirty, was as brittle as dry straw, the nutrients in her body insufficient to sustain its growth. Her tiny arms looked as fragile as sticks and her fingers were long and thin from hunger. But still, her eyes were large and brimming, liquid blue and clear. And full of life and living. Even through the decimation, she was still beautiful.

She hunched against the sycamore tree, saving her strength, then lay down in the mud. It had rained the night before, hard and cold and pelting, and the earth gave way beneath her arms, leaving narrow imprints that looked like they'd been left by bare bone.

She didn't show up on any manifest. History books would never know her name. Children were rare among the colony; there were a few boys but only a handful of girls, most of whom had either been quietly smuggled aboard the ships by their parents or made to pay their passage by acting as domestic servants, an existence that was much closer to that of a slave.

Digging slowly, she pulled the mud toward her, feeling through the soft earth. One . . . two . . . three scoops. She frowned, staring at her fingers. It was too slimy here, the earth thin and gray, the ground too steeped in clay. Moving slowly, she inched down the trail, crawling like an animal deeper into the forest. Hiding behind a low bush, she stopped to listen. The Indians were near, she knew that, and if they found her, they would kill her. But the truth was, she lived with death every day—she saw it, smelled it, knew its constant presence as she knew her own breath. Over the winter she had discovered that hunger was more powerful than fear.

Kneeling, she pushed beneath a mulberry bush and started digging once again. Yes, the earth was rich here, full of rotten leaves and humus. She worked faster, her mouth beginning to water. She lifted the dirt to the dim light—the clouds were still low and the sun had barely risen—then saw the flicking tail. She grimaced as she reached for the earthworm, pulling it from the mud, long and slimy, fat and full. She ran her fingers down the length of it to scrape off some slime, then put it to her lips and sucked it in. She swallowed without chewing—no amount of hunger could make the worm taste anything but bitter—then brushed a spot of dirt from her lips and started digging again.

Some had given up, accepting the inevitable; the only thing to be decided was whether death was quick or slow. But as the meal of worms had demonstrated, she would do anything to live. Besides, earthworms weren't the worst thing she had eaten since the starving time had come.

Half an hour and two dozen earthworms later, she started feeling sick, not so much from the worms as from the dirt she'd taken in. Lying on the wet grass, she rested while she waited for the food to bring her strength, then looked up at the gray skies. In a moment of sudden disorientation, she thought she heard her mother's voice and she rolled onto her side, the horrible memory flashing through her mind: the frozen body, the cry of her brother, the bitter cold, the approaching men, one of them brandishing a knife.

She no longer pondered the things her family had given up. She no longer thought of the life they'd had before. Though it had been only two years, it seemed like a lifetime, and the memories were so dim they were less than dreamlike now. She used to have a mother and a little brother. She had only her father now. Her father had been a gentleman. He had once owned land! He had a title. He'd had barns and horses and a carriage. Now he owned nothing but a mud shack and a gun.

She could read and write! How many of the leaders of the colony could say that?

Her name was Mary Elizabeth, named after the great queen (God save her!). But no one cared about things like that anymore. The eloquence of her name, like everything else, had been sacrificed so they could come to this new world.

She didn't understand it.

And she knew she never would.

Her father was one of the leaders of the colony, and that had some advantages, it was true. But it hadn't saved her brother or her mother. And she didn't know if it would save her.

Lying there, Mary felt their presence before she heard them. Their soft feet made virtually no sound against the wet grass, but the quiet of the morning was disrupted by the moving brush just enough for her to sense that they were drawing near. The fact that she'd been lying flat when they approached was the only thing that saved her—that plus the fact that her tattered dress was brown as earth, making it possible for her to blend into the shadows. Sensing their approach, she moved farther under the brush, rolled onto her knees, then held perfectly still.

The group of Indians walked by her, near enough that she could have reached out and touched them. She heard their voices. She smelled their fur and leather clothing. She counted their ankles as they walked by. They were quiet. They were hunting.

Hunting an animal?

Or hunting her?

She didn't move. She hardly breathed. She felt her stomach rolling as a new fear pushed through her, and for a moment she thought she might be sick. She forced herself not to scream, kept her eyes open, and tried to form some kind of plan.

The four men stopped, one of them squatting down, his back hunched to her. They whispered to each other, the one on his haunches laughing quietly at something one of the others had said.

Easy to laugh when they hadn't eaten a rat for dinner and wouldn't chew on bark for lunch.

She moved her head just enough to see beyond a cluster of dripping leaves. Shadows. Leather and axes. Blood painted across their lips and cheeks and foreheads. Charcoal across their necks. Powhatan warriors. Her heart slammed and she almost whimpered again in fear.

For the past six months, the Powhatan Indians had placed Jamestown under siege, sealing it off completely and waiting for the settlers to starve. Any foreigners they found outside the fortress, they quickly killed or took as slaves, and Mary knew what her fate would be if the Powhatans found her now.

Feeling sick again, she slowly turned her head and prayed that she could hold it in.

Sensing something, one of the warriors stopped and raised his hand, indicating for the others to listen. Like Mary, the Powhatans were extremely sensitive to the natural smells and sounds of the forest, and something had caught him off guard. Noticing the sudden quiet, Mary pushed deeper beneath the brush. One of the Powhatans moved toward her. The brush moved. She closed her eyes and quit breathing. The leaves above her moved, pulled back by an unseen hand, and she felt the painful yank as an Indian grabbed her by the hair and jerked her off the ground. He held her up, her feet reaching for the mud, then turned to his friends.

"Look what I have!" he shouted as if he'd caught a great prize. "A dirty rat. Outside the fortress gates."

Mary twisted by her hair. She didn't understand everything, but she knew enough of his language to get the thrust of what he said. And even if she hadn't understood him, the lust and satisfaction in his eyes told her everything she needed to know. He was going to kill her.

There was not a hint of doubt in her mind.

But it wouldn't be for a few hours. That was what scared her even more.

She kept her eyes low, her heart ready to rupture with frustration and fear. It wasn't supposed to be like this! It wasn't supposed to be so hard! The New Land was supposed to be the Free Land, full of riches and opportunities! The New Land was to be full of promise—full of life and gold. But the only things she'd experienced since landing on the shores of the James River had been deprivation and hunger and a nearly constant fear.

"Why did we come here?" she had often pleaded to her father. "What did you hope to accomplish! What price did you expect to pay!"

Looking at the Indian who held her by the hair, she wondered the same thing now.

Holding her in a steel grip, he looked back at her and growled.

With a jerk—she was so light and empty it was like throwing a cloth doll—he tossed her against the nearest tree. She smashed her head and felt instantly sick and dizzy. The warriors gathered around her. She looked up at them like a trapped animal, her eyes darting all around. She faked a movement left, then scrambled right. The Powhatans easily maneuvered to keep her against the tree. She fell back and started crying, then looked up at the wet sky.

The warriors were laughing. The nearest one reached down and slapped her. She took a breath, her blue eyes flickering in rage, then cleared her mouth and spat.

It landed square between his eyes, brown and thick from her muddy breakfast.

The Indians stared in fury, crying words she didn't know. Grunting, the warrior lunged toward her and raised his fist to crack her skull.

The gunshot sounded from behind him and he dropped instantly, the back of his head shot open with a walnut-sized hole. He was dead before he hit the ground. The other warriors turned around.

Her father was standing in the forest, half concealed, his face glaring at the men. His hand moved and he produced a second weapon, a large barrel of a gun that was as powerful as it was inaccurate. Dropping to his right, he disappeared behind a tree. "Send her to me!" he shouted in their language. "Don't touch her, or you'll die."

Mary cried out and started crawling, but one of the warriors kicked her back.

"I have you in my sights," her father called from the undergrowth.

The Powhatans stared in anger, cursing the wicked weapon that made the colonist so powerful.

"Turn around and go!" the unseen man shouted.

The Indians glanced quickly at each other. There were three of them. One of him. They had flint axes and a dozen arrows. He had the gun, which he wouldn't have time to reload once he had shot it. There was no doubt that they could kill him, but at least one of them would die.

Was it worth it?

Glaring in rage toward each other, they signaled their decision, then turned and slipped into the forest, their shadows fading in the morning light.

Mary didn't move for a long moment. She and her father both waited, making certain they were gone. Then she scrambled to her feet, ran toward her father, and fell nearly unconscious in his arms.

Gently he carried her back to the fortress. Jumping the narrow sewage drain that surrounded the log walls protecting the dying colony, he walked toward the main gate, signaling to the watchmen who waited there. As they passed through the low door cut into the walls, she opened her eyes and looked up at him. "I want to go home, Father," she said.

He motioned to the fortress. "We're home, angel," he told her. She shook her head listlessly. "No, Papa. I want to go home. I want to go back to England."

He closed his eyes and looked away from her. "I understand," he said.

A Long, Hard Road of Failure

The settlement of what would later become known as the United States of America did not happen easily, nor without a significant price paid in human life and suffering.

For the English, it began in what is now known as Virginia on the Chesapeake Bay, which was first sighted by Spanish explorer Pedro de Quejo in 1525. However, all of the Spanish settlement activity in the 1500s occurred to the south, which was much more rich in gold and treasure, and there is no record of the Chesapeake Bay being visited again until 1561, when a Spanish ship was driven off course, ending up at the mouth of the bay. The captain sailed his ship up a river and anchored to take in provisions and make repairs. While there, some of his crew members were approached by a small band of Indians, one of whom agreed, with his servant, to accompany the ship back to Spain. He took on the name of Don Luis de Velasco and for the next nine years spent time in the Spanish court, where he was a favorite of the king, and then in Mexico City. During this time he converted to Christianity, pledging his faith to the Catholic religion.

While Don Luis was spending his time in Spain, learning of the Catholic religion and European ways, the Spanish governor of Florida, Pedro Menendez de Aviles, had been given the task of assuring that no other European power created any colonies from whence pirates could be launched to attack the Spanish treasure fleets. Bent on accomplishing this mission, he established a series of Spanish settlements along the southern coast, among which was Saint Augustine, founded in 1566, the first permanent European colony in the United States.

In 1570, Pedro Menendez de Aviles directed Don Luis to return to his native land, accompanied by a small group of Catholic missionaries. The men sailed into the Chesapeake Bay and disembarked at a location not far from where Jamestown would be established some thirty-seven years later.

Apparently, nine years among the Christians had not quite taken for Don Luis; soon after his arrival back in America, he rejected his Christian faith and rejoined his family. During the coming winter, the small group of destitute missionaries that had traveled with him to the Chesapeake Bay suffered from bitter cold and biting hunger. Three were sent to Don Luis to seek his help. Instead of assisting the starving missionaries, Don Luis killed them, then led a raid against their camp, killing everyone but a small boy who was later rescued by the Spanish.

So it was that the first Spanish settlement along the James River came to an ignoble end.

After learning of the missionaries' fate, the Spanish governor saw no value in further colonizing the area. Still, he remained extraordinarily vigilant against any attempts by the French or English to establish settlements that might pose a threat to Spanish territory or shipments of precious bullion back to the mother country.[1]

The French Give It a Try

Multiple attempts at settling the Atlantic coast by non-Spanish colonists varied only in the scope and timing of their failures.

In the latter half of the 1500s, a group of French citizens known as the Huguenots committed the unpardonable sin of becoming Protestants, members of the Reformed Church established in 1550 by John Calvin. Some Catholic monarchs of France decided they were enemies of the state and demanded their extermination. In March 1562, twelve hundred Huguenots were massacred at Vassy, France. For the next three decades, wars of religion would roil through France.

It was natural, then, that some of the Huguenots might want to find another home.

In the latter half of the sixteenth century, one of their leaders,

Admiral Gaspard de Coligny, won the Queen's permission to establish a Huguenot colony on the Atlantic coast of North America. The Queen's motivation was not simply that she wanted a place to get rid of the Calvinists; she also wanted a base from whence the French could raid the Spanish treasure ships.

Admiral Coligny's first colony, near modern-day Beaufort, South Carolina, failed. In 1564, a second group of three hundred Huguenot colonizers established a settlement at the mouth of the St. Johns River in Florida, the site of modern-day Jacksonville. Fort Caroline was its name and, in typical French fashion, one of its first buildings was a bakery, one of the first crops planted, grapes.

For a short time, the French made out by trading with the Indians. However, they simply did not know how to sustain themselves and either would not or could not learn to farm, fish, and hunt.

When the Huguenots ran out of goods to trade, they began to steal from the Indians or took hostages as bargaining chips. Unfortunately for them, the French proved to be as poor at raiding at they were at hunting and, one year after their arrival, they were living on nuts, roots, and berries. The colony's leader, René de Laudonnière, decided to abandon the settlement.

Then, in quick succession, Fort Caroline was visited by three fleets of ships.

The first was led by the English pirate John Hawkins, who had sympathy for his fellow Protestants and gave them food.

The second was a fleet from France with provisions and new colonists, raising the number of inhabitants of Fort Caroline to about eight hundred.

The third fleet to set upon the colony was manned by Spanish soldiers who came neither as a rescue party nor in peace. Indeed, they came to destroy the colony, for the Spanish governor, Pedro Menendez de Aviles, had taken it upon himself to kill every Calvinist he could find.

After a brief skirmish, the Spanish were forced to retreat, sailing to the south. Most of the French ships pursued them but were blown out to sea by a hurricane. Menendez then attacked Fort Caroline by land with a force of five hundred, and the fort was quickly taken, with only a handful of defenders able to retreat to their ships and flee to France. Menendez slaughtered 142 others, reluctantly allowing, in spite of their "horrid" religion, about fifty women and children to live.

A few days later, Menendez was informed that the French fleet had returned. Marching fearlessly to engage them, he discovered that the French had been shipwrecked and were now at his mercy—mercy he did not possess. He arranged for the Huguenots to surrender and then killed most of them anyway, sparing only those who would confess to being "Christians" (Catholic) and who also had skills that he needed. (Ironically, he did show an interest in the arts by sparing any musicians as well.) He also made a great show of his Christian decency by agreeing to kill his captives quickly by stabbing them or cutting off their heads instead of burning them to death, which was what so many of his men were hoping he would do.

With the Frenchmen killed or captured and the colony destroyed, the Spaniards sailed off.

Another settlement. Another failure. The French didn't return to the mid-Atlantic region again.

For several generations, St. Augustine remained the only successful European settlement on the east coast, a military outpost whose sole purpose was to defend the Spanish treasure ships as they sailed the prevailing currents that would take them back to Spain.[2]

The First English Attempts at Settling the New World

In the last half of the sixteenth century, Queen Elizabeth became enthused about the prospects for English colonization of the mid-Atlantic area. Her reasons for aggressive English colonization were three-fold. First, the Indians could be proselytized. Second, the creation of overseas colonies would provide a source of raw materials as well as an area in which she could disperse England's surplus population. But the most important reason the queen wanted to colonize the New World had nothing to do with missionaries or farming and everything to do with Spain.

Spain had accumulated enormous wealth from the New World. As it became frighteningly powerful, Queen Elizabeth grew more and more anxious. She realized that the primary motivation that drove both countries to colonize was centered in the religious war between the Catholics and the Protestants, and that the Spanish monarch intended not only to spread the Catholic faith in the New World but to use his wealth to stamp out Protestant heresy in the Old World as well. Faced with a growing rival and religious pressure from her people, Queen Elizabeth realized that English colonies along the eastern seaboard could serve as launching points for sacking Spanish bullion ships, a tactic she believed would weaken Spain in both the Old and the New World.

Initially, the English imitated the pattern of failure by non-Spanish Europeans. Off and on during the 1500s, various groups of Englishmen attempted settlements—all of which ended in death and failure.

Two of the more prominent failures occurred in 1576 and 1578, when efforts to find gold and a northwest passage on the southern shore of Baffin Island ended in financial disaster for the sponsors. Those attempts were followed by Sir Humphrey Gilbert's efforts to establish colonies in Newfoundland and along the North American coast, which ended in financial failure and the death at sea of Gilbert.

Gilbert's royal charter from Queen Elizabeth passed to his flamboyant half-brother, Sir Walter Raleigh. A favorite of the queen, Raleigh was a warrior who dreamed of accomplishing what his brother had not. In 1585, Raleigh sent ships with 108 men to settle Roanoke, an island off the North Carolina coast. Under the royal charter, he was entitled to an area that extended 600 miles from his colony—thus he laid claim to everything from the Carolinas to Maine. Raleigh named his colony *Virginia,* after the "Virgin Queen" Elizabeth.

His first effort failed for the same reasons many had before: the colonists' inability to procure their own food except by stealing it from the Indians, the inclusion among the settlers of too many English "gentlemen" unaccustomed to physical labor, and a desire for quick riches that was fulfilled exclusively through pirating Spanish ships. In 1586, the first Roanoke settlement was abandoned except for eighteen men who were left to man the fort. When more settlers returned the next year, they found the fort destroyed and no sign of the eighteen men. Because it was too late in the year to plant crops, the leader of that group, John White, decided to go back to England and return with provisions. He departed for England in August, leaving 113 colonists behind, including his daughter and grandchild, Virginia Dare, the first English child born in Virginia.

White's return to the settlement was delayed for three years, due primarily to the invasion of Great Britain by the Spanish Armada. To his despair, when he finally made it back to America, he found that Roanoke had been abandoned and all of the inhabitants had disappeared.

While the fate of the "Lost Colony" rose up as a dark and unsolved mystery, this much appeared to be clear: the inability to produce food, along with the presence of hostile Indians and the harshness of the environment, made it impossible for European settlements along the mid-Atlantic coast to be successful.

Seventeen years later, Jamestown would demonstrate if that was true.[3]

Jamestown
April 1610

MARY'S FATHER WRAPPED her in a dirty blanket as they hunched by the evening fire, a small glow of wet wood smoldering at the bottom of a pit. An earlier storm had blown off toward the ocean, leaving mud and dripping leaves behind it, but a south wind had taken up, and it was warmer now than it had been in the afternoon.

Her father sniffed the air. "Spring is coming," he said hopefully.

Mary leaned against his arm, her eyes moving to the leather pouch he had placed beside him. She knew what was inside it. His treasure.

His hope. His reason for bringing them to this hell he called the New World. She stared down at the pouch of charts and maps. They used to fascinate her, but something had happened over the past month or two, and she didn't care about them anymore.

Her father reached down and pulled out several leather charts. "I want to show you something," he said as he unfolded them with great care, the mud underneath his fingernails dark and thick. "Do you understand where we are on this map?" he asked her.

Mary glanced at him, a bit insulted by the question. "I do, Father," she answered simply. Near the top of the chart, the James River and Chesapeake Bay ran northwest from the open ocean, and a hand-drawn outline of the eastern coast was depicted by a thin line that ran north and south. She gently touched their location on the map. Her father nodded, then pulled out another map. It contained huge expanses of emptiness and uncharted lands, but the general outline of the east coast and the Gulf of Mexico was clear. The southern tip of Florida was in the corner, Mexico City along the western edge. Pointing, her father grunted, "Do you realize, my little angel, that we're in a life-and-death race against the Spaniards?"

Mary listened intently as her father moved his hand across the map.

"They be our enemy," he continued bitterly. "Have been for a hundred years. Since my grandfather was a baby. Maybe even longer." He glanced down to see that she was listening. "Following Columbus's discovery of the New World, Spain set out to claim every foot of earth, every gold nugget, every vein of silver for their own." He stopped and pointed to a spot on the map. "A hundred years ago, Ponce de Leon claimed Puerto Rico." He moved his thin finger. "Then Jamaica, and then Cuba. Soon after, he walked the southern tip of Florida, the first European to touch this soil.

"After Ponce de Leon, Balboa hacked his way through the jungles here," he tapped the map again at a narrow neck of land in the south, "and found out the Pacific Ocean was just an eight-day walk from the Atlantic shore. The city of Panama was then established, giving Spain another base on this continent." He swept his hand north and south.

"In 1521, they set about to conquer two of the mightiest empires in history, the Aztecs of Mexico and the Incas of Peru, two empires that were awash in gold and silver. For generations now, they have shipped tons of bullion back to the motherland, making Spain the wealthiest nation of us all. But to keep the treasure that makes them rich, they have to ship it. And to ship it, they have to protect it. That is why they have built a series of military outposts along this coast.

"Meanwhile, survivors of the expedition led by the Catholic conquistador Panfilo de Narvaez explored the lands for a thousand miles to the north of Mexico, returning with tales of the Seven Cities of gold. Francisco Coronado went searching for them." He swept his hands across the vast emptiness that would one day be called Arizona, New Mexico, Texas, Oklahoma, and central Kansas. "Two years later he returned with tales, not of gold but of a desert, fertile plains, great herds of animals, and an enormous canyon." Her father made a final gesture across the incredible vastness that would be Florida, Georgia, South Carolina, North Carolina, Tennessee, Alabama, Mississippi, Arkansas, Oklahoma, and Texas. "From 1539 until 1543, Hernando de Soto explored much of the rest of this huge continent, leaving Spain with claims to most of North America as well."

Mary studied the irregular chart, something her father had copied from the king's court back in England. It was rough and certainly not one they could use for navigation, but it gave a sense of what had taken place over the past hundred years.

Her father, an educated man, a gentleman, lowered his voice in awe. "The Spanish kingdom has become the most powerful kingdom in the world. King Philip's reach is terrifying, for he claims more lands than the Romans did at the height of their empire. From the Philippines to Mexico, from Central America to the most southern tip of land, from the central portion of the land upon which we sit to Portugal and Spain, the sun does not set on the Spanish empire. Millions of natives have been converted to Catholicism—converted by the sword or killed. Cities have been established. Universities and cathedrals have been built. More than two hundred settlements have been created in Mexico as well as in the nameless lands that lie just north of there."

Her father's voice trailed off, and he stared at the fire until Mary looked up at him.

"I know that it's been difficult," he whispered as if speaking to himself. "No one of us foretold this." He gestured weakly to the devastation all around him. "But for three years now, we've been fighting to make a run of this place. For three years we've been trying to put England's blessed mark upon this ground. We've paid a terrible price, far greater than any of us should have had to bear. But it's important, Mary, this settlement of Jamestown. And there's a reason we are here. We have to keep on fighting. We have to keep on living. We can't give up and lose our hope."

A New Century, A New Chance in the New World

By 1607, much had changed in both the New and Old Worlds. The Spanish had consolidated their hold on Florida and the southwestern United States—Santa Fe was established as the region's capital in 1610—while, to the north, the French were laying claim to Canada and the northern areas of the future United States.

Although the English were lagging in the New World, the defeat of the Spanish Armada gave them fresh confidence. A new model for colonizing was also developed. The Virginia Company, a stock venture, was formed with investors entitled to share in the risks and profits.

Another change was the emergence of a new kind of colonist—John Smith being the prototype.

Assuming the truth of his own biography, Smith lived an extraordinary life. Raised as a farmer's son, he fled a forced apprenticeship to see the world, became a soldier of fortune and an expert artilleryman, fought the Ottoman Turks, was captured and sold into slavery, charmed his mistress, escaped after killing her cruel brother, wandered Europe, sailed to North Africa, and ended up on a pirate ship, all of this before he was in his late twenties.

When it became apparent that the Old World had nothing new to offer, he decided to venture to the New World.

Smith was part of the Virginia Company's three-ship fleet dispatched to make a settlement in Virginia. During the voyage, he ended up in chains for mutiny but was rescued when, upon arriving in the New World in April of 1607, the colonists opened sealed orders naming the twenty-seven-year-old as one of the seven rulers of the colony.

The 105 colonists chose a site, a swampy peninsula thirty-five miles up the James River from the Chesapeake Bay, a location not far from where the Spanish missionaries had been killed by Don Luis almost forty years before.

They began their adventure with high hopes. But when the spring beauty wore off, the harsh realities of life in the New World hit them hard. Death, hunger, and disease soon followed, setting a pattern for what was to come. Indeed, of the first twenty thousand Englishmen sent to settle in Virginia, it is estimated that an astonishing fifteen thousand of them died premature deaths.[4]

In the case of Jamestown, the location of the settlement forced the settlers to drink from the brackish James River. Dysentery, typhoid fever, salt poisoning, and heatstroke took their toll. Worse, the Indians did not like the Europeans' taking up residence in their hunting domain, and the Jamestown settlers were subject to frequent attacks and acts of thievery.

The colonists also fought among themselves. Leaders were overthrown with regularity. "Gentlemen" who had been afforded royal treatment in England, and who were totally unaccustomed to physical labor or hardship, did not pull their weight and were spectacularly incapable of motivating their lessers to do what was necessary for their survival.

By September, few members of the colony survived. Then, without explanation, the Indians, who seemed to have been killing them for sport, had an unexpected change of heart. After the Indians had visited Jamestown with bread, corn, fish, and meat, the colonists began to realize that they were dependent upon the surrounding Indian nation to survive. Smith was smart enough to see it first. He became responsible for supplying the colony with food and did so over the next two years by a combination of charm and gunboat diplomacy. Using the river system, Smith traveled extensively to trade and acquire supplies. If a village attempted to drive too hard a bargain, a shot from a cannon into a tree helped to hasten more favorable negotiations.

Early on, Smith was captured and taken before the mighty Powhatan. It was during this first encounter that Smith claims to have been saved from having his head smashed when Powhatan's ten-year-old daughter, Pocahontas, threw herself on him. Some question this account, along with Smith's biography in general, but regardless, Smith became the most valuable intermediary between Powhatan and the colony.

Pocahontas helped both Smith and the Jamestown settlement in a number of ways. She brought food, warned of plots to kill Smith and impending attacks on the settlement by her father, and once intervened in saving other captured Englishmen. In 1614, at age seventeen, Pocahontas married John Rolfe and moved to London, where she became a popular figure.

Eventually Smith asserted himself as the leader of Jamestown and proceeded to whip the colony into shape. "He that will not work shall not eat," he ordered, an idea that would shape the developing society that would become the United States for hundreds of years to come. Under his firm control a well was dug, houses built, corn planted, military training conducted, and additional protective structures erected.

A New and Eternal Source of Wealth

Perhaps Smith's greatest contribution to the development of the United States was the fact that he was one of the first Europeans to see that America's wealth did not lie in gold and silver, nor in an easy route to the Orient, but rather in the land's bountiful natural resources. Soon he started demanding that England only send men to his colony who were able to work and who possessed the skills, knowledge, and desire to tap those natural resources, making it clear that he wanted no pampered gentlemen. During his tenure, his men worked not only to grow corn but to produce pitch, tar, soap, glass, and wood products to be sent to England.

Perhaps most unusual for his era, Smith put into action his belief that one had to earn wealth and respect, not inherit it. Merit counted, not birth. But although this belief would ultimately distinguish the America of the future, it didn't, unfortunately, define the English colony of Jamestown in 1609. Smith was too far ahead of his time, and the demands he made of certain gentlemen colonists were his undoing.

By the early spring of 1609, despite Smith's best efforts, Jamestown was in disarray. Promised ships had not arrived with provisions. A number of colonists had deserted to Powhatan and were doing everything they could to encourage others to do the same. Powhatan was becoming more aggressive. There was incessant infighting among the colonists for leadership. Some refused to work at all. Rebellion and mutiny were just below the surface.[5]

The Enemy Comes to Jamestown

In 1609, the Virginia Company arranged for a massive infusion of colonists and provisions for Jamestown. Eventually, nine ships were to sail to Virginia with more than five hundred new colonists bound for the Chesapeake Bay. The first ship, the *Mary and John,* was sent in early May with instructions to find a more direct route to Jamestown than the Southern Passage.

This early departure date, as well as the fact that the ship was to take the most direct route to the New Land, proved to be profoundly important, for the Spanish had already decided that they had had enough of the uppity English and their new colony at Jamestown. A small warship, commanded by Captain Francisco Ecija, was sent from St. Augustine with instructions to spy on the English colony to determine how difficult it would be to annihilate it. Had Ecija found the colony in its current state of weakness and despair, he likely would have destroyed it at that time.

Feeling confident, Ecija sailed north at a leisurely pace, arriving at the Chesapeake Bay on July 14. To his surprise, he spotted a large vessel, the *Mary and John,* that appeared to be guarding the entrance to the bay. Concluding that a victory against the larger ship was unlikely, the Spaniard ran. The English gave chase, but Ecija escaped under darkness of night.

History shows that the English ship in the Bay had arrived *just the day before.*

Had the *Mary and John* not taken the shorter route from England, or had Ecija been just a few hours quicker in his journey, he would have discovered Jamestown in all of its weakness and disarray, allowing the Spaniard to attack the colony at its most fragile time.

Had that been the case, the history of the United States might have proven to be very different.

As it was, for a few months at least, Jamestown was saved.[6]

• • •

In early June, the remaining ships under contract with the Virginia Company set sail. The fleet was led by the *Sea Venture,* which carried Sir Thomas Gates, the newly designated governor of Jamestown. Seven other ships followed.

Near the coast of North America, a fierce storm hit the fleet. The *Sea Venture* was separated from the remaining ships and blown to Bermuda, where it was broken up, the crew forced to remain on the island until the next spring.

In mid-August, six of the remaining relief ships made their way up the James River. The arrival of the ships with their valuable cargo of provisions and new colonists brought the number of Jamestown settlers to five hundred. However, it also brought even more discord among the leaders of the colony.[7]

By the fall of 1609, John Smith had had enough. After an apparent attempt upon his life, he abandoned his hopes for the colony and returned to England.

Without Smith to act as a buffer between the Indians and the colonists, their relationship quickly deteriorated. Powhatan, tired of the settlers' use of terror and aggression, and dealing as well with a severe drought that jeopardized his own people's ability to survive the coming winter, declared war on the colony. Englishmen who were sent to trade for food were slaughtered. Colonists found outside the settlement were hunted. Beginning in the fall of 1609, the Indians undertook a siege of the colony—then watched and waited for the colonists to die.[8]

Jamestown
June 1610

MARY STOOD KNEE-DEEP in the lapping water of the James River. It was brown and murky and cold, the sun creating a thousand shimmering diamonds across the small bay that lay to the west of the fort. Just six weeks before, patches of ice had been floating down the river (later scientists would call the time she lived in the "Little Ice Age"), but the water was warming now, though it still was cold enough to sting. While she bathed, she kept her eyes moving, nervous as a cornered animal, but the afternoon was quiet. Most of the Powhatan warriors had moved up the river in their canoes the day before.

Dipping into the water, she scrubbed and scrubbed, using crushed tree bark as a sponge. As good as the water felt, her stomach, always empty, was taut, and she tired quickly from the work.

Half an hour later, clean for the first time in months, she sat drying on the shore. The sun was low now and losing its heat. She heard a slapping sound and looked upriver, afraid the Indians might have returned, then glanced nervously behind her at the dilapidated fort, gaps in the wood showing where some of the timbers had been pulled down for firewood. She watched movement through the openings in the walls, listened to the familiar voices, then heard the flapping once again. Standing, she shaded her eyes against the setting sun and looked across the river.

A sudden flutter carried on the wind toward her. Fabric slapping in the wind.

She looked south. Down the river.

For a moment she didn't move.

Two ships were sailing toward her, moving slowly against the current. For a long moment she only stared at them in disbelief; then she turned and ran.

An hour later, Sir Thomas Gates moved through what remained of the village, his hand held over his mouth and nose to protect him from the stench. He thought he and his crew had been challenged by being shipwrecked in Bermuda for the winter, but, looking around him, he realized their challenges had been nothing in comparison. The smell of death was everywhere—the fort, if you were gracious enough to call it that, hardly more than a crypt for the dying and the dead. Everyone he saw looked like a skeleton. How had these people survived? A naked woman—at least, he *thought* it was a woman—burst from a dilapidated house and ran toward him, screaming in a raspy voice, "We are starving! We are starving!" When she grabbed one of his sailors, he was forced to push her back, dropping her into the mud.

Standing in the middle of the colony that had been called Jamestown, Gates shook his head in despair. The church was deserted, unused for months. Entire sections of the walls had been torn down. Houses had been moved from their dirt foundations and axed apart for wood. The colony was barely habitable, reminding him of an ancient ruin much more than a fort.

He took a long breath and glanced toward his ships moored in the river, then back to the fort again.

This was the king's colony in the Americas! This was the place they had staked their future on!

He sniffed the rank air, thinking he might throw up, then turned to the desperate survivors, who gazed at him with empty and sunken eyes. "Who is in command here?" he demanded.

The faces stared at him as if he were a vision sent from God. "Food!" one of them muttered.

The captain shook his head again.

After the sun had set, the surviving men of Jamestown, Mary's father among them, met with the newcomers inside the dilapidated church. Forbidden to enter, Mary had snuck into a small crawl space where she had hunted for rodents many times before. Pulling herself up through the tiny compartment behind the firewood chute, she slipped into the corner of the chapel, out of sight but within earshot of everything that was said. The chapel was illuminated by a few candles, which cast the men's faces in shadows that flickered with the dancing flames. A soft draft worked through the open room, and smoke from the outside cooking fires drifted through the holes in the walls. Having feasted on dried fish and bread, those villagers who were strong enough were ready now to talk.

Sir Gates explained how he and his fellow voyagers had been shipwrecked in Bermuda, where they had spent the winter building the two small ships that now sat in the James River. The surviving leaders of Jamestown told of their own winter. The siege of the Powhatans. The starving time. The deaths.

The captain sat and listened, horrified by what he learned.

"How many, then?" he asked.

"Sixty. Maybe fewer." Mary's father answered quietly. "We haven't counted in two or three days."

Sir Gates hesitated, then sadly shook his head. "More than sixty dead . . ."

Mary's father lifted his hollow eyes. "No, sir. Sixty left alive. Four hundred and forty dead."

Gates stared in disbelief and swallowed tightly, his Adam's apple bobbing in his throat. "No . . . no . . . it couldn't be. Sixty of you living! Four hundred and forty dead!"

Mary's father shook his head and kept his eyes down. "There are no more," he said.

Mary peeked around the corner, watching her father. She wanted to cry for him, knowing the pain he must have felt. The room was quiet for a moment as her father pulled his fingers through his beard.

She could hear him breathing. She could hear the night wind blowing through the trees. She could hear the pounding of her heart.

"Four hundred and forty souls lost," Gates whispered to himself. "Four hundred and forty souls . . ."

Mary's father looked away, his face ashamed. "It's been a hard time," he whispered in an understatement that bordered on absurd.

Stealing a glance in her direction—yes, he had known that she was there—he rubbed his hands together as he thought. Cannibalism was surely the lowest point a human being could fall to, and that point had been reached time and time again during the starving time. The colonists had eaten everything imaginable: horses, dogs, cats, rats, mice, excrement, and human flesh, those who died too often consumed by those fortunate enough to discover their dead bodies.

He shivered as he thought, then turned back to Sir Thomas Gates. "We are ready to go home," he said.

Gates stared at him, then looked out into the darkness beyond the partially open door. "Is there any hope?" he wondered aloud.

The desperation in the faces that stared back at him were the only answer he would get.

"The fort will be abandoned," he announced. "You have suffered too much already. It is time to let the dream of Jamestown go."

Over the next few days, the little food that had been brought up from Bermuda was distributed among the surviving colonists. The small ships were loaded with whatever remained of value, which was precious little, and prepared for sailing. On June 7, a little more than three years after the colony had first been settled, four ships set sail down the river, leaving Jamestown behind.

Mary and her father stood near the bow of the first ship as it sailed south. The captain held the vessel in the center of the river, hoping for a stronger current, and the passing breeze brushed the hair away from Mary's face. Her father, standing beside her, turned back to stare at the abandoned colony, which was fading quickly in the haze. His wife was buried there. His only son. His dreams were also buried there. Mary reached out for his hand.

"Like every other English settlement in the New World," he whispered, "Jamestown will be only a memory."

Mary squeezed his fingers, feeling the thin flesh and bone. He looked down and smiled at her, then turned and went to help the sailors prepare the small ship for the open sea.

That night the ships moored at the mouth of the Chesapeake Bay. Morning came. The ships waited for the tides to turn. The day turned quiet and calm, heavy with humidity. The Chesapeake Bay, more than twenty miles wide, had very limited visibility throughout the summer, but the thick haze on this day was going to make it particularly difficult to navigate. Mary stood motionless at the bow of the ship, the waters of the bay slapping gently at the wood below her. She smelled the salty mist, for they had crossed the boundary that separated the fresh water from the sea. Nothing but haze and water spread before her, the grayness of the air melting into the silver waters of the sea that lay just beyond a narrow jut of land. She closed her eyes and almost fell asleep while standing.

For the first time in months, she wasn't hungry. For the first time in months, she wasn't afraid. They were going back to England.

She thought she would be happy. But she wasn't.

The morning passed in silence. Mary remained at the bow of the small ship, staring through the haze. The sun was climbing to its peak when something caught her eye. She leaned across the wooden bow and squinted into the gray mist.

A longboat filled with six men was rowing desperately toward them. Behind the rowboats, barely visible, were three large ships.

She stared, unable for a moment to comprehend just what she was seeing.

Her father walked up behind her. "Do you see them?" he asked.

She nodded hesitantly. Her mind was slowly turning, her heart skipping in her chest.

"Who are they, Father?" she asked.

He didn't answer.

"Where did they come from?"

He didn't know.

They watched the approaching rowboats. "How did they find us?" she wondered. "How did they know that we were here?" She looked out over the vast bay, miles of haze and water, to the open ocean before them. They were the only ships within a thousand miles, perhaps the only ships in this entire hemisphere. "Another hour and we would have slipped into the ocean," she murmured. "We would have sailed away to England. We would have . . . we would have . . ." Her voice trailed off.

Her father looked down at her, shaking his head. "I can't explain it," he said.

Mary pressed her lips together and took a breath.

Minutes passed in silence. The rowboat approached the starboard side, the oarsmen slapping at the water and calling to the sailors who manned the ship. Mary watched their work intently, then turned away. A peaceful feeling settled over her, pushing the anxiety away.

"You understand what this means?" her father asked, his voice heavy with the choice that lay before them.

Mary thought a long moment. "I understand," she said.

"Will you stay with me?" he asked her.

She slowly bowed her head, her blonde hair shining in the mist.

● ● ●

How did the supply ships locate and catch the survivors as they were fleeing Jamestown?

The small ships would have been barely visible, nothing more than tiny spots of gray on the open water. The fact that the two sets of ships, their presence unknown to each other, happened into contact was impossibly unlikely. A few more hours—a few more minutes, even—and the colonists from Jamestown would have passed the supply ships without being seen. They would have continued on their journey, leaving the Americas behind.

But the supply ships *did* find the survivors. And the leaders convinced the colonists to stay.

In the context of their sufferings, perhaps that was the greatest miracle of all. Despite everything they had lived through—despite the fact that almost 90 percent of them had died—despite their suffering, fear, and hunger, *the colonists agreed to stay.*

They turned around, sailed up the James River, unpacked at Jamestown, and started to build again.[9]

• • •

Notwithstanding the settlers' willingness to return to Jamestown, the hardship wasn't over.

Several times over the next fifteen years, the colony almost failed— the most serious challenge occurring in 1622 when a widespread Indian uprising resulted in the death of almost one-quarter of the colonists.

Still, despite these challenges, it wasn't long before Virginia emerged as a resounding success.

A system was devised whereby men of little means could own their own small tracts of land. Agriculture proved to be lucrative, particularly the growing of tobacco, which had taken Europe by storm. English legal and governing practices were also introduced. Beginning in 1618, English common law was adopted. The following year, a representative assembly was established to govern the growing colony. The first meeting of the General Assembly convened in July 1619 and dealt with everything from relations with the Indians to laws governing Sabbath observance to the price of tobacco.

The essential elements of hard work, personal responsibility, ownership of private property, merit over inherited privilege, the rule of law, and self-government took such quick root in English North America that by the time of the American Revolution, the colonies enjoyed a higher standard of living than any other nation on earth.[10]

What If?

What if the Jamestown survivors had sailed a day earlier and not met the supply boats? What if, in the summer haze, the ships had not been seen? What if Jamestown had simply been written off as irrefutable evidence that Englishmen were not intended to live in the New World? What would have happened had the colonists not, despite their incredible suffering, been willing to return?

What if John Smith had not been among the first group of settlers? What if Pocahontas had not saved his life?

What if the Spanish captain Ecija had arrived a single day earlier and had been able to destroy Jamestown as he had the power to do?

What if the earlier Spanish settlements had proven successful, preventing English claim on the mid-Atlantic region?

What if the Spanish governor in Florida had succeeded in killing the English Protestants at Jamestown as he had the Huguenots of Fort Caroline?

What if Jamestown had not paved the way for the Puritans who shortly followed in Massachusetts? The Pilgrims of 1620 considered the option of settling in Guinea, as had previous groups of Puritan believers. Had Jamestown failed, they might have settled there or elsewhere in the West Indies or the Caribbean. Had English colonization been diverted, the vacuum in North America would most likely have been filled by the Spanish, who had already laid claim to much of what is now the United States of America.

It's important to realize that the motivations, attitudes, and practices of the Spanish settlements differed from the English ones in *very* substantial ways.

First, the Spanish ruled their possessions in the New World with an iron fist. All laws governing the New World came from Spain. Conformity in religion and bureaucracy was demanded and largely obtained. On the other hand, beginning with Jamestown, the English allowed for local self-government. The practice of consent and participation of the governed was firmly ingrained in the English colonies. Such an approach to government was never a part of the Spanish settlements.

Second, the Spanish possessions had a monopoly religion— Catholicism. On the other hand, North America was a repository of many religious sects. By the time of the American Revolution, there were seventeen religions with multiple congregations in the United States. Religious dissent nurtured political dissent. The English discovered what the Spanish never did: that the combination of political freedom and religious diversity resulted in the unleashing of economic vitality.

Third, the English colonists brought with them a firm belief in, and experience with, capitalism. They were referred to derisively by their European enemies as a "nation of shopkeepers." The Spanish colonists had neither belief nor experience in capitalism. They were not going to the New World to claim land for farming or to start new businesses, but rather to extract what mineral wealth they could find. They had little motivation to stay, and most did not. The English colonists, on the other hand, after realizing that North America was not blessed with easily obtained gold and silver, were motivated by the desire to own land or businesses. They were there to stay. They were there to produce.

Fourth, in Spanish America, most of the land was controlled by upper-class hidalgos who owned massive estates that were completely dependent on indigenous people for labor. In North America, it was relatively easy for a poverty-stricken Englishman who had made his way to the New World to eventually become "landed."

One other significant difference was the approach to education. In the English colonies, education was deemed to be of great importance, and the responsibility to educate the people was accepted by each new colony as it was established. In the Spanish colonies, education was deemed to be the responsibility of the monopolistic Catholic church, which lacked the resources to educate anyone but the upper classes. Further, the Catholic church actively discouraged education among the poorer people, curbing even the ownership of Bibles. Amazingly, the differences in the views toward education were such that, on the eve of the American Civil War, a higher percentage of black American slaves were educated than the percentage in the general population of almost all South and Central American nations.

Finally, and of greatest importance, the colonial revolts that ended the rule of the English were the result of a long process of evolutionary political thought by which the English residents of North America concluded that the king had no right to rule them. This resulted in a commonality among the English colonies that allowed them to ultimately establish a new, united nation. The Spanish colonies, once freed from the control of Spain, immediately began to break up and engage in petty warfare. They never did unite under a common understanding of the role of government, the rights of the people, and the value of unity.[11]

• • •

The success of Jamestown assured the lasting presence of the English in North America. From its feeble and tenuous beginnings sprang the settlement of the eastern seaboard by English colonists and other Europeans similarly motivated. These English colonies became the hothouse where self-government was nurtured, personal responsibility was rewarded, tolerance of religion evolved, and private property for the masses became the norm.

Jamestown assured the planting of those seeds that grew to become the immensely successful American experiment.

But before all of that happened, it came down to one miraculous day. A deserted colony. A few starving survivors. A handful of ships that happened upon each other at the mouth of the bay. And the courage of the survivors who agreed to set aside their fear and hunger and go back to rebuild the colony again.

Notes

1. Information on the early Spanish settlement of North America comes from Elliott, *Empires of the Atlantic;* Horn, *Land As God Made It,* 1–10; Horwitz, *Voyage Long and Strange,* 86–430; Morison and Commager, *Growth of the American Republic,* 19–35; Schweikart and Allen, *Patriot's History,* 3–12.
2. Information on the early attempts of the French to settle in Florida comes from

Horwitz, *Voyage Long and Strange,* 433–79; Schweikart and Allen, *Patriot's History,* 12–13.

3. Information on the early attempts at English settlements, including the Lost Colony, comes from Horn, *Land As God Made It,* 22–33; Horwitz, *Voyage Long and Strange,* 480–532; Morison and Commager, *Growth of the American Republic,* 35–42; Schweikart and Allen, *Patriot's History,* 13–16.

4. Horwitz, *Voyage Long and Strange,* 538.

5. Information on John Smith and Jamestown can be found in Elliott, *Empires of the Atlantic;* Horn, *Land As God Made It,* 39–171; Horwitz, *Voyage Long and Strange,* 533–52; Schweikart and Allen, *Patriot's History,* 16–18.

6. See Horn, *Land As God Made It,* 152–56.

7. See ibid., 157–64.

8. For information about the events in Jamestown following Smith's departure, including the "starving time," see Horn, *Land As God Made It,* 171–80; Horwitz, *Voyage Long and Strange,* 552–54.

9. See Horn, *Land As God Made It,* 179–180; Horwitz, *Voyage Long and Strange,* 554.

10. McCullough, *1776,* 158.

11. For an analysis of the differences between the Spanish and English methods of colonization and the significance of those differences, see Elliott, *Empires of the Atlantic;* Schweikart and Allen, *Patriot's History,* 14–16; and Stark, *Victory of Reason.*

Chapter 3

The Miracle
of a Summer Fog

Southeastern Shore of the East River,
New York City
July 12, 1776

IT WAS HOT. MISERABLY HOT. Sticky and suffocating and humid and wet. The sun was low, burning through the empty sky and forcing him to squint against the powder-blue horizon. His rough cotton shirt stuck to his ribs, and trickles of sweat made their way down the side of his face. For a moment he thought back almost longingly on the incredible cold they had endured the winter before in Boston, realizing with irony that the summer of 1776 was as hellishly long and hot as the previous winter had been deadly cold.

The American soldier stood in a thicket at the edge of the East River and stared toward the opposite bank, about a mile away. The shore around him stank of estuary and clams and muddy water, for the river was more of a tidal bowl than a river. He had rowed across it several times now, taking men and supplies to the other side, and he knew the river was turbulent with dangerous tides and powerful currents that could force a boat crew to row for their lives. Across the river, the buttes rose steeply above the dangerous water, and though he couldn't see it, he knew the tiny village of Brookline (later changed to Brooklyn) sat roughly half a mile back from the shore, nothing more than a few houses and shanties and proud Tory homes built around a tiny Dutch church along Jamaican Road. From where the young soldier stood, half concealed in the brush, he could clearly see the newly constructed forts that stood guard over the river. Fort Stirling, carved into the rock and earth atop the highest bluff, was the centerpiece of their defenses, but from where he stood he could also see Fort Putnam, Fort Greene, and Fort Box. All of them were designed to protect the river and by extension the city, which was the key to the whole deal.

It really was that simple.

To save their nation, they had to defend New York. To defend the city, they had to defend the bluffs along the Long Island shore.

Looking down, he frowned, then kicked at the mud that oozed between his bare feet.

He was a young man, twenty-three, about average for a Colonial soldier. A Delaware farmer, he had a beautiful wife—slender, with long, dark hair, for whom he longed like he longed for his own breath—plus two babies, twelve acres of hay and twenty of wheat and barley, not to mention a garden designed to feed their family through the winter. Too much work for his wife and father, that was sure, and his crops would rot in the fields if he wasn't back by harvest. Worse, Congress hadn't paid him yet. Though there had been plenty of promises, they had proven hollow to this point, and the economics of serving his nation were becoming as terrifying as the thought of looming battle. What would he and his family do if he couldn't take care of his crops back in Kent County? What would they do if they couldn't feed themselves!

He wanted desperately to go home.

But he knew he had to stay.

He looked down at the piece of rough paper in his hand. He could read well enough, and the words had already been burned inside his brain.

Lifting his head, he looked down the river, then stepped back from the bank and climbed the high ground to his right. The bluff was forty, maybe fifty feet high, just enough for him to see across the bay. And what he saw there terrified him. More massive sails than he could count, a few of them gray cloth, most of them sun-bleached white. The sails were wrapped as the ships sat at anchor, but the Union Jacks fastened at each ship's bow snapped in the wind. They had been coming for weeks now—some days twenty, some days a dozen, some days thirty at a time. A few weeks back, forty additional British ships had set anchor off of Staten Island in a single day, and no one knew for certain how many enemy ships were assembled in the bay now.

The Fateful Summer

On July 2, 1776, the Americans' Continental Congress voted to "dissolve the connection" with Great Britain. Two days later, they adopted the Declaration of Independence, to which fifty-six members of the Second Continental Congress pledged their lives, property, and sacred honor.

Word of this momentous declaration reached the Colonial army defending the city of New York on July 6. As word spread among the troops under the command of General George Washington, spontaneous celebrations erupted. But the celebrations were muted by what these troops were seeing unfold before their eyes—the continued arrival in New York's harbor of the largest expeditionary force ever sent forth by any nation in history.

The American troops were about to fight this well-trained and well-equipped British army under the command of General William Howe, a man who was bitter and embarrassed from his humiliating defeat at the hands of Washington and the Americans at Boston just a few months before. With the British forces gathered, a battle would soon be fought that was likely to bring the foolish rebellion to a quick and violent end.

The American army was led by no ordinary man. A general who'd been commanding soldiers since the age of twenty-two (but who, ironically, had presided over far more military defeats than victories), Washington was recognized as a national hero after the 1755 battle at Monongahela, in which he had shown his courage well, having had two horses shot out from under him and no fewer than four balls pierce his clothing while he sought to rally his retreating troops.[1] At the age of twenty-seven, Washington had married, retired from the military, and settled peacefully at Mount Vernon. Having established himself on his beloved estate, he wanted only to live a quiet life.

But it was not to be.

Some time before, Presbyterian Reverend Samuel Davies had speculated in a sermon about "that heroic youth, Col. Washington, who I cannot but hope Providence has hitherto preserved in so signal a Manner for some important Service to his Country."[2]

The reverend's words turned out to be prophetic, for what he'd hoped for was already proving true.

Under General Washington's leadership, the Colonial army had succeeded in driving the British from Boston in the spring of 1776. After the brilliantly conducted siege, Washington had wasted no time in celebration but immediately marched his army south, for he knew that New York would be the next target of the British forces. His enemy's strategy was fairly straightforward: divide and conquer. Take New York, control the Hudson River Valley, and split New England from the remainder of the colonies. Further, New York's harbor would be the best place for British military supplies and reinforcements to disembark from, as well as an excellent base of operations for the British navy as it carried out its blockade of American sea trade.

New York had another factor dictating its importance—one that was difficult to measure but critically important. It was a hotbed of Loyalists. The year prior, more than half of the members of the New York Chamber of Commerce were Loyalists. Two-thirds of the total property of New York was controlled by those still loyal to the British crown. In the rural areas surrounding New York, in particular on Staten Island and Long Island, Loyalists were in the majority. If the British could take New York and create a major Tory presence in the middle of the country, the rebel nation would be split in two. Recognizing this, John Adams called New York "key to the whole continent."[3]

Understanding (and fearing) the strategic importance as well as the vulnerability of New York, in January Washington had sent one of his best generals, Charles Lee, to begin building its defensive structures.

General Lee recognized it would be utterly impossible to defend New York without controlling the waters surrounding the city. Yet the Americans had no navy, no warships, nothing to defend the city from the rivers or the bay. Still, he hoped that a properly designed line of defense would result in massive British casualties when they finally arrived to conquer the city, casualties of the type inflicted on Bunker Hill, casualties that would decimate the morale of the British army as well as that of the citizens of Great Britain.

Lee devised a scheme that centered on a series of high river bluffs immediately across the East River from New York. There he ordered the construction of Fort Stirling, hoping that it would control naval access up the East River.

Upon his arrival in April, Washington found the defensive efforts to be less than he had hoped. Only about one-half of the defensive structures were completed, and he immediately set about to employ as many men as possible, pressing local residents in the effort. He did, however, endorse Lee's overall defensive plan. He believed that as New York was the key to the continent, Long Island was the key to the defense of New York, and Brooklyn Heights was the key to the defense of Long Island. To ensure their defensive goal was accomplished, he assigned a young but proven leader, General Nathanael Greene, to command the forces on Long Island.

Starting in early May, Greene aggressively prepared for the expected invasion. In addition to Fort Stirling on the highest western bluffs, he ordered the construction of four more forts to the east of the little village of Brooklyn, intended to defend the bluffs and Fort Stirling. These forts were well protected and enhanced by miles of trenches and fields that had been scorched clear by fire.[4]

While the focus was on Long Island, areas all around New York City were being turned into defensive strongholds as well.

The condition of the American army at this time was mixed. On one hand, morale was high, but this was at least partly due to wild misconceptions about its strength. Rumors had it that the army had at least 42,000 soldiers, with one newspaper reporting the number as high as 70,000.[5] But the facts painted a very different picture. Although more soldiers were arriving regularly, desertions were widespread and frequent. The summer of 1776 was seeing bounteous harvests, and many of the soldiers felt compelled to go home to help bring the crops in. Worse, sickness was rampant, including various forms of "camp fever"—dysentery, smallpox, and typhus.

Washington's army knew the British were coming, and they spent their time anxiously preparing for their arrival. Finally, on June 29, it happened. The sails of the first forty-five ships were sighted. Soon after, the British began to disgorge their army onto Staten Island. Upon landing, the British soldiers found themselves very well received, the Loyalists greeting them with joy. The abundance of food and supplies also amazed them. They were even impressed by the beauty of the landscape.

The Americans, in turn, were amazed as well. Unfortunately, their awe was focused on the size of the invading fleet.

Along the Shore of the East River, New York City
July 12, 1776

FROM HIS POSITION ATOP the bluff that looked over the East River, the young Delaware soldier stared at the mighty British ships and thought back on their arrival.

The commander of the Colonial army, General Washington, a

man the soldier would have walked into the very jaws of hell for, hadn't told them yet, but the British had amassed the largest naval armada and landing force ever assembled in the Western world: almost four hundred ships carrying 32,000 men. All of them were well equipped, well fed, highly trained, and combat ready. Perhaps most important, all of them were filled with fury, ready to fight for the kingdom and the crown.

The young soldier looked down at his bare feet. He hadn't worn a pair of boots in months. He ate twice a day on good days, not at all on bad. He looked at his patched trousers, threadbare shirt, and tattered vest. Like most of the Americans, he didn't even have a uniform. The army had no regular supplies to speak of. No waving flags or bugles or fifes and drums. Few cannons. Fewer horses. Some of the American soldiers didn't even have guns, only hunting knives and axes hanging from their belts in ridiculous displays of power. What were they supposed to do, hack to death the entire British army?

The soldier stared in dismay at the mighty navy that was assembling at the mouth of the bay. The British *Centurion* and the *Chatham* were among the ships. Fifty guns apiece. The forty-gun *Phoenix*. The *Greyhound*. The monstrous *Asia*. That was sixty-four guns right there. Hundreds of cannons between the ships. Hundreds more among the armies that had deployed along the southern shores.

The odds, whatever they were, were not in the Americans' favor, he was sure.

The Americans claimed they had 50,000, some said 70,000 soldiers, but the young man suspected the number was much lower than that. And though he was suspicious, he had no idea how bad it really was.

Washington had an army of about 15,000, of which fewer than 7,000 were fit for duty, for a multitude of sicknesses had fallen upon his men like a blanket of death and disease. And although it was true that new recruits were arriving every day, more and more British ships were sailing down from Halifax as well.

The young soldier considered the odds against them, then

thought back to the scene that had played out along the Hudson River earlier that afternoon.

In a brazen display of arrogance and power, two massive British ships, the *Phoenix* and the *Rose,* had cast off from Staten Island and moved up the Hudson River at full sail, carried briskly by the stiff winds and rising tides. As the ships approached, half a hundred Colonial guns within the city, Fort George, and the other batteries along the river started blasting away. The cannons aboard the British ships answered, sending balls of steel exploding through the city streets as women and children and soldiers scrambled for cover.

For almost half an hour, cannonball and thunder hung heavy in the air, the smoke so thick that it obscured both shores. Then suddenly the guns fell silent as the mighty ships moved out of range, hanging to the Jersey shore. Hundreds of Colonial soldiers and their officers stood in frightened awe, watching the mighty ships sail by. It was a humbling display of British power.

The soldier had been told that more than two hundred shots had been fired at the British ships, all without so much as a torn sail or broken mast, as far as he could tell. Indeed, the only casualties in the battle had occurred on the American side: six soldiers killed when their cannons, overpacked with powder, had exploded in their faces. Meanwhile, the ships had sailed up the river and set anchor where they could intercept incoming recruits and supplies.

If there was reason to find hope after the first skirmish in the battle for New York, the young soldier didn't know what it might be.

He looked south a final time, taking in the massive camp of British soldiers—more than the entire population of Philadelphia, the largest city in all the colonies. And all of those soldiers, he knew, were lusting for revenge, anxious to destroy the traitors who had risen up on these American shores.

That was what he was now. The enemy. A mortal traitor. Foe and destroyer of the king. He had crossed the line and there was no turning back, for one couldn't recall a cannonball once the powder had been fired.

But something inside him whispered it wasn't like that. Something inside him whispered that *he was right.*

Looking down, he read the words on the parchment for the hundredth time:

"We hold these truths to be self-evident, that all men are created equal, that they are endowed by their Creator with certain unalienable rights, that among these are life, liberty and the pursuit of happiness. That to secure these rights, governments are instituted among men, deriving their just powers from the consent of the governed. That whenever any form of government becomes destructive to these ends, it is the right of the people to alter or to abolish it, and to institute new government, laying its foundation on such principles and organizing its powers in such form, as to them shall seem most likely to effect their safety and happiness. . . ."[6]

The Declaration of Independence had been written and signed little more than a week before. But holding the manuscript in his hands, a scribbled copy of a few words from the second paragraph, even he, a young man from the farms of Delaware, understood that things were different now. They weren't fighting to get the attention of their king. They weren't fighting over taxes or tea or representation or the arrogance of the crown. They were fighting for their country. Their children. Their present and their future. They were fighting for their freedoms.

And that made it worth it all.

The American Leader

George Washington was forty-three years old when he was appointed commander in chief of the American army. Afterward, he noted the irony of being appointed commander over an army that did not yet exist.

At the time, the major military operation under way was in Boston, and the American army consisted of militias largely from the New England states. John Adams asserted that Washington's appointment was a political compromise—a commander from a Southern state to command soldiers from the New England states—but the simple fact was, Congress had no better alternative. Washington was well-known and highly respected, a patriot dedicated to the American cause. And though his military career had not resulted in military victories, his reputation for valor and his commanding presence were without peer. At six feet, two inches, he weighed about 190 pounds, and when he smiled he displayed a few defective teeth—nothing unusual for his time.

An excellent horseman who carried himself in regal fashion, he was accustomed to being paid respect. And he demanded it, not allowing others to become too familiar. However, he was not arrogant, and those who were closest to him were fiercely loyal. His soldiers loved him, and his appointment as commander in chief was universally hailed.

But for all his strengths, Washington did have his weaknesses. He had developed a reputation for having an explosive temper, though he had largely mastered this tendency. He had been retired from active military duty since 1759, had never commanded an army that was required to fight in the fashion preferred by the British, and had not commanded anything larger than a regiment. As the war progressed, he made many strategic military errors.[7]

Expressing his own reservations about his appointment by the Second Continental Congress, he stated, "I do not think myself equal to the command I am honored with."[8] Such words were not uttered with false modesty. Washington understood his limitations. Still, his extraordinary character made his weaknesses seem of little consequence.

•   •   •

When Washington expressed his concern regarding his ability to guide the country to a successful military victory over the armies of England, he was not only reflecting upon his personal weaknesses but also expressing an accurate appraisal of the difficulties facing the American rebels.

The declaration of independence from Britain was not universally accepted with enthusiasm. Many opposed it outright. One-fifth of the delegates to the Continental Congress of July 1776 had voted against independence. Others had voted in support of it but were never quite sure. Some did not care one way or the other. This combination of apathy and opposition made it nearly impossible for Congress to raise, feed, or supply the armies that were required for success. (Indeed, for the duration of the war, Congress and the states failed to provide the most basic needs of the army: food, clothing, shelter, and men.)

Loyalists were to be found in every colony. In some areas—specifically New York, New Jersey, and Georgia—they were probably in the majority. In Pennsylvania and the Carolinas, they had a very strong presence. Their numbers were particularly high among the political leadership and clergy. The majority of Loyalists stayed and hoped for the defeat of the rebels—however, 80,000 of them left the country during the war. Those who settled in England helped prolong the war by stirring up the public against the rebels, telling of persecution and atrocities committed against those who were loyal to the crown. (Fortunately, though some Loyalist army units did fight beside the British regulars, the king was slow to take advantage of this ready source of manpower.)

Most Americans were dead set against creating a permanent army, believing the war could be successfully conducted by citizen militias. And though most militiamen were brave and well-intentioned, they were poorly disciplined and trained. Many chafed under command unless the commander was a friend or neighbor, competent or not. Many were "summer soldiers" who felt that they had to be home during the fall to handle the harvest. Many of the backwoodsmen of the American colonies, those who made the best soldiers, frequently went even further into the wilderness to avoid war taxes or service in the militia. The end result was that the same feeling of independence that ran through the American personality, leading to the desire for autonomy from the British crown in the first place, was the very thing that almost made it impossible to achieve that independence.

Often entire units would abandon the cause. Frustrated, Washington bemoaned the "dearth of public spirit, and want of virtue. . . . Could I have foreseen what I have, and am likely to experience, no consideration upon Earth should have induced me to accept this command."[9]

The regular army was never large. In the summer of 1776 it reached 18,000, but it fell to 5,000 by the end of that year. At its largest, in the summer of 1778, it was only 20,000 strong, and it quickly dwindled after that. Because the Continental Congress had no legal authority to make laws or levy taxes, it could not force the colonies to supply the urgently needed arms or supplies. Had it not been for foreign assistance, particularly from the French, the war would have been lost.

Congress fought over the appointing of generals, using the positions to pay political favors. Lower-ranking officers were inexperienced and almost completely untrained. Many were selected because they were popular with the troops or had been hometown leaders, and they never understood the need for exercising authority or demanding discipline. During battle, many of these officers were unwilling to make hard decisions that might result in the death of their friends. In addition, camp diseases generated by poor hygiene were unnecessarily rampant.

On the other hand, the British had a professional army and control of the seas. British credit was the best in the world, and their ability to raise and supply that army, including the hiring of feared Hessian soldiers, was never an issue.

Little wonder why John Adams, one of the most vocal and effective voices for independence, expressed the fear that the war might "rage for twenty years, and End, in the Subduction of America as likely as in her Liberation."[10]

New York City
August 21, 1776

THE STORM BOILED OVER them like a cauldron of rain and fire, the skies crackling with so much electricity that the smell of sulfur filled the air.

It had started as a long, low line of blackness against the western horizon just as the sun was going down. But even from a distance, the soldiers could see this was going to be a mighty storm. The dark clouds stretched as far as they could see, and the black mushroom boiled as it grew, flashing constant light from within its mighty bowels as the wind came crashing down. The trees around the soldier strained against the howling wind, the saplings bending almost to the ground. Soon the rain came, then the hail, the moisture pelting with so much fury that the poor man felt it would beat him into the ground.

As the storm rose, the Delaware soldier glanced around in terror, then bent toward the mud and started digging a shallow hole.

It was then that the lightning started.

It buzzed within the black ball and began striking down. It was constant. It was terrifying. It made his skin crawl. At first the darkness was broken by the lightning, but then the lightning became so constant it was the other way around.

The mighty storm rolled over the city and started moving out to sea. Then it stopped and blew back across the river, where it seemed to hover in the sky.

For three hours, the night soaked up the dreadful storm.

Houses within the city exploded in light and flames. Men were cut down by the lightning, sometimes a dozen at a time. Horses fled in panic, some of them drowning in the river. The woods around the encampments seemed to come alive as deer and 'coons and rabbits ran in terror, fires and lightning bursting everywhere. Three men running through the narrow city streets were cut down together, their bodies thrown in opposite directions, instantly charred as black as coal.

The soldier hunkered in his hastily dug hole, but it had filled with rain now and he started shivering in the cold.

Another man, his face white in the constant flash of lightning, crawled toward him and dropped into the hole. The two men didn't talk as cracks of thunder shuddered all around them, strobes of light freezing everything in stilted moments of frozen time.

"Mind if I share your hole?" the stranger finally asked. It was clear from the determined look in his eyes that it wouldn't matter even if the other soldier did.

The Delaware man nodded without really looking up.

Bullets of hail beat upon them until the other soldier yelled above the fray, "You got any Carolina tobacco? I'd like to smoke my pipe one more time before I die!"

The younger man looked at him, then answered sarcastically, "No, but I'll sail down and ask the British if you really want me to."

The two men stared at each other for an awkward moment, then broke into insane laughter. They kept their heads down, but their shoulders shuddered as three hours of utter terror and confusion burst through their emotional seams.

"Going to be a long night," the Delaware soldier muttered when he had finally had a chance to settle down.

The older man slapped him on the back, nodding toward the British army. "I wouldn't worry about that too much, my young friend. Something tells me tomorrow may be worse."

The storm finally passed and the morning broke calm and cool, the sky clear and clean and peaceful, with not a hint of cloud anywhere.

At exactly 8:00 that morning, with a single cannon shot to announce their coming, four thousand British troops marched ashore at Gravesend Bay. By noon, 15,000 men and forty artillery had disembarked on Long Island.

After months of waiting and preparation, the battle for New York City was finally under way.

The Battle Unfolds

In the weeks leading up to the invasion, Washington had stewed over the exact point where the British would attack. He had been advised that Long Island would be the most likely target, due to the ease of landing on its beaches as well as the presence of many Loyalists. But he worried that Long Island might be used as a ruse while the primary assault would be at New York itself.

Undecided, he made a critical mistake. Dividing his men between the two potential targets, he critically reduced their numbers against an overwhelming invasion force.

To make matters worse, as the British moved on Long Island, Washington was led to believe that only eight or nine thousand soldiers had come ashore. This relatively small number of troops reinforced his belief that the invasion of Long Island was in fact a feint, and that either New York City or perhaps a location farther north up the Hudson would soon face the primary attack. Convinced that the invasion of Long Island was a ploy, he sent only a small number of reinforcements across the East River.

Time passed. Washington stewed more. Nathanael Greene, Washington's most trusted subordinate, had fallen deathly ill and had been relieved of command. General John Sullivan was promoted to replace him, but on August 24 Washington relieved Sullivan of command and put General Israel Putnam in his place. These changes in leadership rattled his troops. They were further unnerved when another five thousand Hessian troops arrived on Long Island on the twenty-fifth of August.

Washington crossed the East River to review the situation on a daily basis, traveling to the Heights of Gowan, a high, wooded ridge south of Brooklyn where Putnam and his subordinates, Generals Sullivan and William Alexander (known as Lord Stirling) had their troops digging in. Critically, the high ridge on which these two armies would face off was traversed by three roads, all of which traveled through cuts in the ridge and were easily defendable.

However, in a deadly and unfathomable mistake, a fourth road, known as the Jamaica Pass, was completely ignored. Only five militiamen patrolled it, leaving the door wide open for a British flank attack.

British Headquarters Camp, South and East of Brooklyn, Long Island

THE BRITISH GENERAL DIDN'T trust the man. He was American, after all, and even if he claimed to be a Loyalist, that didn't mean a thing.

He could be lying—all Americans were liars, and those who claimed to be loyal to the crown were only slightly less despicable and untrustworthy than the rest.

He glared at the fat farmer and approached him with clenched fists. "You are loyal to the crown!" he sneered.

"From the day I was born," the local farmer shot back.

General Clinton stared him down. He had only recently returned from South Carolina, where he had failed to take Charleston as commanded, and, like Howe, he was smarting from the ignoble defeat. Still, the experience in South Carolina hadn't passed without effect. First, it had generated in him a greater hatred for the rebels than he had ever felt before. Second, it had created a grudging respect for their guerrilla tactics, which had almost destroyed his army through constant harassment.

But like any professional soldier, he had learned from his mistakes, and this much he was certain of now: Defeating the American rabble didn't depend on taking territory. It didn't depend on capturing their cities or their strongholds or their waterways or forts. It didn't depend on holding landmass, as victory had always been defined before. No, the only path to victory in America lay in killing rebel soldiers. Kill the men. Show no mercy. That was the only way they were going to crush the filthy rebellion that had brought him here.

He sniffed the farmer, then pushed him against the stone wall. "Tell me again," he commanded.

The fat farmer swallowed, his throat tight with fear, then started talking in a trembling voice. "Washington has split his forces. Most of them remain in New York. There are no more than eight . . . nine thousand soldiers defending Fort Stirling. Three thousand of them have been positioned along the Heights of Gowan, spread along a line that has to be at least four miles long. The remaining soldiers are being held in reserve at Brooklyn Heights."

"And you know this how?"

"We walk among them, General Clinton. We see them. We talk to them. We live among them every day. We have eyes and ears, and we love to watch and listen. It is not difficult to know these things now."

"And the condition of their army?"

"It is as I told your adjutant," the fat one answered, nodding toward the colonel who was standing near the door. "They are hungry. Poorly equipped. Rude and drunk and rowdy. My cows are cleaner than the American soldiers, and they smell better too. Great sickness runs among them, which can come as no surprise. They are distrustful, deadly savages who are burning my crops and killing my animals rather than letting them fall into your hands. They are undisciplined and unfaithful, wandering among the battle lines, though we heard that General Washington . . ." here the Loyalist farmer hesitated, his voice softening noticeably, for Washington was respected among them all. "Washington completed an inspection yesterday," he continued. "He reprimanded General Putnam sharply, demanding that he put things in order. But so far nothing's changed."

The British general leaned toward him, his face growing tight. "Tell me about Jamaica Pass!" he demanded.

The farmer smiled, his breath thick with onions. "Five men, sir. Five men protect the pass, and that is all."

"And yet it runs all the way through the highlands?"

"Yes, sir, it does. All the way to Brooklyn. It cuts behind the highlands—"

The general lurched forward, grabbing the Tory farmer by the lapels of his dirty shirt. "I don't believe the rebels could be so stupid! How could they leave the pass so unprotected if it runs right to their flank? Lie to me, and I will cut your tongue out!"

He could feel the farmer tremble as he swayed on liquid knees. "The pass will take you right into the heart of the army. It's guarded by only a handful of rebel soldiers. I swear it on everything we both hold dear."

The general glared. "You will show me!" he finally muttered as he threw the farmer toward the darkness of the night. "Take me to it. I want to see it. Show me now."

Two days later, General Clinton met aboard the *Eagle* with Lord Howe, supreme commander of the British invasion force. The admiral's brother, General Howe, stood beside the table, staring at the roughly drawn map. Clinton presented his plan in mere minutes, speaking with a passion that only the truly converted feel. "It is so simple. So beautifully simple!" He pointed to the rough chart, tapping his finger hard enough to make the leather parchment snap. "There is another road, here, east of the village. It runs through the highlands, then cuts west. It is narrow but clear! We could take our men east to Flatland, then cut north and intercept Jamaica Pass—"

"It *must* be guarded," the commander interrupted in disbelief.

"No, my lord. I have been there myself. There are no men to watch it. A few sentries—boys, it seemed. We nearly walked right up on them without raising their guard. I can assure you, my lord, there are no real soldiers there."

Admiral Howe hesitated.

Clinton sensed his opening and went on. "Let me do as I've proposed, my lord. Let me take our men *tonight,* in utter silence, under the cover of darkness, and I guarantee you victory in this fight. Give me ten thousand men and I will lead them north, intercept the pass, then move west and catch the rebels on their flank."

Lord Howe nodded toward his younger brother. General Howe saw the question with his eyes and nodded. *It could be done,* the eager look on his face said.

Clinton's shoulders tightened. They were seeing it his way! "I could take the men tonight," he urged again. "We'd get there just before dawn. Take a few hours rest," he turned to General Howe, "while you attack at their front and right side. I could allow you time to draw them out, then move in from the east. At that point they'll be surrounded. We'll butcher them on the open plains and marshes behind the highlands. Those who retreat to Fort Stirling will be trapped against the water. But if you, sir," Clinton moved his eyes to Admiral Howe, "if you send your warships up the river to intercept them, we will leave them no retreat, trapping them along the tip of the land."

His voice trailed off, and the three men were silent as they thought.

"This war could be over before the second nightfall," Clinton finished. "We could all be home by Christmas . . ."

Lord Howe seemed to study the map, his eyes unfocused. One

more quick look toward his brother, a slight nod, and it was decided. "Have your men ready," he commanded. "They march tonight. It will be an enormous challenge, moving ten thousand men in silence, in darkness, across uneven and unknown terrain. But if you are successful, we could crush this miserable rebellion. We could destroy General Washington and his army. We could end it all right here."

• • •

That night, August 26, General Clinton did as he had proposed, leading ten thousand British soldiers along the Jamaica Pass. The five soldiers assigned to guard the road were quickly captured not far from the local tavern, and the British continued marching, hardly making any sound. Back at their camp, tents were left in place and fires were kept burning to leave the impression that the British were taking another night's rest. Americans looking down at the fires from the Gowan Heights didn't know that, six miles to the east, 10,000 soldiers with artillery, guided by three local farmers and under the command of Clinton and Cornwallis, were moving toward them through the darkness.

As morning approached, the rest of the British army got ready for their frontal attack. The battle began, and, for a few moments, the Americans actually thought that they were winning. Then General Clinton and his men mounted their flank attack. Sullivan swung his main force to meet them. The battle was fierce and deadly. Deafening sound, blinding smoke, and bloody gore engulfed both sides. Despite their best efforts, the Americans were quickly overwhelmed, realizing too late that the only way to withdraw was through the marsh of Gowanus Bay. To cover his men's retreat, Lord Stirling led a brave attack against the British with militiamen from Maryland who had never fought before. Five times they attacked the Brits—each time suffering heavy losses while allowing other soldiers the time they needed to escape. Finally, Stirling ordered his men to find their way back to the Brooklyn lines. Many were taken prisoner. Many were caught in the marsh and fired upon by the British and Hessians. A good number drowned. Stirling himself was captured.

Outnumbered, outmaneuvered, and out-thought, the American army on Long Island crumbled. What had started as a battle turned into a massacre. The British believed the complete destruction of the opposing army was at hand, but, to their dismay, General Howe ordered them to stop. Sensing a decisive victory, the British soldiers ignored the call to stand down and fought on. General Clinton had to issue "repeated orders" to get his troops to break with the enemy.

As the afternoon passed, what was left of the Continental army struggled into Fort Stirling. By nightfall, the American survivors found themselves hopelessly trapped between 20,000 British soldiers and the East River.

Desperation and Hope

The American army on Long Island was in a desperate situation: massed on Brooklyn Heights, facing a superior force, and with only one route of retreat—over the East River. While they huddled in their strongholds, the British started digging trenches toward their positions, preparing themselves for the final assault.

The next day, August 28, Washington ordered reinforcements from New York. Though their appearance lifted the spirits of the defeated Americans, the elation did not last long, for the fact remained that the Continental soldiers were still trapped inside the Brooklyn defenses.

At this point, there was only one thing that could save them: retreat across the river. But such a retreat would be impossible if the British navy was able to position its warships to intercept them.

That afternoon, the skies grew dark, the temperature dropped ten degrees, and it started to rain, cold and steady. Fires would not burn. Many of the troops had no tents or other shelter. Powder was almost impossible to keep dry. Soldiers slept in place—some while standing. The outer regiments kept up a constant stream of gunfire at the British camps. The British happily fired back. Gunfire, smoke, and blackening clouds filled the rainy skies.

As night fell, the winds shifted and gathered in strength until a forceful northeast wind blew. The nor'easter continued through the next day, making it impossible for the British naval forces to move upriver to intercept the Americans.

Held back by the storm, the British warships anchored at the mouth of the bay.

But how long could the Americans hope the winds would save them?

Long Island
August 29, 1776

"WE HAVE NO CHOICE, SIR. If we stay here, we will die. You. Me. Our soldiers. The heart of our entire army. We have to evacuate Fort Stirling before the British move their ships! We must cross the river and take refuge in New York. That is our only hope."

General Washington stared at his surviving aides and generals. All good men. Many so young. And there were fewer of them now than there once had been. Far too many had been killed or captured.

He sucked in air and held it, almost unable to breathe. It was too painful to think about them, those who had been taken. Looking at his depleted men, he repeated the same words he had cried on that day watching from Brooklyn hill, "Good God, what brave fellows I must this day lose."

General Mifflin stared at his commander. "It doesn't have to be that way, sir. We can get them out. But we cannot wait. The ships we sank in the river will not hold the British warships at bay. They are straining at the reins now, ready to move up the river to intercept us the moment the winds die down."

Even as they spoke, the dark skies howled. Washington looked through the glass of the Livingston mansion situated atop the hills of Brooklyn, staring down on the river. It was late afternoon. He knew he had no time.

"We have to move tonight!" another general offered. "The winds will not favor us forever. This gift from God may be our providence, but we must also act ourselves. The enemy is growing closer by the hour. Never do they halt in their digging, moving their trenches to our walls. They are close enough now that we can hear their shovels scraping, no more than a few hundred yards away."

Still General Washington hesitated. "Move nine thousand men! All of our cannon and equipment! All in utter silence. I don't know if it can be done!"

General Mifflin started to say something, then held back.

Washington looked at him, his voice hard. "Do you understand what a risk it would be to order an evacuation?" he demanded. "It is far and away the most demanding maneuver an army can undertake. It demands constant courage and the utmost discipline, all of which seem to be in very short supply. An organized retreat demands perfect compliance with the letter of every order. Far more dangerous is it than open battle upon the field.

"And think about this, gentlemen. If we begin an evacuation and are discovered, every man left on this side of the river will be in mortal danger. It could be a catastrophe. And to hide our intentions will require a great deception. We won't be able to tell either the enlisted men or the officers, not with so many Loyalists around. We'd have to keep up our campfires, our gunfire, and all the noise, maintaining every appearance of an army that is not there. And as we pull our soldiers back, some will have to move forward to fill the holes."

General Mifflin nodded sadly. "Dying is the other option. And that's what's going to happen if we leave our soldiers here."

Washington thought in silence. "It is too dangerous," he finally muttered as if speaking to himself, "especially for the men who would be the last to leave. If we can't get them over the river before the day breaks, they will be sacrificed. I don't know if I can do that! Who . . . what regiment do I ask to cover our retreat?"

The men didn't speak until General Mifflin finally said, "We will do it, sir. My Pennsylvania regiment will cover your retreat."

A Bitter Wind

On the New York side of the river, General Heath had been ordered to gather up every boat or schooner, every sloop, flat-bottom, fishing ship, or tiny vessel that could be used to move the soldiers. Working under deliberately misleading instructions, he told the sailors and fishermen to get ready to move new battalions from New Jersey to relieve the men on Long Island. As night fell, he was ready to go.

At 7:00 P.M., the American soldiers were told they were to assemble for a night surprise attack and to do so in utter silence. Hungry, cold, exhausted, with wet powder and no hope, they thought the order to attack was suicide. Then, starting at 9:00, some of the rear units were told to fall back to the ferry where they would be relieved by reinforcements.

Only when they had gathered at the docks did they realize that the army was in retreat.

Time passed quickly. More and more soldiers gathered at the docks. Cannons started arriving, their wheels bound in rags to keep them quiet. A hundred. Five hundred. More than a thousand men.

But though the night passed, the nor'easter didn't.

Rowing against the wind, and with the river so rough, not a single boat could pass. Shortly before eleven, General McDougall, the officer in charge of loading the men and equipment at the docks, sent an urgent note to Washington saying the winds were making it impossible to get the boats over from New York and urging him to abandon their plans to evacuate that night.

Shortly after, the northeast wind suddenly died out. There was a peaceful calm for a few minutes, and then the winds shifted gently to the southwest, allowing quick passage across the river.

With the sudden change in wind, the retreat got under way.

Last Man Out

The men labored ceaselessly. It was exhausting work. One by one, with their equipment and their cannons, the Americans were loaded onto boats and rowed across the river. The men were ordered to whisper and to hold their gear so it wouldn't rattle as they moved. Things went slowly. Cannons got mired in the mud, sometimes halting the retreat. The boats were so overloaded, the soldiers were certain they would sink. Back and forth the oarsmen rowed in an exhausting display of determination and seamanship. It was an incredibly complicated task, even under the best of circumstances, let alone at night, in utter secrecy, with few of the men even understanding what was going on.

As more soldiers were ordered to move back to the ferry, General Mifflin and his men moved in to take their places, scattering themselves paper-thin along the battle lines.

Frantic work. Desperate measures. Thousands of soldiers moving through the night.

Yet, despite their best efforts, as the sun prepared to rise, much of Washington's army was still on the Long Island side of the river.

The situation was incredibly dangerous for these men. They were surrounded by 20,000 troops. Most of their cannons were gone. Having abandoned their trenches and other lines of defense, they huddled on the docks. Those still on the front lines faced an even more precarious situation, for when the sun rose—something that would happen in just a few minutes—the British would see that the lines had been abandoned and mount an attack. Those who manned the garrisons would be the first to die as they defended their positions with only a handful of men.

The sky turned pink and the sun started rising on an army that was doomed.

It was then that a dense fog settled over the Long Island side of the river. Thick and heavy, it muffled every sound and made it impossible to see. Trees and men were obscured at five feet and disappeared completely at ten. And though the sun grew higher, the fog didn't burn off. The orderly retreat continued, this time under the cloak not of darkness but of the thick shroud of fog. Working frantically beside his men, Washington offered direction and encouragement until the last of the American troops had made their way to safety.[11]

Eastern Shore of New York
August 30, 1776

THE DELAWARE SOLDIER scrambled off the dangerously overloaded boat. Heart thumping in fear and relief, he jumped in dirty water up to his chest, grabbed a slippery rope, and helped to pull the small fishing boat toward the rocky shore.

Fourteen other men scrambled off the leaking boat, small packs and knapsacks on their shoulders. As they moved around him, the young soldier turned and looked across the river. From where he stood, the skies were clear, the river not obscured by so much as a single wisp of fog. Yet he stared in awe as boat after boat, loaded with his fellow soldiers and friends, emerged from the shroud that still hung over Long Island, gliding quickly toward him to unload along the shore. Rowing furiously, the oarsmen turned their boats again, heading back toward Long Island and disappearing once again into the fog.

For an hour, he sat watching.

By midmorning, the evacuation of Long Island was complete. General Washington commanded the last boat across, not willing to leave until all his soldiers were safely in the boats.

Not until all of the American soldiers had been evacuated did the fog suddenly lift, exposing what had been done.

Fifteen minutes later, the young soldier stared in wonder and relief as hundreds of British soldiers flooded across the walls of Fort Stirling. He imagined their shock and disbelief upon realizing the fort had been deserted, nine thousand soldiers having silently evacuated through the night and the fog.

He watched them for a moment, savoring the victory and new lease on life, lifted a fist in defiance to them, then turned and left the shore.

What If?

What if the nor'easter had not kicked up and the British warships had been able to move up the river, making it impossible for Washington's army to escape?

What if, at eleven o'clock that night, the winds had not suddenly shifted, allowing the waiting boats to finally cross the river and begin evacuating the waiting soldiers?

What if the fog had not appeared, allowing the rest of Washington's army to escape?

In a June 2, 1776, letter to John Adams, Nathanael Greene suggested: "The fate of war is very uncertain. Suppose this army should be defeated, two or three of the leading generals killed, our stores and magazines all lost, I would not be answerable for the consequences that such a stroke might produce in American politics."[12]

Considering that the entire Colonial army in 1776 was only about 18,000 strong, if a significant portion of those American troops—along with their commander—had been captured, Nathanael Greene's great fear might well have come to pass.

The infant nation might have been forced to sue for peace.

As it was, it came close to doing that very thing even with Washington's successful escape!

In the days that followed the Battle of Long Island, morale of the army reached new lows. In New York, discipline evaporated and swarms of marauding soldiers turned to looting. Many quit and went home. Entire units marched out of the city and returned to their states, where they spread the word that the cause was lost. Even the taboo prohibiting criticism of Washington was violated. Some called for his replacement.

Word of the army's defeat reached the Congress on August 31. The leaders there were badly shaken. On September 2, captured General Sullivan appeared in Philadelphia, on temporary parole, carrying an overture of peace from Admiral Howe. The pressure to accept Howe's terms of surrender was enormous. Had the Americans been faced with not only a decisive defeat on Long Island but also the capture of a large number of American soldiers and possibly their commander in chief, they might have had no choice but to accept Lord Howe's terms of clemency in exchange for abandonment of the rebel cause.

Also sobering is the question as to what would have happened had George Washington been killed or captured on Long Island—a possibility that was very likely, since it seems that he was determined to be the last one to leave the scene of his army's defeat. [13]

The question of who would have replaced him cannot be answered with great certainty. When Washington had been selected to be commander in chief, it was not only because of Adams's "political compromise" but because every other possible choice was either too old (Israel Putnam of Connecticut), incompetent and ill (Artemas Ward of Massachusetts), or eccentric and unreasonably demanding (Charles Lee). [14] During the course of the war, excellent leaders did emerge, most notably Nathanael Greene and Henry Knox, but in 1776 they were very young and still maturing. Neither would have been capable of replacing Washington at this stage of the revolution.

Most disinterested observers have reached this one inescapable conclusion: Washington was indispensable to the military success of the young country. True, he was not a perfect general. On occasion he made bad decisions, and sometimes he hesitated too long to make crucial decisions. But the strategy he adopted for winning the war—making it a war of attrition—proved imminently successful, due in no small part to his patience, perseverance, personal courage, and leadership.

Throughout the Revolutionary War, Washington's soldiers suffered the most severe and dreadful hardships, all because civilian leadership failed to provide the most basic supplies: food, uniforms, shelter, weapons, and ammunition. Sometimes the soldiers' pay would be a year in arrears. Twice during the war, there were mutinies by groups of soldiers, both of which Washington was quick to quash. In justifying his actions, he made it clear that, despite their sense of betrayal, hardship, and suffering, civilian authority *had* to be obeyed.

Though he would entreat, beg, shame, and petition the Congress to meet their obligations to the army, he never considered threats and certainly not the use of force. Observing Washington's restraint, a French officer noted, "This is the seventh year that he has commanded the army and he has obeyed Congress: more need not be said." [15]

Washington's deference to civilian authority stands in stark contrast to the countless hundreds, if not thousands, of military leaders throughout history (including the aforementioned French officer's own Napoleon) who could not resist the temptation to use their military might to assume authority over civilian leadership.

And George Washington was indispensable not only when it came to winning our independence but when it was time to establish our constitutional government. The convention that wrote the Constitution likely would not have happened had it not been for George Washington.

Following the Revolutionary War, the new nation struggled to deal with the weakness of the Articles of Confederation. It seemed as if the "united states" would soon become separate nation-states. Wise men such as Hamilton and Madison knew that a new system of government had to be devised.

Washington came out of the war with the reputation of a hero. He could have lived in peace and prosperity on the banks of the Potomac for the rest of his life and been very happy. But he was still a patriot. And he knew that his nation required a new constitution.

When it was decided in the fall of 1786 that the states would convene to consider the "situation of the United States," Washington became conflicted. Any amendments to the Articles of Confederation required the consent of Congress and of every state. Knowing that the men in Congress could never agree to the establishment of a national government powerful enough to solve the myriad of critical problems confronting the new nation, it was understood that the May convention might well be forced to simply start over. And though the stated purpose of the meeting was merely to consider alterations to the Articles of Confederation, Washington knew—along with many others—that the real intentions of those who had proposed the meeting made the convention extralegal, if not outright illegal.

Still, risking his hard-earned and highly treasured reputation, he agreed to attend, a move that removed all serious challenge to the convention's authenticity.

Had Washington refused, it is probable that no convention to consider a new government for the United States would have occurred. But his presence gave the delegates courage, allowing them to attend, even when knowing what the convention was really about. As James Monroe communicated to Thomas Jefferson, "Be assured, his influence carried this government." [16]

Washington was elected to be the convention's president. And though he didn't say much and his votes were rarely decisive, his demeanor, moderation, and overwhelming presence were critical to the convention's success.

Though he did not seek the office and did not want it, he was unanimously elected to be the chief executive under the new Constitution. Knowing that not only the fate of the United States but the entire future of self-government was at stake, he became the new nation's first president.

As president, he set the tone for the leadership of a representative democracy. In everything from how he should be addressed, what manner of entertainment was appropriate, and how exactly a president would receive "advice and consent" from the senate on matters such as treaties, George Washington established a trail of moderation and restraint.

After serving his second term, George Washington set the most important precedent of all—he said farewell to his countrymen. He could have been king, but he preferred the Constitution.

•   •   •

Had George Washington been killed or captured on the shores of Long Island, it is likely that the American colonies would have eventually won their independence. But that they would have been able to do so united and under a governing document as remarkable as the Constitution is simply beyond belief.

Had it not been for a brisk northeast wind followed by a freak summer fog, the future of the entire world would have unfolded very differently.

Notes

1. Ellis, *His Excellency,* 21–23; Brookhiser, *Founding Father,* 23.
2. Ellis, *His Excellency,* 23; Brookhiser, *Founding Father,* 23.
3. McCullough, *1776,* 118. For information regarding the importance of New York, including the Tory presence in New York City, see ibid., 80, 118–19, 132–33; Ferling, *Almost a Miracle,* 120–25, 130.
4. Ferling, *Almost a Miracle,* 120–23, 131; McCullough, *1776,* 121–22, 126–29.
5. For information about the status of the American forces, see Ferling, *Almost a Miracle,* 125–26; McCullough, *1776,* 149–51.
6. The Declaration of Independence, Action of the Second Continental Congress, July 4, 1776.
7. Background information on George Washington is from Brookhiser, *Founding Father;* Ellis, *His Excellency;* Ferling, *Almost a Miracle;* McCullough, *1776.*
8. McCullough, *1776,* 49.
9. Ibid., 64.
10. Ferling, *Almost a Miracle,* 26. For information about the inherent weakness in the American position during the war for independence, see Brookhiser, *Founding Father,* 24–25; Ellis, *His Excellency;* Ferling, *Almost a Miracle;* McCullough, *1776;* Morison and Commager, *Growth of the American Republic,* 191–204.
11. Information on the retreat of the American army comes from Brookhiser, *Founding Father,* 18–19; Ferling, *Almost a Miracle,* 135–36; McCullough, *1776,* 182–91.
12. McCullough, *1776,* 130.
13. McCullough, *John Adams,* 153.
14. Brookhiser, *Founding Father,* 21
15. Ibid., 40.
16. Ibid., 71.

Chapter 4

The Miracle of
Our Constitution

Philadelphia
June 1787

"IT WAS A BITTER WINTER," the older man offered sadly. "An awful winter. Had it not been for the rebellion, we might not have come to this time and place."

The other man didn't answer. In the stifling heat of the Philadelphia summer, it seemed so long ago.

The older man pulled off his bifocal glasses—his own invention—and turned around. Evening was beginning to rest upon the city but the air inside the meeting room was quiet, stale, and stifling. Walking slowly, Benjamin Franklin moved to the nearest window, unlocked it—General Washington demanded that the room remain secure—and pushed the wooden shutters back.

James Madison walked to his side, and the two men breathed the cooler air. Less than half his age, Madison was quicker than Franklin and certainly as thoughtful, but he wasn't nearly as experienced, and it showed.

Franklin put his back to Madison, replaced his spectacles, and stared out the open window. "Daniel Shays was a fool and traitor. I curse him every day! If he had just contained himself, we might not be in this mess today."

Madison frowned. The winter of 1786–87 had indeed been a hard one for their infant country. Feeling crushed by debts and taxes, the rebel Daniel Shays had led a revolt of farmers in western Massachusetts. The uprising had faltered, but not before four of the rebels had been killed by the state militia, the leaders arrested and tried for treason. And though small in scope, the rebellion had struck a universal chord, resonating far beyond what anyone could have predicted.

He answered Franklin carefully. "The rebellion might have shocked us into action, but it was coming either way. It only accelerated what was inevitable. There's not a literate man inside our nation who doesn't believe the Articles of Confederation are doomed to fail."

Franklin took a breath and folded his hands behind his back. "For a moment, I viewed it as a race to see who could die first, the Confederation or myself." He faked a sigh. "Frankly, it makes me angry. If we could have waited another handful of years, I might have passed away peacefully in my bed."

Madison couldn't help but smile. It was impossible that Benjamin Franklin would have chosen to miss this time. Not even for eternity. He would have fought angels and grim reapers to stay and fight for this day. But the battle might still kill him, for it was proving far more difficult than either of them had ever dreamed.

The two men, both of them exhausted, were content to stand by the open window, savoring the cool air and the sounds of life that filtered up to them from the dimness of the moonlit streets outside.

Minutes passed. A wooden mantel clock above the fireplace marked the passing time.

"Are we doing the right thing?" Benjamin Franklin finally mumbled. His voice was soft and inward-seeking, and Madison knew he was mostly talking to himself. And it wasn't the first time he had asked the question. The truth was, every man working at the Convention asked himself the same question every day.

"History will tell if we are," Madison offered, "but this much we know. We have to do something. The Articles, as they exist, are fatally flawed. Like a slow-acting poison, they will destroy us in the end. How many times was General Washington driven to outbursts of wrath during the war because the Congress was too weak to supply his soldiers even the most basic of supplies, leaving them naked and starving on the battlefield? Congress had no power to pass laws or regulate commerce, leaving us with more trade wars between the states than with all the nations of Europe. We have no unified international policies, no single voice or representation overseas. Our ships are captured by pirates in the Mediterranean, our sailors enslaved, and we have no means to stop them. Poverty leaves us powerless. Yet with no power to impose taxes, all we can do is beg for contributions from the states. Think of when the messenger came to announce Washington's defeat of the British at Yorktown. There we were, the final victors, yet Congress had not a penny to pay the messenger for the cost of his official travel. Do you remember what had to be done? Members of Congress dug into their pockets and provided him whatever they could pay. Is that any way to build a nation?"

"Some of the states have been diligent in their contributions," Franklin offered weakly.

"But many of them have not! Now those who have been diligent have grown resentful. And how are we to blame them if they do?"

Franklin reached into his pocket and extracted a bill of currency printed by a southern state. Madison looked down and scowled. "It is worthless here in Philadelphia. All that southern money is. Some of the states print far more money than is good for them, then wonder why it won't buy them anything. Little wonder we find ourselves in the middle of an economic depression. And that's not the only thing we fight about. The dire financial condition of the states is leading to instability within their borders. There are coming battles over boundaries. And it's sure to get much worse. It seems the only difference between us and the warring nations of Europe is that they've had more time to learn to hate each other, I think."

Franklin shrugged and pushed the money back into his pocket. "We may be making up for lost time," he added sarcastically.

Again they fell into silence. Franklin took off his spectacles, breathed on them, cleaned nervously, then placed them in his breast pocket once again. "I heard a rumor . . . I don't believe it . . . but I heard that New York officials are making overtures to the leadership of Canada for a reconciliation."

Madison nodded slowly. "And Georgia has declared martial law."

Franklin closed his eyes. "Do you know what Article III of the Confederation states?"

Madison thought a moment. "Article III specifies that the states have entered into a 'firm league of friendship with each other.'"

"It seems then, my friend, that friendship has its limits."

Madison actually huffed. "We see that here, in this room, every day. Jealousy, envy, and competition are the norm. The small states hate the large ones. The Southern States are suspicious of the Middle Atlantic States, and both of them hate the North. They all place tariffs on each other and operate individual customs services at the borders. Nine states have their own navies! This from the same men who refused to send Washington what he needed for the war!"

Franklin's eyes narrowed slightly, though his smile remained. "Your people may be the worst, my friend. Your own Virginia has imposed duty on her seaports, sometimes even confiscating ships. And who is their target? Ships from England? Maybe Spain? No, my friend, they target ships from New York and Boston. It's a foolish way to move forward; work with your enemies and tax your friends."

Madison looked down. "This is no way to grow a nation," he repeated with a strain.

"It is no way at all. Men swear allegiance to their states but not their country, too many insisting they are from the 'country of Virginia' or the 'great nation of New York.' My friends claim they are citizens of Massachusetts and nothing else!"

"Washington said we are thirteen sovereignties pulling against each other. Any way you look at it, we have a very long way to go."

Franklin didn't answer. The clock ticked and the wind blew, billowing the sheer white curtains from the window like a passing ghost.

"I'm afraid we're going to fail," Madison said in a tired voice. "We've been working here for weeks, and we're not any closer to resolution than we were when we started negotiating in May. Most are ready to surrender. None knows what to do. If we can't find a way to move forward, this nation will descend into chaos and anarchy. Everything that we have fought for will be for nothing. All of it in vain. But the simple truth is, I don't know what to do! I don't know how to proceed. And I'm quickly losing hope."

Franklin looked away before he offered, "Maybe all we can do is pray."

It Was Possible to Fail

The two leaders' presumption of failure was completely justified.

Other than sporadic cooperation during the war for independence, the thirteen "sovereign colonies" had no history of unity or sense of country beyond their own states. Few citizens had any sense of being an "American." Fewer still understood the sacrifices and compromises it would take to forge a nation from thirteen individual states.

The new nation's weakness made it impossible for America to counter mischief from foreign powers. For example, the British still occupied military forts south of the Canadian border and were continually encouraging hostilities between the Indians and the Americans. The Spanish harassed the southern border—with the ready help of the Creeks, Choctaws, and Chickasaws—from their outposts in New Orleans, Natchez, and Florida, effectively controlling the lower Mississippi River. This led to serious problems in the western territories (the massive areas between the Appalachian Mountains and the Mississippi River that would one day become ten states), where it was prohibitively expensive for settlers to move their goods and products to market by any other way except the river. This geographical reality, along with Spanish intrigue and insensitivity on the part of politicians in the East, led some of the leaders in these areas to seek alliances with if not outright governance by Spain.

Both the British and Spanish were convinced that the concept of a United States of America was a failed experiment. John Adams, acting as the nation's representative in London, had recently been told that His Majesty's government intended to negotiate with each state independently, the Confederation having proved to be unreliable.[1]

It appeared that the American experience in self-government, brief though it was, was doomed. And this nation was not alone. Throughout most of Europe, governments "of the people" were in solid retreat. Only England had a record of a viable Parliament. In Spain, Denmark, Germany, and Hungary, legislative bodies that ostensibly represented the people were dying or already dead. And history gave no reason for optimism. Apart from a few Swiss cantons and Greek city-states, there was no example of a successful republican self-government in the history of the world. And there certainly was no example of a republican government that was capable of governing such a huge geographical area as the new United States. (An exception to this observation might be the Roman republic under Cicero, but even that was short-lived and quickly replaced by the reign of Julius Caesar.)

Making matters worse was the fact that America was far from thinking of itself as a whole and single nation. States and regions were much more important to the average citizen than the "United States," and, with the exception of the lust for freedom, there was little held in common between the country's citizens.

If some way wasn't quickly found to bind these disparate and independent peoples, the states would inevitably dissolve into open conflict over boundary and trade disputes. Jealousy and rivalry would replace any sense of commonality, leading the United States to become nothing more than a northern version of the future republics of Central and South America.

Little wonder, then, that early in the summer of 1787, in a letter to his friend the Marquis de Lafayette, George Washington pronounced what was at stake: Either the United States was going to create a new and functioning government or it was going to drift into anarchy, confusion, and rule by demagogues.[2]

Who Were We?

What was the United States like in 1787? Relying primarily on the census of 1790, the first conducted in the new nation, we can postulate that its population was nearing four million, about 700,000 of whom were slaves. And it was a very young nation, with one-half of its people younger than sixteen.

The people were widely dispersed, with only six cities (Philadelphia, New York, Boston, Charleston, Baltimore, and Salem) having a population of 8,000 or more.

The new nation was huge, with more territory than the British Isles, France, Germany, Spain, and Italy combined. The land was rich: abundant fish in the rivers and the ocean, plentiful game in the forests, fertile soil, bounteous forests for wood products. The nation's incredible mineral wealth, as yet untapped, was there for the taking.

A far greater percentage of the population owned land than did the people in Europe. Because land was abundant and relatively cheap, anyone who wanted it and was willing to undergo the toil of clearing it had it available. Yet the forests were not yet conquered, with only a few areas in southern New England and the Middle Atlantic States having more cultivated land than forest.

Yet even among those who owned large amounts of land, very few had any disposable income. Graphic examples of this can be found among the nation's leaders. Despite his land holdings, when George Washington left Mount Vernon to go to New York for his inauguration as the first president of the United States, he had to borrow money for his expenses. One of Virginia's delegates to the Constitutional Convention, George Mason, owner of a great plantation, had to borrow money in order to even attend. On the flip side, there was very little extreme poverty, and little to distinguish between the maid and the mistress, the farmer and the mayor, the workman and the foreman. Indeed, European visitors were continually struck by the absence of the savage poverty that beset the cities in their homelands.

Newspapers and journals were numerous. Everyone read at least one, often two per day. The Americans of that day were well-informed, especially considering the distances between the cities and the wide dispersion of the population.

All of these factors led to an extreme sense of independence among these new Americans. European visitors (who were mostly royalty) were also amazed at the equality among the people. And it rattled them how Americans gave so little deference to their own elected officials and virtually no deference to their visitors' royal station.

In short, America was on the cusp of a degree of greatness, but *only* on the cusp. Accomplishments in science, architecture, music, medicine, and the arts were in the future still.

This was understood by one of the wisest of the Founders. In a letter to his wife from Paris, John Adams observed: "I must study politics and war, that my sons may have liberty to study mathematics and philosophy, geography, natural history and naval architecture, navigation, commerce and agriculture, in order to give their children a right to study painting, poetry, music, architecture, statuary, tapestry and porcelain."3

• • •

By 1786, it had become painfully obvious that the Articles of Confederation were inadequate and needed to be either reworked or superseded. Although many called for reform—some with great passion—most of the leaders of the era saw no way of accomplishing serious reform in light of the five years it had taken just to get the states to agree to the weak and ineffective Articles.

There were some, however, who would simply not give up in their quest to actually *unite* the United States. Three stand out: George Washington; his former aide-de-camp, Alexander Hamilton; and James Madison of Virginia. And though they were not alone, they were the key players. Heeding with hesitance the urgent calls for change, Congress acted with typical caution. It took until February 1787 to issue an invitation to the thirteen states to send delegates to Philadelphia in May. And even then, the delegates were told they were gathering "for the sole and express purpose of revising the Articles of Confederation."[4] To suggest that they move beyond the Articles, let alone to advocate they scrap the Articles and create a central and unified Constitution, would have bordered on treason, guaranteeing the Convention's failure before it even began.

• • •

The eighth president of the United States, Martin Van Buren (1837–1841), is reported to have called the writing of the Constitution "an heroic and lawless act."[5] And it is true. Though the delegates knew that the Congress had instructed them, with rare specificity, to do nothing more than suggest revisions to the Articles of Confederation, from the very beginning it was understood that the Constitutional Convention was an effort to supplant those Articles. That made the Convention, if not outright illegal, assuredly extralegal.

Understanding this, one of the first rules enacted by the delegates was the secrecy rule. No discussion of the affairs of the Convention was to take place outside of the State House. Sentries were placed at the doors to the building. The windows were kept shut for privacy, despite the stifling heat. Copies of the daily journal could be made with permission only.

On one occasion, a delegate dropped a piece of paper containing his notes of the proceedings, which was given to the president of the Convention, George Washington. When the Convention was about to adjourn for the day, Washington confronted the delegates, warning them of the consequences if such information were made known to the press, and tossed the paper onto a table. "Let him who owns it, take it," he demanded.

The paper was never claimed.[6]

• • •

In what turned out to be the hottest summer in more than thirty years, delegates to the Convention began to gather to the State House in Philadelphia in May. Things did not start well. Rhode Island refused to send any delegates at all. While seventy-four delegates were appointed by the other twelve states, only fifty-five would participate. Eleven days passed before the Convention could even start, it taking that long for a quorum of seven states to show up.

When they finally did, it was clear they were a youthful group. Benjamin Franklin, at age eighty-one, was the senior member of the Convention. Only four members were older than sixty. Five were younger than thirty. But their youth did not accurately reflect their experience. Twenty-eight had served in Congress and almost all of the others had been in state legislatures. Two were college presidents, twelve had taught school, thirty-four were lawyers, and eight of them were judges. Most were planters, landowners, or merchants. Eight of the delegates had signed the Declaration of Independence eleven years before. Twenty-one had been soldiers of the Continental Army.

Two men who were not in attendance, John Adams and Thomas Jefferson (Adams was in London and Jefferson in Paris), nonetheless exerted their influence through their long-held views and their surrogates.

Also conspicuous by their absence (arguably evidence of Providence's influence) were some of the firebrands of 1776, the "Violent Men": Patrick Henry and Sam Adams, Richard Henry Lee and John Hancock. Irreplaceable in bringing about the war for independence but suspicious of the power of a national government, their role in the Convention might have been disruptive beyond measure. It will never be known whether the spirit of compromise would have fallen on these men in sufficient degree to allow them to be positive contributors to the efforts of the Convention.

As the Convention gathered, one thing became very clear: Opposition was strong from north to south. As mentioned, Rhode Island boycotted the gathering altogether. It was not alone in its fear that its recently hard-won independence might be threatened. Anxiety about a strong national government rippled from Maine to Georgia. *Let the states govern themselves!* was the dominating feeling of nearly everyone.

As an example, William Blount, a member of Congress from North Carolina who disapproved of the Convention, prophesied, "I still think we shall ultimately and not many years [hence] just be separate and distinct governments perfectly independent of each other."7

• • •

As the Convention unfolded, the intensely held views of the various delegate factions were laid bare. There were disagreements over so many issues: Should we have a single chief executive? Wasn't that too close to a king? How should the president be elected? Would he be selected by the Congress or elected by the people? How long should he serve? Was there any reason he couldn't serve for life? How much power should the executive branch have? Should the president have the power to veto acts passed by the Congress? What should the terms of office be for those in the executive and legislative branches? Some demanded they serve no more than three years. Some insisted they serve for life. Should senators be selected from the Congress or elected by the people? Who should pay the salary for the members of Congress—the states? What should be the power of the judges?

The matters to be decided were critical and long lasting and great in number. But by far the most intense struggles centered on three main issues:

1. *National Government versus States' Rights.* Those who favored a strong national government contended against those who wanted to protect the sovereign rights of the states. This proved to be the most critical and contentious issue, overpowering other critical questions such as how to safeguard the rights of the individual (which had been so eloquently set forth in the Declaration of Independence) from the encroachment by a too-powerful government. It was presumed that the

best way to protect the inalienable rights of individual citizens was to retain more sovereignty in the states, where the government was more answerable to the people.

2. *Finding Equity among the States.* Almost equal in intensity were the differences between the states with the largest populations—Virginia, Pennsylvania, and Massachusetts—and the smaller states. The large states feared they would become the primary source of revenue to the government, and they wanted to be assured that they had an equal say in the legislative branch. On the other hand, the small states feared that if the large states achieved their goal, a coalition of the three large states would totally dominate the national government.

3. *Slavery.* The slave states of Virginia, Georgia, and North and South Carolina were intent on protecting their right to own slaves. Antislavery delegates felt just as strongly that the Convention was obligated to condemn the practice. Assuming that slavery remained, other questions followed: How should the slaves be counted for purposes of proportional taxation of the states? How should they be counted for purposes of allocating membership in the House of Representatives?

Beyond these three critical and emotionally charged issues, there were many other factional and regional concerns. The interests of the merchants sometimes varied with those of the farmers. Those who held the debt of the United States demanded that the government have sources of revenue to repay them. How would the members of the Congress be allotted? How would interstate commerce be regulated? So many issues of concern!

As president, Washington said little. But his calm demeanor kept the debate civil. Kindly and wise Benjamin Franklin used his well-known humor and pithy anecdotes to calm troubled waters. Madison, Hamilton, and other wise and thoughtful men introduced major principles to keep the Convention focused on the big picture. Yet despite their best efforts, the Convention teetered on the edge of failure. For weeks, and then months, the delegates debated among themselves. Tempers flared. Angry exchanges were shouted across the room. Decisions were made, only to have the issues raised again. Over and over, the most difficult and controversial issues were put off. Some delegates were forced to leave for long periods of time to deal with personal business, sickness in the family, or duties in the Congress, bringing the Convention to a standstill because of the absence of a quorum.

As spring wore into summer, it appeared the Convention was doomed to end in deadlock.

Four members abandoned the Convention altogether and became leading opponents to the Constitution, or Anti-Federalists, as they were called. Two of these were delegates from New York, leaving Hamilton (one of the major forces behind the Convention) alone to represent his state. Left to his own accord, and at odds with the political forces in New York, he was forced to leave the Convention frequently.

Though the members were able to reach agreement on some of the minor issues, the major obstacles remained.

How to balance power between the federal government and the states?

How to balance power between the states?

Would the new nation outlaw slavery?

By the time it adjourned for the Fourth of July—an anniversary that passed with very little celebration between the members—the Convention was in danger of failure. Delegate Luther Martin of Maryland wrote that "we were on the verge of dissolution."[8] A Frenchman visiting George Washington described his gloom to be akin to that which he had observed in the general at Valley Forge. Washington wrote to Hamilton of his despair that the Convention would fail.[9]

Philadelphia
July 1787

JAMES MADISON ROLLED in his bed, moving from one side to the other, feeling occasional lumps of feathers underneath him. A light sweat coated his body, but he didn't notice, having grown used to the humidity and heat. The room was bathed in white light, and he knew from the position of the moon that it was very late—or maybe it was early, closer to sunrise than sundown—and yet he hadn't slept.

They had been struggling for weeks now and still they were so far from success.

They had negotiated in good faith, worked vigorously together. All of them had. He no longer doubted the intentions of his fellow Convention members. Some of them he loved like brothers, and even those he fought against he respected, for he had come to realize they were fighting out of conviction, just as he was. But despite the forceful arguments and battles, they were no closer to an outcome than they had been months before.

He rolled over and cursed the darkness.

Power.

Sharing power.

It all came down to that.

Between the central government and the people. Between the larger and smaller states.

As he thought back on the endless deliberations, his mind seemed to settle on one thing. It had been several weeks since the "Connecticut Compromise" had first been presented, but the essence of the proposal was still clear in his mind, mostly because he had opposed it so adamantly.

How could they not base representation on population? How could he go back to his people in Virginia and try to convince them of that? It was the essence of democracy! The essence of fair government! Yet the Connecticut Compromise proposed a weighted option that took so much of it away. He had fought such ideas from the beginning and he would continue fighting now.

Yet, sometimes he wondered . . .

The Connecticut Compromise had been presented by Roger Sherman, dark-haired and lanky, a good friend, a good man. Everybody seemed to respect him, but when he had first proposed the idea on June 11, it had been outright rejected, having very little support.

Personally, he hated it. Why should a state with half the people lead a much larger state around? Why should the smaller states have equal power to a state with two or three times the population! It stood against everything he had fought for. The Senate should be proportional to the people.

Yet again, sometimes he wondered. Maybe it was the answer.

He sucked in a breath and held it.

If it was the answer, it would kill him to swallow the bitterness of it down.

He rolled over again and closed his eyes, blocking out the shadows in the small room that were created by the moon. He tried to clear his mind, forcing his thoughts back to his friends and family, back to his beloved home, the peacefulness of Virginia, the rolling hills and bright green countryside.

Maybe it is the answer! a voice in his head seemed to say.

He sat up on the side of his bed.

Maybe it's the answer. Maybe it's the compromise that you've been looking for.

He shook his head as he remembered the verbiage of the Connecticut Compromise: "That the proportion of suffrage in the 1st. branch should be according to the respective numbers of free inhabitants; and that in the second branch or Senate, each State should have one vote and no more."

The numbers of the lower house would be represented by the proportion of the population. The numbers of the upper house would be the same for each state, regardless of its size or population.

It would bring balance.

It would share power. And it might be the only way.

As he sat there in the dark, he realized he had been forced to change his heart. For the first time he would support the idea.

It was time to save the Convention. And if that meant he had to compromise on something he opposed so strongly, then maybe others would be willing to compromise as well.

And maybe the idea of the Constitution might be pulled back from the grave.

The Sun Breaks Through

On July 16, the Convention agreed on what was to become known as the Great Compromise, in which the small states were protected from the influence of the larger states by being given two seats in the Senate, and the large states were protected by proportional representation in the House. Further, it was agreed that all revenue bills would begin in the House—that body where the large states would have the greatest influence—thus allaying the fear that the large states would be held responsible for too great a share of the national government's cost of operation.

Although the Convention was to continue for almost two more months, by and large this compromise ended the major crisis. The issue that Madison described as "the most threatening that was encountered in framing the Constitution"[10] was overcome.

The second great issue, state sovereignty versus the powers of the national government, was solved by agreeing that the Constitution would be the "supreme law of the land." However, the national government possessed only those powers that were enumerated in the Constitution, only those powers granted by the people. The rest of the powers were retained by the people and the states.

The issue of slavery proved to be thorny. Benjamin Franklin had decided to make the abolition of slavery his last great cause. He wanted to introduce a resolution that would have the Convention condemn slavery but was persuaded by other delegates from Northern states not to do so. After agreeing not to condemn slavery outright, the Convention fought over whether to allow a slave to be counted as a "full person" for purposes of deciding representation in the House of Representatives, eventually agreeing to count each slave as "three-fifths of a person." Some wanted the importation of slaves to be outlawed, but it was agreed that it would be permitted until 1808, after which it would be forbidden.

Many contemporaries and opinion makers since have denounced the Convention for its failure to bring an end to slavery. How could those who had fought a war based on the belief that "all men are created equal" fail to end the odious practice of slavery?

But had abolition-minded members of the Convention succeeded in forcing antislavery measures, the Convention would almost certainly have collapsed, sealing the nation's doom.

The best evidence of this reality is the fact that a number of the proposed compromises regarding slavery came from abolition-minded delegates from Northern states. They understood how important slavery was to the economic interest of the South and that it was a deal-breaker for them.

It is also irrefutable that many of the Convention delegates believed that slavery was dying of its own accord. At the time, it was becoming more and more uneconomical to own slaves, for the crops the South relied on to justify the cost of slavery were becoming economically unviable. The view, both within and without the Convention, was that compromises on slavery could be made to hold the Southern states in the Union because the evil of slavery would soon fade away.

Sadly, the invention of the cotton gin by Eli Whitney in 1793 changed the economics dramatically. Suddenly, cotton production became so profitable that slavery became an economic boon and a necessity. Larger and larger plantations became the norm in the South. Slavery was not to end for another seventy-eight years.

• • •

Even after the Great Compromise, the delegates continued work week in and week out. A total of 560 roll-call votes were to be taken on various resolutions and amendments.

Earnest and contentious debate continued up to September 15, the final working day of the Convention. Throughout the last day, members stood to expound on everything that they found wanting in the Constitution while suggesting things that they would change. A serious motion was made for a second Convention to follow, allowing the people an opportunity to review the results of the first Convention and provide further amendments and clarifications, a certain recipe for deadlock and disaster.

At the end of the day, a final motion was made to agree to the Constitution as it was written. With the outcome utterly uncertain, an anxious air settled over the hot and crowded room as each man was given an opportunity to vote.

At the end of the process, every state had voted aye.

Two days later, the Constitution was signed and sent to the Congress.[11]

The Fight Goes to the States

After only eight days of consideration, the Congress passed the Constitution on to the states, where the battle for ratification would be fought state by state.

Wanting to avoid the problems they had encountered in struggling to get the unanimous consent of all thirteen states to the Articles, the new Constitution provided that it would become effective upon ratification by just nine states. Further, the Constitution was to be ratified by "THE PEOPLE," not the Congress nor the states, a task that could require extraordinary effort on the part of the Constitution's supporters.

Many people, including leading citizens, opposed the Constitution. These Anti-Federalists, as they were known, had five significant objections, including:

- the loss of state sovereignty
- the absence of a Bill of Rights to protect all citizens from expansive federal power
- having already rejected a king, an overwhelming fear that the president was too powerful
- alarm over the independent federal judiciary
- significant fears about the power of taxation

The Anti-Federalists organized opposition in every state: Patrick Henry and Richard Henry Lee in Virginia, Samuel Adams and General James Warren in Massachusetts, the Clintonians and General John

Lamb in New York. Anti-Federalists included members of the Convention, members of Congress, generals and other officers in the war for independence, governors, judges, and a future president of the United States, James Monroe.

On occasion, the debate became violent. In December, following Pennsylvania's ratification of the Constitution, a rally was held to celebrate. A mob of Anti-Federalists attacked the rally and almost beat the featured speaker to death.

On December 6, Delaware became the first state to ratify. It was followed by the first of the large states, Pennsylvania, and then in turn New Jersey, Georgia, and Connecticut. The next large state to consider ratification was Massachusetts. With its relative wealth and sophistication, industry, and highly progressive educational system, not to mention the critical role the state and its leaders had played in the Revolution, Massachusetts was considered one of the keys to ratification.

On January 9, 1788, the Massachusetts state legislature convened a convention to consider ratification. The debate raged for more than a month, the reputations and futures of many good men placed on the altar.

Andover, Massachusetts
February 1788

WILLIAM SYMMES APPROACHED his home on foot. The narrow lane was dark and empty, the only sound the bark of lonely dogs from down the street. There would be no grand homecoming or celebration of his return, and he was grateful for the anonymity of the night.

She was waiting at the doorway, a cotton shawl around her shoulders. Walking the frozen road, he studied her demeanor, his steps slowing just a bit. He knew her well, and her body language was as clear as any spoken word, but something in her face confused him now. Was she angry or just frustrated? It was too dark to tell. Moving closer, he studied her dark eyes, the shadows from the parlor lamp falling through the window, then finally recognized the look on her face. Confusion and bewilderment. She simply didn't understand. A surge of relief ran through him. He was exhausted, and the last thing he wanted was to have to justify himself again.

Neither of them spoke as he opened the wooden gate and walked toward her.

"I'm not angry at you," she said as he approached.

He glanced up at the moon that was barely rising into the hazy winter sky and muttered a grateful "thank you."

He was a young man, handsome and articulate and intelligent, his youth coming with great ambition and a bright future. But standing in the light of the partially obscured moon, both of them wondered if he had thrown it all away.

She shook her head and pulled him tightly to her, resting his brow upon her shoulder. "What were you thinking, William? You had so much to lose. So much to lose. The price you will pay may prove to be very high indeed."

He started to pull away, then leaned into her. "There are a few here who still support me."

She shrugged, nodding vaguely at their surroundings, the neat houses, churches, narrow streets, and small stores that made up the town in which they lived. "There may be some, but they are very few now."

"But we don't know what their dispositions might become once the Constitution has been accepted . . ."

"This much we know. You were sent to represent the feelings of the township. Now they feel that you've betrayed them. When you left here a month ago, you were firm in your opposition to ratification. You claimed nothing would change your mind. Now you stand here, not only a supporter of the federal Constitution but one of its strongest advocates." Her voice was picking up now, taking on the sharpness of the emotion she was fighting to hold down. "You not only changed your mind, but you changed the mind of many others. You are too good! Too persuasive! Others follow where you lead. Worse, you've turned against the wise men of our community, the influential men of Andover—those who chose to send you! You've disregarded the wisdom and the counsel of their years. It galls them terribly. They are angry. And they stir that anger up among the others, calling you opportunistic, saying you did nothing but sniff the wind, then pitch your vote to the winning side. We have seen the price of traitors. We know about that here in Andover.

"And it matters not the outcome. If the Constitution is ratified or defeated, it matters not to us any longer. You've been branded. We've been branded. And we have nowhere else to turn."

William shook his head and looked away. "But these people know me. They believed in me. These people are our friends."

"They trusted you, and you've betrayed them. You left here as a staunch opponent, yet look now where you stand."

He lowered his voice, his words pained. "I didn't switch out of political opportunity! I didn't switch just to be on the winning side!"

She almost scoffed, her dark hair blowing in the cold winter breeze.

"I didn't. You *know* I didn't." He quickly shook his head. "I will say to you the very words I told the delegation as we prepared to cast our votes. I stand acquitted of my conscience. I hope I stand acquitted of my constituents, but I know I do before my God."

She looked at him, then forced a smile and pulled him close again. "We'll have to move, you know that. We have to leave this place. We have no friends here any longer. It is intolerable that we stay."

He glanced back to the empty road that they would soon travel down again.

"We can do it, though," she concluded. "We can move from this place and start over. We have no future here, but yes, we can start somewhere else."

He nodded his head, determined. "If that happens, then I accept it. It is an acceptable price to pay."

• • •

Eventually, the Federalists in Massachusetts prevailed, but only because they agreed to allow recommendations for amendments to the

Constitution. One delegate, the courageous William Symmes (whose biographer noted as having surrendered "his chosen prospects in life, the hope to acquire wealth and honor in his native town, for the sake of the people . . ."[12]) bravely voted for ratification against the wishes of his constituents, for which choice he was forced to move from his town upon his return from the convention.

In April, Maryland joined the states approving the Constitution. In May, South Carolina brought the number of ratifying states to eight. On June 21, New Hampshire ratified. Nine states had now voted for ratification. Technically, the Constitution was now in effect. But Virginia, a state with one-fifth of the nation's population and a huge geographical area that included what would one day become the states of Kentucky and West Virginia, was not yet on board.

Everyone recognized the significance of getting Virginia's approval of the Constitution.

The Virginia ratifying convention was the height of drama. Patrick Henry, the leader of the opposition, was joined by some of the state's most famous men. The Federalists were led by the "Father" of the Constitution, James Madison. George Washington stayed at Mount Vernon but remained in constant communication.

In the end, by a very narrow margin, Virginia ratified.

Patrick Henry, ever the patriot, offered the final argument against ratification, but ended by saying that should he lose, he would be "a peaceful citizen." That night, after losing the vote, he addressed a mass meeting where some called for resistance to the new government. Henry, true to his word, told the angry crowd that the matter was now settled and "as true and faithful republicans you had all better go home."[13]

With Virginia's vote secured, opposition in New York began to crumble. As noted, two of New York's three delegates to the Constitutional Convention had quit to become leaders of the Anti-Federalists. Standing alone, Hamilton had voted for the Constitution, despite knowledge that his position was highly unpopular in his state. Undaunted, he and Madison, along with John Jay, had written eloquent defenses of the Constitution in anonymous letters that were later compiled as *The Federalist Papers*—the finest exposition on the Constitution ever written. Ultimately persuaded, New York narrowly ratified on July 26 by a vote of thirty to twenty-seven.

North Carolina and Rhode Island came along in due time.

The Constitution was now the law of the land.[14]

Was It a Miracle?

One might ask how the compiling of 4,400 words on a piece of paper can be considered evidence of God's hand. We would answer that the crafting of the Constitution of the United States was a miracle for three reasons.

1. *Timing.* The window of opportunity for the writing and ratification of the Constitution was very small. But the window *did* open for a short time, and the men of the age were wise enough to take the opportunity.

Every effort to make the Articles of Confederation workable between 1776 and 1787 had already failed. But then suddenly, in May of 1787, a group of fifty-five patriots came together with both the wisdom of the ages and enough youth to energetically fight for the ratification of the Constitution. The reasons why prior efforts to create a working central government had failed were multitudinous, but this much is clear: they did in fact fail.

Any attempt to create a Constitution any later than 1787 would have almost certainly resulted in failure as well. Just two years after the Convention finished its work, France became embroiled in its own Revolution, which lasted a full decade and degenerated into a bloody, violent affair. During the course of that Revolution, England and France went to war with each other. This ended up splitting many of the Founders, as they were divided by their support or opposition to the French Revolution, then between the French and British in the war.

The French Revolution was particularly bloody as "the people" rose up against their king. Having disposed of him, the French set up a series of dysfunctional and brutal republican governments, most of them more violent than the ones they had replaced, each of which failed in turn. In the meantime, thousands died at the guillotine, and private property was confiscated. Surely this example of failure would have frightened the Founding Fathers, giving them reason to think very differently about the degree of power to be retained by "the people." Had the Founders met to decide on the form of a new government of the United States with the radicalism of the French Revolution hanging over them, the Constitution would likely have been crafted in a very different way. Would the Founders, for example, ever have agreed to a House of Representatives that was elected by the people when they feared that it might duplicate the fanatical nature of the French National Assembly?

Making matters worse was the fact that the Founders split into two distinct political camps in the years that immediately followed the Convention. Old allies became political enemies. Adams's and Jefferson's long friendship, nurtured by serving together in Paris during the war for independence, could not survive their differences over the French Revolution, the war between the French and the British, and viewpoints as to the role of government versus the people. Jefferson and Hamilton had a highly partisan clash that split the cabinet under Washington in which they both served. Madison sided with Jefferson against his comrade-in-arms of *The Federalist,* Hamilton. Hamilton conspired to prevent his Federalist ally, John Adams, from obtaining the presidency in 1796. Hamilton and Aaron Burr, then vice president of the United States, allowed their differences to turn into bloodshed.

Today, it is hard to comprehend the partisan differences that erupted in the decade that followed the Constitutional Convention. Founders who had stood side by side through every step of the Revolution and the creation of the Constitution became bitter enemies.

Had the Constitutional Convention been called just a few years later than 1787, many of these men would have been unwilling to stand together. And without their input, the Convention would never have had a chance of success.

2. *Miraculous Compromise.* The second way in which the Constitution is demonstrably a miracle is the manner in which it came about—specifically, the degree to which the delegates were willing to listen, to learn from one another, to compromise, and, when defeated, to accept the wisdom of their fellow delegates.

Famed historian Catherine Drinker Bowen, in her great work *Miracle at Philadelphia,* described her conclusions after her in-depth study of the record of the proceedings of the Constitutional Convention: "Yet in the Constitutional Convention the spirit of compromise reigned in grace and glory; as Washington presided, it sat on his shoulder like the dove. Men rise to speak and one sees them struggle with the bias of birthright, locality, statehood—South against North, East against West, merchant against planter. One sees them change their minds, fight against pride, and when the moment comes, admit their error."[15]

But one does not have to rely on the observations of a historian writing two hundred years after the Constitutional Convention to reach this same conclusion. Listen to the thoughts of those who were there for those fateful months.

James Madison, as he wrote in *The Federalist Papers #37:*

> The real wonder is that so many difficulties should have been surmounted, and surmounted with a unanimity almost as unprecedented as it must have been unexpected. It is impossible for any man of candor to reflect on this circumstance without partaking of the astonishment. It is impossible for the man of pious reflection not to perceive in it a finger of that Almighty hand which has been so frequently and signally extended to our relief in the critical stages of the revolution.[16]

George Washington, in a letter to his friend Lafayette of February 7, 1788: "It appears to me, then, little short of a miracle, that the Delegates from so many different States (which States you know are also different from each other), in their manners, circumstances, and prejudices, should unite in forming a system of national Government, so little liable to well founded objections."[17]

On the last day of the Convention, Benjamin Franklin, the oldest, some say the wisest, and certainly the most experienced of the delegates, pleaded with the delegates to support the product of the Convention:

> Mr. President:
>
> I confess that there are parts of this constitution which I do not at present approve. But I am not sure I shall never approve them. For having lived long, I have experienced many instances of being obliged by better information or fuller consideration, to change opinions even on important subjects, which I once thought right, but found to be otherwise. . . . Sir, I cannot help expressing a wish that every member of the Convention who may still have objections to it, would with me, on this occasion doubt a little of his own infallibility—and to make manifest our unanimity.[18]

During the course of the Convention, every delegate had to give up on some cherished principle.

James Madison, who had come to the Convention more prepared than anyone and was primarily responsible for the general outline of government established by the Constitution, lost on many issues. Most dear to him was his belief that both the House and the Senate should be based on proportional representation. The Great Compromise was a bitter pill for him, but he swallowed it. He also initially objected to the House of Representatives being elected by the people, the length of terms of office for the Senate, the absence of a power in the national government to veto state laws, and other items.

Alexander Hamilton's view of the new government, as expressed by him in a six-hour speech that took almost an entire day, was very different from what emerged from the Convention. He favored a president who was chosen for life with the power of absolute veto, senators with life tenure, governors of states appointed by the national government—in sum, a national government and a ruling class with far more power than the Constitution provides.

Despite having their viewpoints rejected in so many significant ways, these two joined with John Jay to become the most potent and convincing advocates for the Constitution.

Franklin wanted an executive council, voted for life, rather than a single executive. He did not want the chief executive to have the power of the veto. He did not want anyone in the executive position to receive a salary. He lost on all counts. Most important to him, however, was his desire for the Convention to condemn slavery. He lost on that issue as well.

As we review the results of the Convention and compare them to the expressed desires of each delegate, we cannot help but be impressed by how often they lost on key votes. But during the course of the 560 roll calls, no man lost every time, and everyone was part of a winning vote on some occasion.

The "Spirit of Compromise," which prevailed not only during the course of the Convention itself but just as importantly thereafter, when the delegates disappointed in the product of the Convention put aside their displeasure and returned to their states to secure ratification, is remarkable!

These men of social stature, political and business success—"demigods" all—swallowed their pride, accepted defeat of personal agendas, and went forth and convinced a nation to accept the product of the Convention.

Anyone who observes the political processes today, at any level of government, knows that such nobility of spirit does not seem to exist in this modern world.

It is doubtful that this nation of more than 300 million people could ever produce fifty-five men or women of the caliber and character of those who arose from the ranks of the four million Americans of 1787.

3. *Forty-Four Hundred Miraculous Words.* Perhaps the greatest miracle of the Constitution is the document itself. As ratified in 1787, it

contained 4,400 words. Within seventeen years, twelve amendments were made, ten of them being the Bill of Rights. Since the passage of the Twelfth Amendment in 1804, the Constitution has been amended only fifteen times. Two of those amendments, the Eighteenth and the Twenty-First, are "throw-away" amendments, establishing and then abolishing Prohibition. In essence, the Constitution has had only thirteen substantive amendments in over two hundred years.

The genius of the Constitution is that it created a government capable of governing a massive geographical area containing a huge population, affording that population the most security, freedom, and opportunity of any people on earth. It has granted the people of the United States opportunities to flourish economically, educationally, and culturally. It has adapted to the changing conditions of this nation over the past 220 years and has actually expanded the liberties and freedoms enjoyed by its citizens. More, it has been a light and example to the world, its impact felt in one way or another in nearly every nation on earth.

The genius of the Constitution is found in the fact that, unlike every other major revolution in history (the French and Russian Revolutions being prime examples), the United States did not simply replace one despot with another. History has proven that the Constitution creates a system that defies despotism and tyranny.

How is it able to do this? Primarily through the underlying premise, part of Madison's gift to the world, that the Constitution comes from the people. Madison coined the phrase "We the People." These words are far more than a clever phrase. They restate the principle, first asserted in the Declaration of Independence, that God gives man rights and that the only legitimate purpose of government is to protect those rights.

Men create governments by consciously surrendering a portion of their God-given rights to government with the charge that such government is to protect the bulk of their rights. As Madison said, "Individuals entering into society must give up a share of liberty to preserve the rest."[19]

The danger that arises is that the government might go beyond the voluntarily granted powers and begin to exercise powers not granted, creating tyranny.

Madison set forth the dilemma in *The Federalist Papers #51:*

> If men were angels, no government would be necessary. If angels were to govern men, neither external nor internal controls on government would be necessary. In framing a government which is to be administered by men over men, the great difficulty lies in this: you must first enable the government to control the governed; and in the next place oblige it to control itself.[20]

To make certain that the government they created would control itself, the Founders devised a system with the following mechanisms to protect the citizens of the United States in the exercise of their God-given rights:

1. The Constitution is the supreme law of the land, yet it is granted only those specified, enumerated powers that are actually set forth in its pages. It can do only certain things and nothing beyond.

2. The states retain their sovereignty, and those powers not granted to the federal government are reserved *in the people.* The states provide a check against the federal government, and vice versa.

3. The federal government has three separate branches, the executive, the legislative and the judicial, each with its own independent power, creating a powerful but delicate "balance." In addition, the Constitution provides a means by which the power of one branch can be countered by another, creating a "check" on the other's power. As examples: the president can veto legislation passed by the Congress. Congress can override that veto. The courts can declare legislation unconstitutional. The executive and legislative branches can limit the jurisdiction of the courts. These checks and balances have nearly perfectly endured the test of time.

4. The Constitution creates a republic, where the people elect men

and women to represent them, while rejecting the creation of a democracy, where majority rule can allow the rights of the minority to be repressed.

5. Two of the branches of the government are accountable by way of regular elections. The third branch, the judicial, is independent and hopefully insulated from mob rule and changes in the popular mood.

6. The Constitution contains a means by which it can be amended in order to adapt and adjust to a changing nation and world.

This framework of government has worked incredibly well. Consider the following:

When the Constitution was devised, it created a government capable of governing a nation of about four million people. Today, that same Constitution governs a nation of more than 300 million people.

When the Constitution was ratified, the United States consisted of thirteen states massed along the eastern seaboard. The same Constitution today governs a nation that is strung through six time zones.

Originally, the Constitution governed a nation that was generally of the same language, religion, and culture. Today, that same Constitution governs a nation with an amazing diversity of religions, cultures, and even languages.

The original Constitution governed a nation that was still primarily agrarian. Today, it successfully governs a nation with a plethora of industrial, manufacturing, agricultural, and service-oriented sectors.

The Constitution has survived this nation's wars with foreign nations: England (twice), Mexico, Spain, the Central Powers (Germany and Austria-Hungary) of World War I, the Axis Powers (Germany, Italy, and Japan) of World War II, communist Korea and China, North Vietnam, and Iraq.

Most notably, it survived the great Civil War, in which there were more than 600,000 American casualties.

The Constitution has survived incompetent leadership and, on occasion, thoroughly corrupt leadership.

It has survived slavery, Jim Crow racism, and mistreatment of Japanese-Americans in World War II.

In short, the Constitution not only survived the evolution of this great nation but permitted the American people to exercise the greatest level of individual liberty in history. It has flourished in every way imagined by John Adams when he wrote to his dear wife regarding his desire to "study politics and war" so that his sons could study the sciences so that his grandchildren could study the arts.

●　●　●

When fifty-five men gathered in hot, humid Philadelphia for four months in 1787, they devised not only a system of government agreeable to the people but a form of government that has been the foundation of the greatest country the earth has ever known.

Further, it has been the "shining light on the hill" that has provided the inspiration for peoples all over the earth to seek liberty and freedom for themselves.

Is that not a miracle?

Notes

1. For information about the struggles of the United States under the Articles of Confederation, see Bowen, *Miracle at Philadelphia*, 3–31; Ellis, *Founding Brothers*, 10–12; Johnson, *History of the American People*, 177–84; Kennedy, Cohen, Bailey, and Piehl, *Brief American Pageant*, 107–11; Madison, *Notes of Debates in the Federal Convention*, 13–16; Morison and Commager, *Growth of the American Republic*, 1:255–73; Schweikart and Allen, *Patriot's History*, 88–110.
2. Bowen, *Miracle at Philadelphia*, 77.
3. McCullough, *John Adams*, 236–37. For information about the status of the young United States, see Bowen, *Miracle at Philadephia*, 141–84; Ellis, *Founding Brothers*, 10–11.
4. Bowen, *Miracle at Philadelphia*, 4.
5. Ibid., 62.
6. Ibid., 99.
7. Ibid., 12.
8. Ibid., 140.

9. Ibid.

10. Ibid., 187.

11. For information about the Constitutional Convention generally, see Bowen, *Miracle at Philadelphia;* Johnson, *History of the American People,* 183–90; Kennedy, Cohen, Bailey, and Piehl, *Brief American Pageant,* 111–14; Ketchum, *Anti-Federalist Papers and the Constitutional Convention Debates;* Madison, *Notes of Debates in the Federal Convention;* Morison and Commager, *Growth of the American Republic,* 1:274–89; Schweikart and Allen, *Patriot's History,* 106–19.

12. Bailey, *Historical Sketches of Andover,* 398; Bowen, *Miracle at Philadelphia,* 289–90.

13. Bowen, *Miracle at Philadelphia,* 305.

14. For information about the process of ratification, see Bowen, *Miracle at Philadelphia,* 267–310; Johnson, *History of the American People,* 191–95; Kennedy, Cohen, Bailey, and Piehl, *Brief American Pageant,* 114–18; Ketchum, *Anti-Federalist Papers and the Constitutional Convention Debates;* Morison and Commager, *Growth of the American Republic,* 1:289–94; Schweikart and Allen, *Patriot's History,* 119–26.

15. Bowen, *Miracle at Philadelphia,* xiv.

16. Hamilton, Jay, and Madison, *The Federalist,* 193.

17. Bowen, *Miracle at Philadelphia,* xvii.

18. Ibid., 255–56.

19. Madison, *Notes of Debates in the Federal Convention,* 627.

20. Hamilton, Jay, and Madison, *The Federalist,* 281.

Chapter 5

The Miracle of Abraham Lincoln and the Battle of Gettysburg

Little Pigeon Creek, Indiana
October 5, 1818

THE ROLLING LANDSCAPE stretched along the northern edge of Kentucky, making Spencer County a natural geographical, economic, and cultural border that differentiated the North from the South. Protected from the chill winds that swept down from Lake Michigan, the tiny, frontier town wasn't quite in the hill country, but it was close and the people were as simple and as rural as any in the United States.

Fall in southern Indiana was a beautiful time of year. The hardwoods along the streams burst into bloom, explosions of orange and tan and red. The October skies were clean and clear, the moisture adding a little texture to the air. And, like the streams that meandered through the black earth around the county, the days were calm and cool.

But the little boy who stood alone in the corner of the tiny log cabin didn't see any of the beauty that was around him. He didn't feel the cool air blowing through the roughly crafted window. He didn't hear the quail, or see the hummingbird hovering just outside the open door. He didn't see the slanted autumn sunshine breaking through the cracks in the tar used to seal the logs that ran underneath the roof.

The only thing he saw was his dead mother lying on the makeshift table in the center of the room. Her face was pale. Her eyes were closed. Her hair, brushed back by his father, was uneven and hastily combed.

One day before, his entire world had consisted of three things: his home, his older sister (who was weeping in the corner now), and the woman who lay motionless upon the table.

Abe Lincoln stared at her, his heart breaking. A crushing weight seemed to fall upon him. At that moment, he felt more alone than he'd ever felt in his life.

His father was a hard man who'd lived a hard life, and he made no bones about the fact it was going to be impractical for him to take care of the children by himself. Thinking of his father, the little boy looked through the open window. Not far from the cabin, the forest was thick. Between the cabin and the forest, a couple of acres of dry corn stalks protruded from the ground, cut down to their nubs. He remembered the unbearable work it had taken to prepare the fields and plant the crop: clearing the trees, pulling and leveling and hauling off rocks, digging for hours, planting, toting a thousand buckets of water, hoeing in the summer heat, fighting varmints who would come to eat their precious crop at night. But all the work had proven worth it. The golden kernels had turned out to be their family gold. Not only would corn be their primary source of food throughout the coming winter, it also had provided them with a commodity they could use to trade. More, the boy had learned to be skillful with his ax, and lately he'd come to realize that some of his neighbors were willing to let him borrow books in exchange for an hour or two of splitting logs.

Thinking of his closest neighbors, another frontier family almost half an hour's walk away, he moved his eyes toward the path that led off through the forest, then turned back to look at his dead mother. The table was about the same height as he was, and his face was even with hers. Her skin was thin and off-colored, almost a bluish hue. Milk sickness, they had called it, poisoned milk from a poisoned cow.

The boy took a small step toward her. Thirty-four and slender, this woman, who had not a day of formal schooling in her life, had always encouraged him to learn to read and write. She had even tried to help him with his arithmetic, a subject she clearly didn't understand. No matter where they'd lived or how poor they were, she'd always found a way to get him books.

And though only nine, the boy was wise enough to see the world for what it was. His mother was gone. His father, remote and unfeeling, had shown little interest in his children. He seemed to look at them with the same eye with which he looked at his chickens or a calf, measuring their stature and wondering when they'd be strong enough to contribute to the cause.

Standing in the dim light of the one-room cabin, Abe wondered pitifully what was going to happen to him and his sister now. Who would feed them, clothe them, nurse them when they were sick? Would they move on or stay here in this cabin on the edge of the frontier? Who was going to teach him? Would his father let him go to school?

He didn't know it yet, but two years of squalor lay before him—two years of painful loneliness until his father would remarry, followed by more loneliness and a lifetime of stunning challenges few men would be called on to endure.

But, as he would acknowledge later, the influence of his mother would help sustain him through it all.

An Incredible Man, a Horrible Time

Among all the gifts this nation has been given, Abraham Lincoln would have to be among the most supernal. Were it not for his leadership during that dreadful period in our country's history when

Americans fought their Civil War, we would not be living in the nation that we enjoy today. Further, the history of the entire world would likely have unfolded in a very different way.

The forces that were at work to tear this nation apart during the late 1850s and the Civil War cannot be fully appreciated today.

In 1860, the United States of America was the foremost, some would argue the *only* democracy on the earth. The world was full of dictatorships, noble monarchies, fledgling parliamentary governments, and military tyrannies, but there wasn't another functioning example of a democracy outside of the United States.

Because of this, governments and people all around the world—but especially in western Europe—watched with intense interest as the great experiment of democracy began to tear itself apart. Would the United States survive? Which direction would its people turn? The outcome would have profound influence on the rest of the world, for there were only two alternatives: either the United States would survive, allowing it to lay the foundation for democracy throughout the rest of the world, or it would die, taking the concept of a *people's* government to the grave. And if this noble experiment in self-government failed in the United States, could it possibly succeed elsewhere?

Simply put, the Civil War was one of those extraordinarily rare moments when the future of mankind literally hovered in the balance.

At this critical moment, Abraham Lincoln walked onto the stage.

The Man Who Started It All

Dred Scott was a black slave born somewhere in Virginia in the late 1790s. In 1830 he moved with his owner to St. Louis, Missouri. In 1833, he was sold to an army surgeon named John Emerson, who took Scott to posts in Illinois and the territory of Wisconsin. While at Fort Snelling in the territory of Wisconsin, Scott married a young teenage slave named Harriet.

Over the next few years, the Scotts accompanied Emerson back to St. Louis, Louisiana, and Iowa before winding up in St. Louis after their master died. In 1846, the Scotts sued Emerson's widow for their freedom, based on the fact that they had previously resided in the free state of Illinois and the free territory of Wisconsin.

Their case was strong. For years, the courts of Missouri had been granting such petitions, emancipating slaves who had been taken by their owners to free states. In 1850, a jury found for the Scotts. Upon appeal, however, the state Supreme Court, ignoring its own precedents, reversed the jury's decision.

In a wonderful twist of fate, about the same time, the Scotts became the property of the widow of Mrs. Emerson's brother from New York. This permitted the Scotts to renew their claim for freedom in the federal courts.

It began to appear that this case might become destined for consideration by the United States Supreme Court, and high-profile attorneys took over representation of both sides in the dispute. In February 1856, the Supreme Court heard the case over four days, a very long time for oral argument. It was held over for reargument in the 1856–57 term— likely to avoid having a decision affect the highly charged presidential election of 1856.

It became apparent to the nation's insiders that Dred and Harriet Scott had become pawns in a controversy that had taken on national consequence.

As the case unfolded, five Supreme Court justices with Southern sympathies agreed to a ruling that would reach far beyond anything imagined by the Scotts or their sympathizers. Sensitive to the politics at stake, the majority justices felt an urgency to have at least one of the Northern justices join in their proslavery decision. To accomplish this, one of the Southern sympathizing justices undertook an unprecedented maneuver. He prevailed upon President-Elect James Buchanan to use his influence to convince his fellow Pennsylvanian, Justice Robert C. Grier, to join the majority opinion, which Justice Grier did.

This extraordinary plot was furthered by an apparent communication to Buchanan of the Court's unannounced decision before his inauguration. He used the occasion of his inaugural speech to reference the forthcoming Supreme Court decision as one that would settle the issue of slavery in the territories. Feigning ignorance of the coming decision, he hypocritically encouraged the American people to "cheerfully" abide by the Court's ruling, whatever that decision might be. Two days later, the Court announced the outcome of the case.

The first part of the decision rendered by the Supreme Court was that the Scotts, being black, were not and never could be citizens of the United States. In fact, the majority ruled, no black, slave or free, was ever intended by the Constitution to be a citizen of the United States. Accordingly, they were not entitled to sue in federal court.

Further, the fact that the Scotts had been taken by their owner into the state of Illinois and the free territory of Wisconsin did not entitle them to freedom. Chief Justice Taney's opinion went on to conclude that the Wisconsin territory never was a "free" territory of the United States because Congress did not have the authority to designate an area "free."

The opinion held that the Missouri Compromise of 1820, which had been repealed by Congress in 1854, was unconstitutional. Slaves were property, and an owner of a slave could not be deprived of his or her property by an act of Congress.

The majority opinion, only the second Supreme Court ruling to declare as unconstitutional an act of Congress, was amazing in its scope and audacity as well as filled with gross misrepresentations of fact and law. Two members of the Court filed stinging dissents, revealing the corrupt nature of the majority opinion—but the ruling remained.[1]

Northern Democrats supported the Court's decision, but only with trepidation. In the South, the decision was hailed as a great victory. Slavery had been granted respectability by the highest court of the land. Indeed, Taney's majority opinion was broad enough to prohibit any state from forbidding slavery.

The Republican Party, just in its infancy, was energized by the decision, calling it a "politicized abomination."[2] Republicans, claiming that the judiciary had now joined the other branches of the federal government to force slavery on the entire nation, were determined to win the White House and replace the members of the Supreme Court who had rendered the "anti-constitutional, anti-republican, anti-democratic" decision.[3]

Among the most affected and most motivated by the *Dred Scott* ruling was the successful lawyer from Illinois, Abe Lincoln.

Why *Dred Scott* Mattered

To give context to the *Dred Scott* opinion, it is important to understand what had occurred elsewhere in the United States in the ten years leading up to the Civil War.

The decade of the 1850s began with secessionists in a fever pitch over the question of whether or not to admit California to the Union as a free state. Slave sympathizers felt that Northern radicals were engaged in war against the South—a war with the chief aim to stop the natural and inevitable expansion of slavery into the Western territories. Creating new states that forbade slavery was the primary weapon of the Northern radicals.

California's admission became entangled with questions of abolishing the slave trade (not ownership, just trade) in the District of Columbia, passing a fugitive slave law, solving a border dispute between Texas and New Mexico, paying the debts of Texas, and organizing the territories of New Mexico and Utah. When Southern radicals talked of secession, overwhelming the voices of moderation in the South, a crisis was at hand. The longtime masters of the Senate—Clay, Calhoun, and Webster—led the debate. In the end, the so-called Compromise of 1850 was passed, and joy erupted in Washington. The moderates had seemingly won a great victory. The Union was preserved.

But the Compromise of 1850 had only postponed critical decisions about the expansion of slavery and was, in fact, not a compromise at all. The three distinct sections of the United States, the North, the South, and the Border states, had each voted their special interests, leaving the nation more severely divided than before.

One of the important pieces of the Compromise of 1850 was an enhanced fugitive slave law that permitted slave owners to go into other states to find and return slaves who had escaped. Over the next few years, there were a number of high-profile episodes in which abolitionists in Massachusetts and Pennsylvania tried to prevent the discovery and return of slaves. Their Southern owners relied on the powers contained in the Compromise of 1850 to pursue, arrest, and return these fugitive slaves. Civil disobedience to the fugitive slave law was organized. Mobs assembled. Lives were lost.

The reaction in the South was swift and furious. How dare the uppity Northerners flaunt the laws of the land! And the Southern slave owners were not alone; many in the North turned against the abolitionists as well.

In 1854, legislation was introduced in Congress to deal with the territories of Nebraska and Kansas. The brainchild of Senator Stephen Douglas of Illinois, it called for a vote of the people within the proposed new states to decide the issue of whether they would permit slavery or not. The highly controversial legislation passed, roiling the nation even more.

Antislavery voices called for emigration from the East to guarantee a slave-free Kansas. Proslavery "bushwhackers" from Missouri poured across the Kansas border to counter their influence and to stop the influx—by force where necessary. Passion soon turned to violence. In May of 1856, proslavery Missourians stormed and ran wild through the town of Lawrence, Kansas. Homes were burned, antislavery newspapers destroyed, businesses ransacked. Two days later, a group of violent antislavery activists, led by the infamous John Brown, hacked to death three proslavery settler families on Pottawatomie Creek.

Not only were life and property at risk, but Missouri proslavery activists arranged for the rigging of elections in Kansas. United States Senator David R. Atchison of Missouri bragged, "We had at least seven thousand men in the Territory on the day of the election, and one-third of them will remain there."[4]

Years of violence followed in "Bloody Kansas," particularly along the border with Missouri. Bands of wild men roamed the land bringing death and destruction, rampage and revenge. This random violence continued in eastern Kansas and western Missouri through the rest of the 1850s and into the Civil War years.

The presidential election of 1856 pitted the infant Republican Party, led by John C. Fremont, against the established Democratic Party, led by James Buchanan. The election turned on the issue of slavery— the old issues of tariffs, immigration, and internal improvements being largely cast aside. Fremont and the Republicans ran on the slogan of "Free Speech, Free Press, Free Men, Free Labor, Free Territory, and Fremont." The Democratic Party, now dominated by proslavery forces, claimed that the Republicans were bent on destroying the Union and imposing equality between white and blacks, inflaming racist fears, particularly in the Border states.

In the end, the South proved that the belief in the superiority of the white Anglo-Saxon was not exclusive to Southern slaveholders. Buchanan won enough Northern votes to be elected president.[5]

Defending the Indefensible

Looking back, it's hard for us to understand how citizens of this country ever countenanced the ownership of their fellow human beings. How could reasonable people defend such a despicable practice?

Among the most mysterious excuses for slavery was that the practice was justified by Christianity. Because slavery was seen as a means of removing slaves from the barbarism of Africa, both the Protestant and Catholic churches justified it as a method of converting the heathens.

This rationale lost some of its appeal after the 1831 slave rebellion led by Nat Turner in which fifty-seven whites were murdered. It seems that Turner felt that his rebellion was inspired by the "Holy Spirit" and triggered by a "sign appearing in the heavens."[6]

Thereafter, many of the Christian churches that had tagged slavery as a necessary evil to reach a righteous end abandoned the notion in favor of the view that slavery was essential for social control and, perversely, as a means of ensuring freedom. This rationale found expression through the South's most consistent advocate for slavery, John C. Calhoun, a senator from South Carolina. In 1838, he argued, "Many . . . once believed that [slavery] was a moral and political evil; that folly and delusion are gone; we now see it in its true light . . . as the most safe and stable basis for free institutions in the world."[7] This rationale contended that all blacks were morally and intellectually inferior to whites—therefore, as slaves, they were simply doing what God intended for them to do. Further, the dispersion of slaves among the population broadly permitted for greater equality among the white population— even the poorest white could be lifted out of drudgery, freed to join the ranks of the wealthy elite.

This view was further enhanced by the popular propaganda in the South (which was somewhat true) that the North was a hellish place for its poorest workers. Only in the South could the poor be truly equal, and that equality was fueled by slavery. The *Richmond Enquirer* stated in 1856 that "Freedom is not possible without slavery."[8]

In addition to such inexcusable moral arguments for slavery, there were, of course, purely economic justifications as well. Before the slave trade into the United States ended in 1808, approximately 661,000 slaves had been imported. By 1860, the South had a population of 3.84 million slaves. Slaves represented 60 percent of the "agricultural wealth" in Alabama, Georgia, Louisiana, Mississippi, and South Carolina. An estimate, based on the census of 1860, put the total value of slaves at about $3 billion—more than the value of railroads and manufacturing combined. A field hand in the 1850s could cost $1,200. As the cloud of Civil War approached, the price of a male slave rose to $3,000, as much as the price of 500 acres of prime land.[9]

It was a simple fact that a huge percentage of the "wealth"—that is, the property—of the South was in the form of human beings. Slavery was profitable. The larger the plantation and the more slaves on that plantation, the more profitable it was.

Yet it has to be recognized that all of the religious and economic arguments for slavery ignore this basic human fact: Slave ownership created an atmosphere that fostered the most despicable of human passions.

The system legitimized rape. No female slave could refuse the advances of her master.

Slave families were subject to being ripped apart and destroyed for economic gain.

Runaway slaves who were caught were often tortured horribly. Whipping on farms and plantations was common. Some Southern states allowed for the murder of slaves. In other states the penalties were minor.

In the end, in addition to dehumanizing the slaves, slavery dehumanized the slave owner and everyone who witnessed or benefited from these evil acts.

Many of the people of the South knew that their society and practices were wrong and not morally sustainable. But as the decade of the 1850s unfolded, these voices of moderation were completely lost in the fray.

A Political Platform of Evil

One radical voice that grew in popularity was that of Robert Barnwell Rhett of South Carolina. Following the election of 1856, he began to espouse independence for the South. He had a vision of the South achieving its "high mission" as an independent slaveholders' republic, larger in geographical size than all of Europe and enriched by its production of cotton. And Rhett had a vehicle to broadcast his views: control of the *Charleston Mercury* newspaper.

He and others who embraced radical views were known as the fire-eaters. Their creed was not just the protection of the right to own slaves but a view of democracy that was very foreign to that of most Americans. The fire-eaters believed not only in the superiority of whites over blacks but in the superiority of a handful of whites over all other whites, teaching that the inalienable rights of life, liberty, and pursuit of happiness were endowed to white Anglo-Saxons alone. They believed that men's natural condition was to be subjected by their betters, and that civilization rested on the ability of the superior few to enforce such inequality. In order to see this happen, they were willing to completely reject the notion of democracy and majority rule.

L. W. Spratt expressed the fire-eater position in this way:

It is obvious that two distinct and antagonistic forms of society have met for the contest upon the arena of this Union. The one assumes that all men are equal and that equality is right, and, forming upon that theory, is straining its members to the horizontal plain of a democracy. The other assumes that all men are not equal, that equality is not right, therefore, and forming upon this theory, is taking upon itself the rounded form of a social aristocracy.[10]

Early on, the fire-eaters were a distinct minority, most Southerners believing in the relative equality of all whites. However, they were not without influence. And their influence grew. As the majority of the Northern states turned against slavery, there was a coalescing of Southern opinion around the view that popular democracy was out of control and could not be trusted.

It is critical to understand that the threat of the Southern philosophy was not just that it justified ownership of human beings, but that it rejected the concepts of freedom, liberty, and self-government that were the very foundations of this nation. Of this fact there is no doubt: *The rise of the South had as much to do with the stifling of democracy as it had to do with the owning of slaves.*

And while it is true that not all members of the Confederacy shared these antidemocratic views—the average soldier on the battlefield and most of the Southern leaders, such as Robert E. Lee, were not fighting for an antidemocratic government—it is also true that the views of the fire-eaters were shared by many of the political class. Perhaps such antidemocratic beliefs are best illustrated by the fact that when South Carolina voted to secede from the Union, it did so by declaring in its

"Address to the People of South Carolina" that the Constitution of the United States was a failed "experiment."[11] Antidemocratic sentiments eventually drove the South to practices common in modern police states. Mail and newspapers from the North were censored. Free speech and the right of assembly were curtailed. Free whites were subject to being conscripted to form slave patrols.

This antidemocratic mentality was also expressed in the Constitution adopted for the Confederate States, which stated: "Our new government is founded . . . upon the great truth that the negro is not the equal of the white man. That slavery—subordination to the superior race, is his natural and normal condition." Not only were slaves to be deprived of liberty and freedom, but free blacks were subject to being enslaved at the whim of the government. In fact, in response to President Abraham Lincoln's Emancipation Proclamation, Confederate President Jefferson Davis declared, "On and after February 22, 1863, all free negroes within the limits of the Southern Confederacy shall be placed on slave status, and be deemed to be chattels, they and their issue forever." Further, Davis declared than any free blacks who would be taken during the course of the war were to be reenslaved. [12]

The Constitution of the Confederate States granted subsidies to slave owners. Censorship was enshrined. Because the Confederate Congress never created a Supreme Court, the executive and legislative powers of the Confederacy were without a check and balance and, as the war unfolded, the executive power of the Confederacy expanded without restraint.

No knowledgeable person could see the Constitution of the Confederate States as a mirror image of the Constitution of the United States. The Confederacy was not a clone of the United States with the simple addition of humans being viewed as property. It rejected the American Constitution. It rejected the Bill of Rights. It rejected the very foundation of democracy.

It was *not* a government of the people, by the people, or for the people.

Abraham Lincoln understood this. But his ability to do anything about it would not come without a very long and uncertain fight.

How It Began

Abraham Lincoln reentered the political arena in 1858, at a time when the nation was starting to come apart.

The national stage was occupied by an increasing radicalism in both the South and the North. The majority of the Northern population was still conflicted on the issue of slavery. There was no consensus that the nation could not continue "half slave and half free," no consensus on what rights the black man was entitled to, and certainly no widespread view that war would be justified to preserve the Union.

Lincoln had served one term in the U.S. House of Representatives in the 1840s before building a reputation as a lawyer. For most of his life, he, like many others from the North, had objected to slavery but tolerated it. For example, in a speech delivered in 1854, Lincoln had articulated a condemnation of slavery without attacking the slave owner:

> The spread of slavery, I cannot but hate. I hate it because of the monstrous injustice of slavery itself. I hate it because it deprives our republican example of its just influence in the world; enables the enemies of free institutions with plausibility to taunt us as hypocrites; . . . and especially because it forces so many good men among ourselves into an open war with the very fundamental principles of civil liberty, criticizing the Declaration of Independence. . . . Before proceeding let me say that I think I have no prejudice against the Southern people. They are just what we would be in their situation. If slavery did not now exist among them, they would not introduce it. If it did now exist among us, we should not instantly give it up. This I believe of the masses North and South.[13]

But during his time as a lawyer, his hatred of slavery became intense. He had strenuously opposed Stephen Douglas's "popular sovereignty" as reflected in the 1854 Kansas-Nebraska Act, recognizing it as a backhanded way of allowing slavery to expand into every remaining territory of the United States. When the *Dred Scott* decision was announced, he was finally motivated to action. When he challenged Senator Douglas in 1858, their campaign became one of the classic political theaters in the history of the United States.

In his inaugural speech following his nomination as the Republican candidate for the United States Senate, he articulated his evolved position on slavery: "In my opinion, it will not cease until a crisis shall have been reached, and passed. 'A house divided against itself cannot stand.' I believe this government cannot endure, permanently half slave and half free. I do not expect the Union to be dissolved—I do not expect the house to fall—but I do expect it will cease to be divided. It will become all of one thing, or all the other."[14]

Lincoln expressed confidence that freedom would triumph over slavery and those men, such as Senator Douglas, who aided and abetted its evil. He then threw down the gauntlet to his Republican Party, pleading for it to become a more powerful voice for ending slavery, a challenge that he then extended to the entire nation.

Douglas met Lincoln's basic assertions with a challenge: Where was the evidence that this large and diverse nation could not survive with both slavery and freedom? How did Lincoln respond to the obvious fact that the Founding Fathers accepted the coexistence of both? Did not Lincoln, in effect, pronounce that war was inevitable? For himself, Douglas preferred peace!

The stage was set for the famous Lincoln-Douglas debates. Over the late summer and fall, in seven different towns scattered across Illinois, the two engaged in a verbal war that captivated not only the people of Illinois but the entire nation.

Early on, Douglas put Lincoln on the defensive by his assertions that Lincoln's positions were "revolutionary" and would lead to war. Most effectively, he characterized his opponent's real motive as an intent to give blacks the rights of full citizenship. Lincoln asserted that Douglas's efforts to frame him as an advocate for both war and black equality were "false issues." The real issue was whether slavery was wrong or not:

> That is the issue that will continue in this country when these poor tongues of Judge Douglas and myself shall be silent. It is the eternal struggle between these two principles—right and wrong—throughout the world. They are the two principles that have stood face to face from the beginning of time; and will ever continue to struggle. The one is the common right of humanity, and the other the divine right of kings. It is the same principle in whatever shape it develops itself. It is the same spirit that says, "You work and toil and earn bread, and I'll eat it."[15]

Through the debates, Lincoln carved out a position for the Republican Party that framed the slavery issue in terms that could be understood and were agreeable to the majority of Northerners: the position that, even if the black man was not the white man's perfect equal, he was still entitled to freedom, life, liberty, and the pursuit of happiness.

But it would not prove to be enough.

Springfield, Illinois
1858

HE WAITED IN HIS OFFICE. The night passed and then most of the morning. Shortly after five, his partner and close friend trudged into the office. Lincoln greeted him in a tired but cheerful voice, which the other man ignored. The man took off his coat and hat, folded his arms across his chest to warm himself, and sat down wordlessly, stamping the mud from his boots on the floor.

Both of them waited in silence, wrestling with an uncertain strain.

Finally, the message came. Slow steps on the wooden sidewalk. The door pushed open. A young man standing there.

Lincoln could tell from the look on the messenger's face that he hadn't won the Senate race. He took the letter, cut the seal, took a breath, and read. His partner waited, knowing the outcome too.

"What was the count?" he finally asked him.

Lincoln tossed the message across the table.

The other man took it and read, then was silent for a moment.

Lincoln stared out the small window across his wooden desk. If he was distraught, he didn't show it. Quite the opposite. He looked calm and satisfied.

His partner suddenly thrust himself from his chair and started pacing. "We've got to keep fighting!" he announced. "You've got to keep on with the battle! It's too important . . . too important! You can't just give up now."

Lincoln pulled on his chin as he thought, his hair a shock of black strewn in all directions. He considered the great debates that had taken place between himself and Senator Douglas, debates that had thrust him onto the national stage. They'd been hard-fought and intense, capturing the attention of the nation unlike anything before. Thousands of people had come to listen to them, many of them traveling for miles. Their words had been reported in every newspaper in the country and many overseas. He was one of the few men of his time—and part of this was because his features were so difficult to forget—who was recognized almost everywhere he went now. No longer was he anonymous, and never would he be again.

Which was why he wasn't overcome with disappointment. He valued his privacy. He'd never sought to be famous. He'd only sought to do the right thing.

That was the thing about him. He didn't *need* this. Unlike other men, he didn't *have* to win. He was perfectly content with his life: his children, his wife, his law practice, his friends. He had opportunity to travel on the judicial circuit from time to time and he loved the time he had to read. He was satisfied with his health. He loved his hometown. There were plenty of reasons to still be happy.

Was his life perfect? Not in any sense of the word. Had he everything he'd ever wanted? Nothing could be further from the truth. He had suffered through many more disappointments than most other men his age. Over the past few years, his relationship with Mary had come under a constant strain. Financial hardship had come upon them and he struggled to pay the bills. He'd lost his mother, his sister . . . others who were even closer to his heart, including little Eddie. But through it all, he'd kept his sense of humor as well as a deep appreciation for the blessings in his life.

"I thought we had it won," his friend went on.

Lincoln didn't answer. By most reckoning, he *had* won the great debates. Indeed, he'd spent himself preparing, pouring his heart and soul into the outcome, calling on every ounce of intellect he had to win not only each debate but the election.

But the people now had spoken. And it was not to be.

His law partner seemed to double his pace, his face angry, his steps heavy on the wooden floor. "It isn't over!" he said again. "This is too important! We will fight them. We will fight them . . ."

Lincoln lifted a hand to stop him.

Too much emotion. Too much passion. Too much anger on every side. Like the oxygen around him, bitter feelings had permeated the very air. Every family and every friendship was being affected by it now, the pride and hatred becoming almost impossible to confine. It was a poison to the country. No, it was worse than that. It was alive and growing, foul and full of potential death. And though he'd spent the last year building up his following, he had to find a way to bring them down now or, like an infected wound, the ill feelings and disappointments would fester and infect them and eventually lead to war.

"We lost it fair and square," he said, trying to get his friend to relax.

His partner turned and glared into his eyes. "This isn't a battle from which you can simply walk away! The time is ripe. We are ready! If we have to, we will fight to the death!"

Lincoln leaned back and placed his feet up on the table. He seemed to stare up at the ceiling as he thought; then he nodded toward his friend. "Fighting to the death is a bit premature at this point, don't you think?" he smiled.

His partner instantly recognized the look on Lincoln's face and braced for what he knew was coming. He didn't want to hear it. Not here and not now.

Lincoln continued smiling, making it impossible for the other man to keep on pacing with the scowl on his face.

Lincoln was a master storyteller; once he started talking there was no way to avoid being drawn into his tales. And his good humor wasn't feigned or unnatural. He was always quick to laugh. He'd recently sat for an ambrotype photograph, a process that required thirty seconds of holding his face in a serious pose, which had proven almost impossible for the smiling Lincoln to do. Three ruined plates into the process, the photographer had expressed enough frustration at his subject that Lincoln had finally settled down long enough to hold a serious pose—an overly serious one, as it turned out, making him look like an austere and stern man, the one thing he was not.

The smile lines around his eyes crinkled as he watched his friend. "Your words about fighting to the death remind me of a story I heard several years ago."

"Abe, this isn't the time to wander off."

"No, no, this one is worth telling . . ."

"Please, Abe." His partner tried to frown.

Lincoln crossed one leg over the other and continued. "It was the dark days of the War of 1812. There was a beautiful young woman who was making a leather belt to present to her lover before he went to war. After long consideration, she'd decided to engrave 'Liberty or Death!' upon the belt. When he heard her plans, he considered for a moment, his face falling. 'It seems a little strong,' he finally told her. 'Maybe you'd consider, "Liberty or Be Crippled!"'"

The partner stared in a determined frown.

Lincoln broke into a laugh. "Liberty or Be Crippled! Now there's a call to war!"

His partner finally smiled, though not so much from the story— he'd heard it several times before—as from the sound of Lincoln's laugh.

"Liberty or Be Crippled!" Lincoln laughed again. "If only our

Founding Fathers had worked that into our Declaration of Independence . . ."

The partner shook his head and turned away, wanting to hide his smile.

A long moment passed between them, and then Lincoln spoke again. His voice was low and serious now. "We did our best. That is all that we can do. I'm not discouraged. All is well."

• • •

Senator Douglas took the oath of office. Abraham Lincoln went back to practicing law.

Over the next two years, the different sides on the slavery issue moved further apart as the debate reached a fever pitch. One of the events that fueled the division included the attempt, in the fall of 1859, by the ardent and violent abolitionist John Brown to generate a slave revolt by attacking a federal armory at Harpers Ferry, Virginia. His efforts to ignite a war failed miserably, but he became a hero to many abolitionists. His dying words, uttered just before he was hung, "the crimes of this guilty land will never be purged away; but with blood,"[16] struck a chord with many.

In the North, Brown took on the status of a Christ figure, his death provoking images of a hero willing to die for a righteous cause, his hanging generating fury against slavery and slaveholders. Notables such as Ralph Waldo Emerson, Henry David Thoreau, and Victor Hugo praised him as a hero and tried to obtain a pardon for him.

The response in the South to the hero-worship of a "murdering madman" was predictable. To the fire-eaters, it reinforced their argument: Democracy was not meant for those crazy enough to worship John Brown.

The fire-eaters became even more belligerent. They demanded that Congress pass a law guaranteeing slavery's protection in all of the Western territories as well as, unbelievably, the renewal of the slave trade. Legislation was introduced in Congress to accomplish these two goals, a move that resulted in a number of longtime political heavyweights, such as Jefferson Davis, succumbing to the fire-eaters and joining their cause.

For those who were working to tear the Union apart, one final act had to be accomplished—the destruction of the Democratic Party and the guarantee that a Republican would be elected to the presidency. Such an outcome would assure victory of their ideas and aspirations.

The Democratic convention of 1860 was orchestrated so that the hard-liners from the South had no choice but to walk out when their issues on slavery were denied. After Democrats in the North nominated Senator Stephen Douglas, Southern Democrats nominated their own candidate for president, John C. Breckinridge from Kentucky, effectively splitting the Democratic ticket.

The Republican convention, held in Chicago, was a classic political contest. The favorite going into the convention was William Seward, senator from New York. His long-standing reputation as a radical Republican caused many to question his ability to win, however. Other candidates were put forward, including Governor Salmon P. Chase of Ohio, Edward Bates of Missouri, and a favorite son, the great debater Abraham Lincoln.

Lincoln won the nomination on the third ballot.

That fall, he carried every free state except New Jersey. And though the Republican nominee won only 40 percent of the popular vote, the electoral college tally was a solid victory for Lincoln.

For the fire-eaters in the South, their strategy had worked. Popular democracy had resulted in the election of a man who spoke openly of freedom for the slaves and who would, inevitably, put the United States on a path to eradicate slavery, proof that self-government was a failure. Secession and disunion were inevitable.

The Coming of War

The fire-eaters in South Carolina moved quickly. On December 20, 1860, a secessionist convention approved an ordinance pronouncing that "the union now subsisting between South Carolina and other

States, under the name of the 'United States of America' is hereby dissolved."[17] The other Deep South states soon followed. On March 11, 1861, a new Constitution was adopted for the Confederate States of America.

Although historical revisionists, including Jefferson Davis, have attempted to frame the cause of the Confederacy in terms of "states' rights," disputes over tariffs, and cultural differences between the North and the South, such was not the case. The Constitution of the Confederacy, in sum, defined *liberty* as the right of a white man to own a black man and to take such black man wherever he wanted. The vice president of the Confederacy, former Congressman Alexander Stephens of Georgia, stated as much:

> The prevailing ideas entertained by [Thomas Jefferson] and most of the leading statesmen at the time of the formation of the old constitution were that the enslavement of the African was in violation of the laws of nature; that it was wrong in principle, socially, morally, and politically. . . . Our new government is founded upon exactly the opposite idea; its foundations are laid, its corner-stone rests upon the great truth, that the negro is not equal to the white man; that slavery—subordination to the superior race—is his natural and normal condition. . . . This, our new government, is the first, in the history of the world, based upon this great physical, philosophical, and moral truth. . . . It is upon this, as I have stated, our social fabric is firmly planted; and I cannot permit myself to doubt the ultimate success of a full recognition of this principle throughout the civilized and enlightened world.[18]

In addition to defense of slavery, the new government of the South posed a challenge to the entire concept of self-government. President James Buchanan, who had been elected in 1856 based on his coddling of Southern sympathizers, acknowledged that fact in his final annual message, delivered in December 1860. In that message, he stated that secession over the election of Abraham Lincoln was illegitimate. Further, he declared that the dissolution of the Union "would be quoted as conclusive proof that man is unfit for self-government."[19]

The European elites, who had managed to crush every major effort at democratization by their own people, looked upon events in the United States with glee. They believed that the fact that the people of the secessionist states would simply pack up and leave the Union when the election of 1860 did not go their way was proof positive that democracy in the United States would fail. America would soon descend into anarchy and be replaced by a government of the strong and the elite. After all, the Confederate States were already proceeding down such a path.

In 1861, the United States of America was at a critical crossroad. Would it remain a united nation under the Constitution, dedicated to the lofty principles of the Declaration of Independence? Or was it going to become two nations, with one rejecting the Constitution and adopting instead the principles of inequality and slavery for millions of human beings?

Such were the stakes when Abraham Lincoln assumed the presidency of a dis–United States in March 1861.

Springfield, Illinois
February 1861

HE WALKED ACROSS THE county square, tall, with drooping shoulders. His legs moved awkwardly, as if he were in pain. He took his time, grateful for a few moments to finally be alone. The moon was dim, the sky overcast, the wind cold, the blowing mist snapping away his frozen breath. Making his way up the wooden steps, he stepped into the cramped office he had shared with his partner for more than twenty years. Books, papers, briefs, and folders were piled high in a T-shaped table arrangement in the center of the room, letters and legal correspondence crammed in every pigeonhole, some of the most important documents scattered in loose arrangements on the floor. He stopped in the doorway, taking in the scene. The darkness of the night was nearly unbroken, but he didn't need to see. The room hadn't changed in years; he knew every chair, every table, every knick-knack on the shelves. He stood a long moment, watching the shadows from the flickering oil lamps outside while listening to the wind blow through the wooden shingles.

Closing his eyes, he took a breath, his mind drifting back.

So much had happened to him in this town. So much good, so many significant events, so many joys, it overwhelmed him to think of them now. A summer night. Walking along the river. The scent of lilac in the air. The first time he had seen his wife. He was young. She was younger. Beautiful and sure. "I want to dance with you in the worst way," were the first words he had ever spoken to her. A turbulent courtship was to follow, but they'd been together ever since. All of his children had been born here. The friends he'd made here! He would be grateful to them for the rest of his life.

Yes, much good had happened to him in Springfield.

But the good hadn't come without a price.

There had also been pain and disappointments, heartaches so acute they hurt him even now, pains he'd never gotten over and knew he never would.

Starting his law practice, almost completely bankrupt. Two lost elections. A few enemies made along the way. Other failures he'd experienced here as well.

He thought back to his son, little Eddie. Three years and ten months may have been all the time he'd been on earth, but the impact he'd had on his father was undying and powerful.

In his mind, he pictured the feathery-haired child slipping through his grandmother's kitchen, a stranded kitten cradled in his hands. Moments before, he'd pulled the kitten from his older brother's arms and taken off, shielding it from his grandmother's eagle eyes. A practical woman, she had no soft spot in her heart for any animal she couldn't eat—most of all she hated cats!—and she scolded him the moment she caught sight of the scraggly animal.

Lincoln smiled as he remembered the reaction of his child. Barely taller than his grandmother's knees, he shook his head, clutched the tiny kitten, and ran. For weeks he secretly fed it table scraps and water until it was old enough to fend for itself.

His child was gone now, buried not far from where he stood. Thinking back, he remembered the day he realized that his son was going to die, the feeling of despair, the fear and overwhelming grief. But there had been more in his heart than pain. There also had been acceptance. A sudden and peaceful sense of relief. The child had suffered for weeks, and it was time to let him go. Though the thought of losing his boy almost brought him to his knees, he had known then— as he knew now—that there were some things worse than death. Watching his son suffer had been one of those things.

Shaking his head, he finally moved into the dark room, lit two oil lamps, and sat down at his cluttered desk.

He was a tall man, six foot three, and his gangly knees jutted at an awkward angle as he sat down in his wooden chair. His face was creased, his eyes deeply set. He was far better-looking up close than far away, for there was something relaxed and inviting about his eyes that drew others in.

Raised on the frontier of a frontier nation, he'd known what it meant to live off the land, work with his hands, fight for his survival, struggle for what few things he could acquire. With no more than eighteen months of formal schooling, he'd fought to educate himself. His mother having passed away when he was just a child, with an estranged father he hadn't seen in many years and a grandfather who'd been killed by Indians, he was as strong and independent as any man from the frontier. But there was a more thoughtful side to him as well. Much more thoughtful. He hated killing animals, even if he needed to for food. He didn't like to garden; it reminded him too much of farming with his father. He had no formal religion but as great a faith in God as any man.

And this was how he felt now. This was what he really believed, deep in his soul: A long road lay before him. But God had always walked beside him. And He wouldn't leave him now.

Rummaging across his desk, he found a pen, then began looking for his half-written speech but didn't see it. Remembering, he lifted the stovetop hat he'd placed on the desk, reached in, and extracted the partly finished work from the rim. Staring at the paper, he thought for a moment, then wrote the last few lines of his farewell:

"My friends—no one, not in my situation, can appreciate my feeling of sadness at this parting. To this place, and the kindness of these people, I owe everything. Here I have lived a quarter of a century, and have passed from a young to an old man. Here my children have been born, and one is buried. I now leave, not knowing when, or whether ever, I may return, with a task before me greater than that which rested upon Washington. Without the assistance of that Divine Being who ever attended him, I cannot succeed. With that assistance, I cannot fail. Trusting in Him who can go with me, and remain with you, and be everywhere for good, let us confidently hope that all will yet be well. To His care commending you, as I hope in your prayers you will commend me, I bid you an affectionate farewell."[20]

Two days later, standing at the back of a private railroad car, Abraham Lincoln read these parting words to his friends who had come to the railway station to bid him good-bye.

Then he departed his beloved town of Springfield and never came back again.

Black Days and Lonely Nights

Oh, the woes that lay ahead of Abraham Lincoln!

During the brief four years of his presidency, he would preside over a war that would cost the people of the United States more than 600,000 lives. The political pressures were immense. Within the Democratic Party were a large number of "Peace Democrats," also known as Copperheads, who objected to the war and appealed to those citizens in the Union who grew weary of the war. And besides those who were generally antiwar, the Northern states also contained many Southern sympathizers. That was particularly true in the Border states where slavery existed but the states had not seceded because of strong pro-Union sentiment. These states—Missouri, Maryland, Delaware, and Kentucky, along with the region that became the state of West Virginia in 1863—stayed in the Union, but every major decision that Lincoln was to make during his presidency had to consider the effect that it would have upon those key states.

Early in Lincoln's presidency, July 1861, Congress passed the Crittenden-Johnson Resolutions, which declared that the purpose of the war was not to interfere with slavery, but "to defend and maintain the supremacy of the Constitution, and to preserve the Union with all the dignity, equality, and rights of the several states unimpaired."[21] But on the other side of the political extreme, Lincoln had to contend with the radical Republicans—those who viewed the war as a way not only to protect the Union but, more importantly, to carry out the righteous cause of ending slavery. These radicals became indignant whenever the president did anything that was considered conciliatory, even if the conciliatory move was necessary to keep the Border states aligned with the Union. They also constantly criticized Lincoln for not being aggressive enough in publicly asserting that the ultimate goal of the military conflict was to end slavery.

While president, he suffered personal tragedy, including the death of another beloved son. Three of his wife's brothers died fighting for the *Confederate* side. His wife, Mary, didn't ever recover from those losses, her sense of grief making worse her general tendency to be morose and negative.

He was surrounded by a cabinet with split loyalties, forcing Lincoln to sort through the egos and divisions among his most trusted confidants.

He had incompetent, sometimes malicious generals, outnumbered only by those who were disloyal or disobedient. Personal jealousy and ego-driven decisions led to far too many Union defeats.

Most of the media despised him. Many public officials held him in open contempt. He was constantly being criticized. During the dark days of the spring of 1863, one visitor to Washington, D.C., observed that there did not exist *any* personal loyalty to the president. The editor of the *Cincinnati Commercial* called Lincoln "an awful, woeful ass," contending that "If Lincoln was not a damn fool, we could get along yet."[22] He was characterized by a fellow Republican as "so vacillating, so week [sic] . . . so fearful . . . and so ignorant . . . that I can now see scarcely a ray of hope left."[23]

That criticism led Lincoln to make one of his most astute observations:

> If I were to try to read, much less answer, all the attacks made on me, this shop might as well be closed for any other business.
>
> I do the very best I know how—the very best I can; and I mean to keep doing so until the end.
>
> If the end brings me out all right, what is said against me won't amount to anything. If the end brings me out wrong, ten angels swearing I was right would make no difference.[24]

Of no small consequence was the fact that this war was between Americans, resulting in brother against brother, friend against friend, former comrades in arms now against each other. As noted above, three of Mary Lincoln's brothers fought and died for the Confederacy; Jefferson Davis's wife had relatives fighting for the Union; Senator John Crittenden of Kentucky had one son serve as an officer of the Confederacy, another son as an officer of the Union army; Robert E. Lee had a nephew who was an officer in the Union navy; Edward Bates, Lincoln's attorney general, had one son serving in the Confederate army and four sons serving in the Union army or navy. Sam Houston, governor of Texas, wanted the South to stay in the Union; Union General George McClellan preferred that the South be allowed to go.

How did Abraham Lincoln survive? How did he find the strength to continue under the excruciating pressure?

For one thing, he was simply a good man. He was amiable and kind. He was patient. He loved people, especially the Union soldiers.

He knew how to use humor to calm and to teach. He was honest. He had self-confidence, believing in his own abilities.

Above all, he believed in the rightness of his efforts to save the Union, to protect the Constitution, to achieve equality for black slaves, and to preserve the United States as a democracy for itself and as a beacon for the rest of the world. This confidence was based in his belief in the American destiny. In an address to the New Jersey Senate in February 1861, Lincoln compared America with God's chosen people of the Old Testament. After describing his feelings about the Founders, he said:

> I recollect thinking then, boy even though I was, that there must have been something more than common that those men struggled for. I am exceedingly anxious that that thing which they struggled for; that something even more than National Independence; *that something that held out a great promise to all the people of the world to all time to come;* I am exceedingly anxious that this Union, the Constitution, and the liberties of the people shall be perpetuated in accordance with the original idea for which that struggle was made, and I shall be most happy indeed if I shall be an humble instrument in the hands of the Almighty, and of this, *his almost chosen people,* for perpetuating the object of that great struggle.[25]

In a speech to Congress in 1862, Lincoln encouraged his colleagues not to become discouraged: "We know how to save the Union. The world knows we do know how to save it. We—even we here—hold the power, and bear the responsibility. In giving freedom to the slave, we assure freedom to the free. . . . *We shall nobly save, or meanly lose, the last, best hope of earth.*"[26]

Finally, Abraham Lincoln had faith that God ruled the world. He believed that God cared whether the United States was destroyed or survived.

During the many, many dark days of the Civil War, he pondered deeply why the war was not ending more quickly. He wrote often of his ruminations, expressing his views of God's direction. On one occasion, after a congressional delegation had encouraged him to make certain that America ended slavery so that God could continue to bless America, Lincoln replied:

> My faith is greater than yours. . . . I also believe He will compel us to do right in order that He may do these things, not so much because we desire them as that they accord with His plans of dealing with this nation, in the midst of which He means to establish justice. . . . I have felt His hand upon me in great trials and submitted to His guidance, and I trust that as He shall further open the way I will be ready to walk therein, relying on His help and trusting in His goodness and wisdom.[27]

These traits helped Lincoln succeed, but they did not inoculate him from suffering as the Civil War took its toll on the nation and its people.

• • •

Both sides of the conflict expected it to end quickly and in victory for their side. One bold Confederate official boasted that he would be willing to drink all of the blood that would be shed on his side before victory was obtained.

And the South did have one distinct advantage—they knew that they did not have to invade the North; they only had to provide a strong defense of their own lands. They learned the lesson from the American Revolution—from the type of war that George Washington had fought so successfully—that to win, all you have to do is avoid major defeats and wear the other side down.

The South believed that support for the war in the North was shallow. If they could just hold out, inflict maximum damage to invading Northern armies, and let their sympathizers in the North maximize their influence, the war would end quickly and they would have their own nation.

From the very beginning, the North suffered significant defeats.

The first major confrontation occurred at Manassas Junction, Virginia—the First Battle of Bull Run—in July 1861. The battlefield was close enough to Washington, D.C., that citizens from the District traveled out to watch the expected Union victory. After a disastrous defeat, these spectators were forced to join the Union army as it dashed pell-mell back to Washington.

The war continued to go badly for the Union army. Confederate General "Stonewall" Jackson defeated Union forces in the Shenandoah Valley and drove them across the Potomac. Fear that Washington, D.C., was at risk required immediate reinforcement of troops guarding the nation's capital.

In the "Peninsular Campaign" (May to August 1862), the Union made a major effort to take Richmond and failed. In August, the Union was defeated at the Second Battle of Bull Run. General Stonewall Jackson then took Harpers Ferry, obtaining major stocks of supplies and arms.

It appeared the North was facing imminent defeat.

It is particularly interesting, then, that at one of the most desperate and uncertain times in the war, Lincoln made a decision that had the potential to demoralize the Union even more.

Washington, D.C.
September 1862

"YOU CAN'T DO IT!" William Seward almost shouted. "You can't do it, not right now. It will destroy everything that we've been fighting for! It will tear our people apart!"

President Lincoln only stared at his secretary of state. The rest of the cabinet sat in silence, the air so strained each man could almost hear the sound of his own heart. Their hostility toward each other was obvious in their body language, their glaring eyes, their bitter words. With their enormous egos, hidden agendas, and frustratingly diverse levels of competence, it was nearly impossible for the members of the cabinet to endure each other anymore. Indeed, they had become so alienated that they rarely even met—almost a ghost cabinet they'd become.

Hunched in the corner, the postmaster general almost huffed. One way or another, he didn't care. The war had been one long and unmitigated disaster, interrupted by just enough success to convince Lincoln to continue killing soldiers on both sides. Other members of the cabinet sat in silence, unwilling to voice even the weakest indication of support. Salmon Chase, the secretary of the treasury, kept his eyes on the table. Considering Lincoln a far inferior man, he had never accepted his presidency and wouldn't accept it now. "Go ahead and do it," he almost muttered to himself. "Do it, then see if you can maintain the presidency!" Chase had already had enough conversations with Lincoln's enemies—other members of the cabinet, senior members of the Congress, a couple of members of the press (oh, the press, his secret weapon, those who'd do anything to bring the hated Lincoln down!)—to know that if Lincoln proceeded with his absurd proposition, he was certain to fail. And when he did, Chase would be there to step into his place.

Seward glanced around him, then leaned across the wooden table that separated him from Lincoln. "Please, sir." His voice was softer now. "I'm begging you . . . we're all begging you . . . don't do this. Not right now." He wasn't pleading for himself. He wasn't pleading for his own agenda or some hidden purpose. He was pleading for his country, convinced that the president was making a deadly mistake.

A former rival, a man who'd battled for the presidency himself, Secretary Seward was now one of Lincoln's only friends. The president knew that. But he was neither naïve nor stupid about the other members of his cabinet, knowing they would desert him like rats jumping from a sinking ship.

Seward leaned forward once again. "Look at our recent history,

Mr. President. McClellan was consistently defeated throughout the Peninsular Campaign. His enormous ego, combined with the battlefield tactics of a child, assured our defeat at the Second Battle of Bull Run. Even if we are to claim a victory at Antietam—something that is possible but certainly not likely—it would be foolish to conclude we've turned the corner in this war.

"And we can't ignore the fact that Lee is on the offensive now and has deserted the tactics of a defensive war. His invasion has the potential to change the outcome! One more Union defeat, and he believes the British and French will recognize the Confederacy, which would be our death knell."

Seward fell silent. The room was quiet. Lincoln continued staring at his men.

Seward cleared his throat and then concluded, "I've said ever since last summer, you can't announce the Emancipation Proclamation until we know this war is won. To do so would demoralize our army. It is nothing but a fantasy." He looked away. "But I have told you that before."

Lincoln finally nodded. "The last measure of an exhausted government"[28] had been the secretary's very words. Seward's argument had hit him with great force and, up until this moment, he had believed that it was true.

The president looked the secretary in the eyes. "I have always made the argument for freeing the slaves as being a military necessity," he started. "The disastrous Peninsular Campaign has brought home to us the distinct military advantage slavery provides the Confederacy. Slaves are used to dig trenches and build fortifications, as teamsters, cooks, and hospital attendants. They are down south farming, allowing more white soldiers to be available for the front. Divesting the Confederacy of their slaves is a military necessity. And you know I have the authority under the president's constitutional war powers to announce the Emancipation Proclamation."

"You do, sir, but not right now! The country isn't ready. We are as fragile as an egg. Please, don't drop this on our people now."

Lincoln clasped his hands across his lap but didn't answer.

Twenty minutes later, still unable to resolve the conflict, the cabinet meeting broke up.

• • •

The Battle of Antietam, September 17, was the most bloody day of the Civil War. Six thousand American soldiers were killed and 17,000 wounded, four times more than died on D-Day in World War II.

But the Union was victorious. General Lee was forced to withdraw from Pennsylvania back to Virginia.

Soon afterward, Lincoln announced his intention to issue the Emancipation Proclamation, declaring to his assembled cabinet, "I made a solemn vow before God, that if General Lee was driven back from Pennsylvania, I would crown the result by the declaration of freedom to the slaves."[29]

God had answered Lincoln's urgent plea for a victory at Antietam. True to his word, he did what he had promised God he would do.

Should the North Surrender?

As critical as the victory at Antietam was, McClellan failed to follow up—despite Lincoln's desperate urgings. The perception that the war was going to linger on, as well as the negative reaction to the Emancipation Proclamation, resulted in major Republican losses in the midterm elections in November, with the Peace Democrats making major gains in Illinois, New York, Pennsylvania, Ohio, and Indiana.

Gloom from further military defeats was quick to follow. In December, a Union attack on Fredericksburg proved disastrous, with 13,000 Union casualties, twice the Confederate losses.

These events led to a revolt from radical Republicans in the Senate. Fearing that the Fredericksburg defeat might lead to the Peace Democrats obtaining their peace-with-slavery objectives, they confronted Lincoln, demanding that William Seward be dismissed from the cabinet. Fuel for this revolt came from Secretary of Treasury Chase, who had been secretly telling the senators that it was Seward who was responsible for the tepid pursuit of the war.

It required all of Lincoln's skill, patience, and compassion to end the crisis over Seward, who was the most important of his cabinet members as well as a trusted friend. Although this was a political contest of seemingly small impact, Lincoln described the fight to retain Seward as leaving him more depressed than any event in his life.[30]

The fears of the radical Republicans were justified. In the early months of 1863, it began to appear that the coalition of Republicans and Democrats who had provided tenuous support for the war would collapse. In New York, the new Democratic governor denounced emancipation in his inaugural address. In Kentucky, the governor recommended that the legislature reject the Emancipation Proclamation. Democratic majorities in the legislatures of Illinois and Indiana debated whether to reject ties to the New England states and to join with states of the South to assure an end to the war—with slavery intact.

Lincoln, and the war, were made even less popular when Congress instituted a military draft in which one could avoid conscription by paying a fee or finding a substitute. Poor people in the North saw this as terribly unfair. Violent riots resulted in some cities, New York City being particularly wracked.

As the Congress was coming to the end of its session in March, Peace Democrats used extreme measures to obstruct all types of legislation. They hid out in various Capitol retreats during votes, attached unacceptable amendments to key legislation, and used the filibuster in the Senate with great success.

In the House, Clement Vallandigham, a congressman from Indiana, spoke what some considered treason. "Ought this war to continue? . . . No—not a day, nor an hour!" The war had been initiated to save the Union; now it was a "war for the negro."[31] Vallandigham called for the soldiers on both sides to just go home. If the New England states did not want to join in a peaceful nation, with slavery intact, let them go make their own nation.

Debate over the power of the president to suspend the writ of habeas corpus resulted in one Delaware senator calling Lincoln an "imbecile" and the "weakest man ever placed in a high office." When the senator was called to order and refused to yield, the sergeant at arms was called on to remove him from the floor. The senator pulled out a pistol and threatened to shoot the sergeant at arms.[32]

Lincoln was accustomed to such feelings toward him in the Congress, but he was not prepared for the reaction of his soldiers to the Emancipation Proclamation. As had been suggested by Peace Democrats, Lincoln began to receive reports that many soldiers felt betrayed. They had joined the army to save the Union. Now they were being asked to fight "for the negro."

These matters became secondary, however, as Lincoln followed the movements of his army, now under the command of General Hooker. Wanting to draw Lee's army away from Fredericksburg and into an open battle, in late April Hooker moved the Union army across the Rappahannock River. There he got his desire. But the outcome was humiliating. Outmaneuvered, he was crushed in the Battle of Chancellorsville, with 17,000 Union soldiers killed, injured, or taken captive before the Union army was able to withdraw.

Secretary of the Army Edwin Stanton called it the "darkest day of the war."[33] In Washington, D.C., secessionists were openly joyful.

The weeks after the battle of Chancellorsville were among the most desperate of Lincoln's presidency.

The Final Hammer Holds Ready

General Lee decided not to permit time for the Union army to recover. In June, he began a second invasion of the North, setting the stage for one of the most critical battles in the war—indeed, in the history of our nation.

Lee had a number of reasons for abandoning the defensive war strategy in favor of going on the offensive once again. For one thing, he knew that an invasion of Pennsylvania would halt another invasion of the South—in particular, an invasion of his native Virginia.

He also believed that if he could lure the army of the Potomac into a final battle, he could defeat it, a move that would result in British and French recognition of the South, widely regarded as the final step in winning the war.

Finally, Lee and Jefferson Davis were convinced that the people in the North were ready to break. With one more decisive Southern victory, they felt certain the Peace Democrats would demand the end of the war—even if that meant "peace with slavery"—especially if Lee was able to capture Washington, D.C.

Davis was sufficiently convinced of coming victory that he boldly sent his vice president north under a flag of truce with secret instructions to convince Lincoln to surrender before the entire Union army and Washington, D.C., were destroyed.

As the Confederate vice president traveled toward Washington from the south, Lee and his army were moving toward the city from the north, having crossed the Blue Ridge Mountains, proceeded up the Shenandoah Valley, crossed Maryland, and moved into Pennsylvania.

As word of the movements of Lee's army filtered into Washington, Secretary of the Navy Gideon Welles recorded that "something of a panic pervades the city."[34] Government officials packed up and were ready to leave at a moment's notice.

Summer's stifling temperatures settled upon Pennsylvania, the tiny village of Gettysburg suffering tremendously under the heat. As the two armies moved toward each other, more than 165,000 men, the great battle was made ready.

The future of the nation lay in the balance. Indeed, the future of the entire world would be decided in this place.

Washington, D.C.
Late June, 1863

THE CITY WAS SIMMERING in a broth of doom and fear. *Invasion from the north! The city is going to burn!* Terrifying rumors had led to panic that the leaders had barely been able to control. Thousands were set to flee before Lee's army. Many had already gone. Some of Lincoln's cabinet had slipped up north, and most of those who remained in the nation's capital were insisting that he leave. "You cannot wait here for Lee's army to capture the city!" a few of them had cried. "You can't humiliate yourself, our army, or the Union by remaining here. Think of the repercussions if you are captured! If you want to keep on fighting, you are going to have to go!"

Abraham Lincoln had listened to their arguments, sometimes sympathetically nodding his head. Yes, it would be a disaster if the Union army were to fall—and how much worse it would be if Lee were to surround the capital and capture the president inside.

If that happened, the war would be lost.

But it would also be a disaster if he were to tuck his tail and run.

Hearing all of their arguments, Lincoln had inexplicably excused himself. Standing, he had left his cabinet in the middle of the meeting and slipped into his private office. There, alone, he closed his eyes and took a long breath. His body ached. He was so tired. He wished with all his might that he could just walk out into the countryside and leave it all behind.

"I'm not strong enough," he almost prayed. "I'm not strong enough to do this. I can't do this alone!"

But he was alone. He *was* alone.

He opened his eyes and leaned over his desk, looking down at the battle map of Gettysburg.

The tip of the Chesapeake and Delaware Bays lay on the south end of the map; Washington, D.C., was depicted at the bottom; the Blue Ridge Mountains lined the western edge. The small village of Gettysburg lay in the middle of the hand-drawn map, rows of small hills depicted to the north, west, and south. The Southern army had moved quietly up the Shenandoah River Valley, gathering north and west of Gettysburg. They were moving now toward the village as the Union soldiers marched toward it too.

Lincoln thought for a long moment, gently tapping the cartographic symbols that depicted the hills lying west of the village. The high ground. Forested clumps of black earth above the meadows. How important these small hills were going to be!

In his mind, he pictured the coming battle, his gut crunching into knots, the painful ball of anxiety all too familiar to him now.

He knew this was the tipping point. After hundreds of thousands of dead, untold wealth and treasure wasted, who knew how many injured, how many suffering, how many families, loves, and friendships destroyed, it all came down to this. Win here, win now, claim a victory against the Confederacy, or the nation would be lost. It really was that simple. They had to win this battle or everything they had fought and bled for, every sacrifice and hardship they had suffered, was going to be for naught.

Lifting his eyes, he looked out. The sun was going down now, and muted shadows were beginning to form outside. Across the cluttered fields that surrounded the White House, the narrow streets of the city were almost quiet. They had settled the general panic, but only barely, and he knew they were just a breath away from losing control of their own people, faith in the Union ebbing to an unbearable low.

He took another breath and held it, his heart thumping in his chest.

This was it.

The future lay in the balance.

Which way would it turn?

Feeling overwhelmed with the crushing responsibility, he stared ahead, the office quiet, then fell to his knees.

What Happened in Lincoln's Private Office?

On July 1, the first shot at Gettysburg was fired. A million other shots soon followed as, over the next three days, one of the most momentous battles in the history of the world unfolded upon the green fields of southern Pennsylvania.

Who was winning? No one could really tell. Could the Union hold the high ground? The first day, it seemed unlikely. The second day, it seemed impossible. How many soldiers had the Union army lost?

Thousands lay upon the ground. Had Lee ordered Longstreet to attack the Union's III Corps on the left flank? Reports were sparse and faulty. No one really knew what was going on.

Amazingly, throughout the battle, Abraham Lincoln remained unexplainably calm. During the entire episode at Gettysburg, while his Union army faced the possibility of a final and crushing defeat, he was described as being "in excellent spirits."[35]

Only later did Lincoln confide why he was possessed of such calm.

One of the wounded of the battle was General Daniel Sickles, a man whose injury led to his leg being amputated. Shortly after the battle, he was moved to a house in Washington, where he was visited by his president. During the conversation, Sickles asked about the level of concern in the capital when Lee's army was approaching. The president acknowledged that measures had been taken to evacuate the city, but that he personally had remained confident of the battle's outcome. When asked why, the president related:

> When Lee crossed the Potomac and entered Pennsylvania, followed by our army, I felt that the great crisis had come. I knew that defeat in a great battle on northern soil involved the loss of Washington, to be followed perhaps by the intervention of England and France in favor of the Confederacy. I went to my room and got down on my knees in prayer.
>
> Never before had I prayed with so much earnestness. I wish I could repeat my prayer. I felt I must put all my trust in Almighty God. He gave our people the best country ever given to man. He alone could save it from destruction. I had tried my best to do my duty and had found myself unequal to the task. The burden was more than I could bear. I asked Him to help us and give us victory now. I was sure my prayer was answered. I had no misgivings about the result at Gettysburg.[36]

This discussion was observed by General James Rusling, who gave the following account of the conversation:

> In reply to a question from General Sickles whether or not the President was anxious about the battle of Gettysburg, Lincoln gravely said, "No, I was not; some of my Cabinet and many others in Washington were, but I had no fears." General Sickles inquired how this was, and seemed curious about it. Mr. Lincoln hesitated, but finally replied: "Well, I will tell you how it was. In the pinch of the campaign up there, when everybody seemed panic-stricken, and nobody could tell what was going to happen, oppressed by the gravity of our affairs, I went to my room one day, and I locked the door, and got down on my knees before Almighty God, and prayed to Him mightily for victory at Gettysburg. I told Him that this was His war, and our cause His cause, but we couldn't stand another Fredericksburg or Chancellorsville. And I then and there made a solemn vow to Almighty God, that if He would stand by our boys at Gettysburg, I would stand by Him. And He did stand by your boys, and I will stand by Him. And after that (I don't know how it was, and I can't explain it), soon a sweet comfort crept into my soul that God Almighty had taken the whole business into His own hands and that things would go all right at Gettysburg. And that is why I had no fears about you."[37]

Union Victory

The Union's triumph at Gettysburg was a great but dreadful victory. The two armies suffered almost 50,000 casualties. Nearly 8,000 soldiers died in the three-day battle.

But still, the North had won.

The political consequence of the South's defeat was enormous.

Upon hearing of the outcome, Lincoln refused to allow Vice President Stephens a pass through Union lines to engage in peace discussions. When news of the defeat reached London, any hope of European intervention in the war ended. The value of Confederate war bonds in Europe fell precipitously over the next several months.

Gettysburg turned out to be the turning point. Though the war was to continue for two more bloody years, the tide had turned.

By the fall of 1864, a series of timely Union military victories at Mobile Bay, Alabama; Sherman's taking of Atlanta; and General Philip Sheridan's victories in the Shenandoah Valley assured Lincoln of re-election. After Atlanta, General Sherman engaged in "total war" in the South. In February 1865, his army entered Columbia, South Carolina. Fort Sumter was retaken. Elsewhere, General Grant pursued military victories relentlessly.

Facing starvation and increasing ruination, in April, General Robert E. Lee surrendered at Appomattox, bringing to a close the most brutal, bloody, and significant episode in our nation's history.

The nation was reunited, the cause of democracy pulled back from the brink.

What If?

What if there had been no Abraham Lincoln? What if he hadn't had such faith as to declare the Emancipation Proclamation and, more important, hold strong at Gettysburg while seeking God in prayer? What if a lesser man had occupied the White House in the years 1861 to 1865?

In seems likely—in fact, a certainty—that the Union would have failed. The Confederacy would have prevailed either through outright military victory or through a negotiated peace, achieving its independence with slavery intact.

In that event, how would the history of this nation, and the world, have unfolded? Although it's impossible to predict everything with a certainty, this much seems probable:

1. Slavery would have continued indefinitely. The industrial revolution might have altered the South's dependence on slave-produced agriculture, specifically cotton; however, it would not have taken much for emerging industrialists to figure out that slavery worked quite nicely in factories and mines. For an unknown period of time, the Confederate States of America would have continued to operate under the guiding principle that, for the black man, "slavery—subordination to the superior race, is his natural and normal condition."[38] It also seems inevitable that the Confederacy would have expanded slavery to the West. For some unknown period, the elite of the Confederacy would have reveled and grown fat off the sweat of other men's labor.

2. Equity would have been denied. The fact that the leaders of the Confederacy rejected the universal idealism of the Founders would have dictated their postwar actions. Beyond expansion of slavery to the West, their belief in the superiority of the white Anglo-Saxon would have justified colonialism in Cuba, the Caribbean, Mexico, and Central and South America.

With the elitist attitudes of the fire-eaters, would democracy have survived in the Confederate States of America? The success of the fire-eaters in contending for and achieving secession would have given them great credibility. Over time, their philosophy of liberty for the few might well have prevailed. It has been throughout history, and remains so today, the dominant philosophy of the world. There is no reason to assume that the Confederacy would not have evolved in that direction.

3. The Constitution would have been dismissed as a failed experiment. The principle of constitutionalism—the notion that people can come together, create a government, allocate powers to the different levels of government, institute forms within that government to protect the rights of its citizens, and remain bound by that agreement even when a minority or a majority find themselves aggrieved—would have failed.

4. Freedom would have been halted around the world. The nations of the earth would have taken a lesson from the brief history of the

United States—the lesson being that a democratic republic is not a suitable alternative to a monarchy or dictatorship.

5. The nation would have been balkanized. It is presumed by many that history would have unfolded with two nations sharing what is now the United States. But would the divisions really have stopped there? How long would it have taken before Texas left the Confederacy and joined other territories in the Southwest to create its own nation, perhaps joining with Mexico? Would California have stayed in the United States? What about Brigham Young and the Mormons in the Rocky Mountains? Would the states of the Northeast have declared a separate union—a break that almost *did* occur during the height of the Civil War?

The United States would most likely have been completely balkanized, becoming like the nation-states of Central and South America and Europe at that time.

Wars over territorial claims would have been inevitable. Such wars would have allowed European powers a toehold in the various nations that then existed in the United States. Britain would have welcomed invitations to support one side or the other in order to reestablish its links to its former colonies. Even France, under the leadership of Ferdinand Maximilian, longed to reestablish itself on this continent and took advantage of preoccupation with the Civil War in a quest to conquer Mexico.

Separated into warring parts, what remained of the U.S. would never have been as powerful and rich as it was in its united form.

6. The future would have been changed. Would a balkanized nation have been strong enough to settle the massive and rugged West? Would it have had the vision and courage to build the transcontinental railroad? What would the next century have been like without the power and moral leadership of a *united* United States? What would have happened during the two World Wars of the twentieth century? Who would have been available to save Europe from fascism, or the entire world from communism?

Perhaps most important: What would have been the reaction to the failure of the United States throughout Europe and the rest of the world? Even if the North had prevailed as a nation, how much dimmer would have been its light with its reduced size and wealth? How much would its image as a beacon of freedom have been dimmed as it was forced to live side by side with a nation committed to the abuse of basic human rights?

How many efforts at achieving freedom and self-government for nations throughout the world would have failed without the brightly burning light from the United States of America, a united nation from coast to coast, proving that constitutionalism works, that people of all nationalities can govern themselves, and that the liberties spoken of in the Declaration of Independence were God's gift to every man and woman on the earth, not just a chosen few.

In 1870, as the French sought to build and defend a democracy of their own, the great French author Victor Hugo was addressing a massive crowd in Paris when he pointed to the American flag flying in front of the nearby embassy of the United States and said, "That banner of stars speaks today to Paris and France proclaiming miracles of power which are easy to a great people, contending for great principle, the liberty of every race and the fraternity of all."[39]

If the Civil War had been lost by the North, such a call to arms in the name of the flag of the United States would not have been justified in 1870, nor ever since.

• • •

In November 1863, Lincoln was asked to speak at the dedication of the Gettysburg Cemetery. The address there given is one of the most famous speeches ever delivered. In the brief span of a few minutes, he summed up the first eight decades of the American experience, ending his speech with a plea: "It is for us the living, rather, to be here dedicated to the great task remaining before us—that from these honored dead we take increased devotion to that cause for which they gave the last full measure of devotion—that we here highly resolve that these dead shall not have died in vain—that this nation, under God, shall have a new birth of freedom—and that government of the people, by the people, for the people, shall not perish from the earth."[40]

If it had not been for Abraham Lincoln, those great dreams and goals might very well have perished, not only from this nation but from the earth.

But God *did* intervene to save His nation. During the darkest and most oppressive days of the war, when the battle hung in the balance and the outcome was anything but assured, God answered Lincoln's urgent prayer, giving him the strength to carry on.

In his Second Inaugural Address, Lincoln begged, "With malice toward none; with charity for all; with firmness in the right, as God gives us to see the right, let us strive on to finish the work we are in; to bind up the nation's wounds; to care for him who shall have borne the battle, and for his widow, and his orphan—to do all which may achieve and cherish a just and lasting peace among ourselves, and with all nations."[41]

He was not to live to see this lofty goal achieved.

On April 14, 1865, God called his servant home.

Notes

1. Information on the Dred Scott case can be found in Morison and Commager, *Growth of the American Republic*, 1:651–53; Schweikart and Allen, *Patriot's History*, 278–81; Wilentz, *Rise of American Democracy*, 707–15.

2. Wilentz, *Rise of American Democracy*, 713.

3. For a description given of the opinion by the Ohio Republican state convention, see ibid., 714.

4. Morison and Commager, *Growth of the American Republic*, 1:649.

5. For information about the years immediately before the Civil War, including the election of 1856, see McCullough, *Truman*, 26–28; Morison and Commager, *Growth of the American Republic*, 1:643–61; Schweikart and Allen, *Patriot's History*, 256–83; Wilentz, *Rise of American Democracy*, 677–767.

6. See Schweikart and Allen, *Patriot's History*, 263; Wilentz, *Rise of American Democracy*, 338–39.

7. Morison and Commager, *Growth of the American Republic*, 1:537–38.

8. Wilentz, *Rise of American Democracy*, 731.

9. Statistics on the number and value of slaves came from McCullough, *Truman,* 27; Schweikart and Allen, *Patriot's History,* 256–61.

10. Wilentz, *Rise of American Democracy,* 745.

11. Schweikart and Allen, *Patriot's History,* 299.

12. Ibid., 302. For a discussion of the antidemocratic nature of the fire-eaters and the Confederacy generally, see ibid., 261–64, 299–302; Wilentz, *Rise of American Democracy,* 725–34.

13. Mason, *Free Government in the Making,* 529.

14. Wilentz, *Rise of American Democracy,* 738.

15. Ibid., 741.

16. Ibid., 749–50.

17. Morison and Commager, *Growth of the American Republic,* 666–67.

18. Wilentz, *Rise of American Democracy,* 774–75.

19. Ibid., 779.

20. Wolf, *Almost Chosen People,* 114.

21. Schweikart and Allen, *Patriot's History,* 315.

22. Donald, *Lincoln,* 424.

23. Ibid., 425.

24. "Visitors from Congress," in *Mr. Lincoln's White House.* August 5, 2009, http://www.mrlincolnswhitehouse.org/inside.asp?ID=11&subjectID=2.

25. Wolf, *Almost Chosen People,* 13.

26. Ibid., 158–59; emphasis added.

27. Ibid., 146.

28. Goodwin, *Team of Rivals,* 468.

29. Wolf, *Almost Chosen People,* 17.

30. Goodwin, *Team of Rivals,* 486.

31. Ibid., 503.

32. Ibid.

33. Ibid., 520.

34. Ibid., 531.

35. Ibid.

36. Wilson, *Intimate Memories of Lincoln,* 574.

37. Wolf, *Almost Chosen People,* 124–25.

38. Wilentz, *Rise of American Democracy,* 774–75.

39. Lind, *What Lincoln Believed,* 304.

40. Wolf, *Almost Chosen People,* 172.

41. Ibid., 183.

Chapter 6

The Miracle at Midway

Japanese Submarine I-17,
Off the California Coast
February 1942

THE JAPANESE COMMANDER was on a personal mission that had nothing to do with battle orders, tactical advantage, or the strategies of victory. Indeed, his actions had precious little even to do with the war. His only purpose was to avenge a broken ego from an incident that had happened years before.

The black, diesel-powered submarine ascended slowly, her propellers and leveling planes pushing her gently upward and to the east. Fifty feet below the surface, the sub leveled, drove west for two miles, then started ascending once again. Twenty feet. Ten. "All stop," the commander called. He braced himself to keep from tipping forward as the powerful engines rolled to idle power, the submarine coming to a stop against the wall of water pressing at its nose. "Forward periscope," the commander ordered. The smaller of the two periscopes aboard the long-range sub slipped up, and the captain moved toward it, pressing his eyes against the hooded lens. He studied the scene for several minutes, slowly walking from side to side, taking in the California coast, which was little more than a mile off the submarine's starboard side.

The hills above the oil refinery were cluttered with dry brush and low trees. The sky was clear. The sun had been down for half an hour, but it wasn't quite dark yet. Visibility was nearly unlimited, although a few high clouds obscured the moon. Farther south along the coast, he could barely make out the small town of Santa Barbara, most of the city hidden behind a sharp elbow of land that jutted into the bay. The city was dark, for they were under a curfew and there were no lights allowed. He stepped slowly to his right, bringing the refinery into view again. Everything was familiar. He had been here many times before. As the skipper of a Japanese oil tanker, Commander Nishino Kozo, now commander of the Japanese submarine I-17, had taken on fuel at the Bankline Company oil refinery just a few years before. It was here he had witnessed for himself how arrogant and disrespectful the hairy-faced Americans could really be. His cheeks flushed with embarrassment as he remembered what had happened: Walking up the sandy pathway that led to the oil refinery from the beach, he and his tanker crew were outfitted in their formal dress to greet the American welcome party waiting at the top of the ridge. Tripping over a rut in the trail, he had fallen into a prickly pear cactus. While he scrambled to stand, feeling the pain of cactus spines in his buttocks, the Americans had pointed and laughed, a few of them actually rolling on the ground.

Yes, Commander Kozo remembered the humiliation very clearly.

Now he would enjoy a personal moment of revenge.

Smiling, he took one last look at his target, then completed several circles with the periscope, looking up and down the coastline before searching the open ocean to the west. Stepping away from the periscope, he tugged down on his submariner's cap.

"Take her up!" he ordered. "Man the forward guns!"

Minutes later, the shelling started. Almost twenty deadly warheads from the 5.5-inch guns were sent toward the shore. Some fell short. One went long. Only a couple hit their targets, but Commander Kozo didn't care. It felt good to see the American soil torn up by his Japanese shells. It felt good to feel the thunder of his guns. It felt good to smell the smoke and see the balls of white-hot gases bursting from the barrels of his weapons as they fired in the dark. It would be worth the entire trip across the Pacific if he could kill a single American on American soil.

The shelling continued for almost thirty minutes; then the submarine slowly turned around. Cruising arrogantly across the bay, still exposed above the waterline, it exited the south end of the Santa Barbara Channel, Commander Kozo standing proudly beside the small mast, the banner of the Rising Sun flapping in the wind.

A Season of Lost Hope

Such was the state of the war at the beginning of 1942: Japanese commanders free to skulk around in the waters of the U.S. western coast, attacking when they wanted for no more reason than that they could.[1]

The winter of 1941–42 was a dark time for the people of the United States. The attack on Pearl Harbor had rocked the nation's psyche. The country tried to stagger to its feet after the devastating defeat in Hawaii, but it was battered repeatedly as the United States and its allies suffered blow upon blow under the hands of the Axis powers.

In Europe, the German army was knocking at the door of Moscow. The Russians had barely held on through the brutal winter and appeared to be within a battle or two of being thrown back to the Urals. Stalin had already moved his headquarters and much of his diplomatic staff away from Moscow. In February, Great Britain was humiliated by the successful move of the German battle cruisers *Scharnhorst* and *Gneisenau* and the heavy cruiser *Prinz Eugen* through the British Channel in broad daylight—this despite British foreknowledge and plans to prevent it. In the Atlantic, German submarines operated at will, destroying massive amounts of Allied shipping. Hundreds of ships. Thousands of men. The sinking of a merchant supply ship was almost a daily occurrence, severely threatening the economy and war-making power of both Great Britain and the United States. In late May, Rommel was besting the Allied forces in the battle of Gazala in North Africa.

Day after day, it was the same thing. Another defeat. Another loss. Not a piece of good news could be found anywhere. Some were calling for surrender. A few were demanding that FDR resign. One of the nation's leading papers summed up the mood: "The nation needs to understand that *it is possible for the United Nations and the United States to lose this war and suffer the fate of France—and that this possibility may become a probability if the present tide does not change.*"[2]

Grim as things were looking for the United States and her allies in Europe, it was in the Pacific that the world was absolutely shocked by the Japanese juggernaut.

The day after Pearl Harbor, Japan invaded Malaysia and Thailand. Two days later, Japanese troops landed on northern Luzon in the Philippines and also began the taking of Guam. The same day, the British battleship *Prince of Wales* and its partner battle cruiser *Repulse* were sunk by the Japanese off Malaya. More than eight hundred men lost their lives.

The next week, Japan invaded Burma, followed quickly by invasions of British Borneo and the Netherlands East Indies.

Wake Island had come under attack within hours of the attack on Pearl Harbor. The undermanned U.S. troops initially drove back the Japanese invaders; over the next two weeks, they sank six Japanese warships, shot down twenty-one airplanes, and killed nearly a thousand Japanese troops. But, on Christmas Eve, the island surrendered.

The next day, Hong Kong fell to the Japanese. Six weeks later, the same fate befell Singapore. Australia came under attack from the air in February and by submarine in May.

The Allies suffered a major defeat in the Battle of the Java Sea in late February. Ten Allied ships were sunk; the Japanese lost two. The Allies failed to stop the invasion of Java.

With the U.S. Pacific Fleet incapacitated at Pearl Harbor, the Japanese were free to venture into the Indian Ocean and run amok—attacking shipping at will, mounting bombing raids on various ports, and inflicting major damage on the British fleet.

In early May, the Philippines fell. This was followed by a victory for the Japanese in the Battle of the Coral Sea. One of the casualties of this engagement was the U.S. aircraft carrier *Yorktown*, which had to limp back to Pearl Harbor. It was expected to take up to three months to repair its damage.

Japanese submarines operated between the west coast of the United States and Hawaii—much to the humiliation of the once-powerful American navy. The shelling of the Santa Barbara oil facility by a vengeful Japanese submarine commander added insult to the fear.

No one realized that when the Japanese started their Pacific campaign with the invasion of Manchuria in 1931, in ten short years they would have conquered more land and people than the Roman, Mongol, or Muslim empires ever did.[3]

The White House, Washington, D.C. Early March, 1942

THE PRESIDENT OF THE United States sat alone in the Oval Office, his glasses reflecting the semidarkness around him, a single Tiffany lamp with a forty-watt bulb illuminating the corner of his desk. The room was cool—he'd ordered the White House staff to cut back on the amount of fuel they used to heat their offices—and a soft brown sweater was draped around his shoulders. His circulation wasn't good anymore, and from October to March it seemed that he was always cold. He looked at the military summary. A few of the items had turned him even colder. The Russians weren't going to make it if something didn't change. Seventy-five thousand Filipino and

American troops were being decimated in the Philippines. How many of them were they going to lose? And what was this thing out in California? A submarine blasting at the coast! Thinking of the situation, he felt his chest grow tight.

Sometimes he wondered if he was getting too old.

As the clock chimed midnight, he heard a light knock on the door. He grunted, wanting to be left alone—this was the only time he really had time to think—but the door moved back. His primary military adviser, the army chief of staff, hesitated as he looked into the room. Tall, thin, salt-and-pepper hair, handsome face with brooding eyes. The four-star general stood a moment without moving, knowing he had interrupted the president.

"Come in, George," Roosevelt said.

General George C. Marshall moved toward the desk.

"Sit down," the president offered.

Marshall glanced at the leather chair on the opposite side of the desk but didn't move. "You were asking about the incident in California?" he said.

Roosevelt lifted a knee and pressed it against his desk. "Does it bother you?" he wondered.

Marshall hesitated before he answered, "Not much, sir."

"Not much!" Roosevelt shot back. "We've got a Japanese submarine prancing up and down the bay of Santa Barbara, half of California in a panic, and you're not bothered by that, George?"

Marshall stared into the president's eyes. He understood what his leader was asking. In the heat of the battle, sometimes even the president needed to be reassured.

The general stood firm, his back straight. He'd grown up in Pennsylvania, a small-town kid from middle-class America, but his education at Virginia Military Institute had trained him, and the army had steeled him into the leader he was now. And though he wasn't royal, he was as dignified as only a man with the lives of two million troops and the future of a nation resting on his shoulders could ever be. "Sir," he started, "the submarine attack in Santa Barbara was a meaningless gesture. Very little damage has been reported. Truthfully, it's a bit confusing, there was so little value in the attack. Psychologically it sets us back a little and it's embarrassing, but we don't think there's any danger. It's not like the Japanese are ready to sally forth across the ocean. Both of us know there is no danger of an imminent attack."

The president searched the general's face, seeing the assurance in his eyes, then leaned forward and rested his arms across the desk. "It hurts us in ways you have not mentioned yet," he answered.

General Marshall knew immediately what the president was talking about.

The president gestured to the window and the dark streets of D.C. "If you were to go out there and ask the first person you met, 'Who is our enemy?' how do you think they'd answer? Germany? The Italians? No, that is not what they'd say. Japan is our enemy! Japan, not Germany! They've seen the pictures from Pearl Harbor. They've seen the fires and destruction, rows and rows of sunken battleships, thousands of young men dead. Japan has destroyed more U.S. blood and treasure than any nation on the earth. You and I know that's going to change soon, but it's the Empire of the Rising Sun that they want to fight right now."

Marshall listened but didn't answer. He was tired and wanted a cigarette and a couple of days to sleep.

Turning, he looked off. He knew Roosevelt was walking across a canyon on a tightrope that was being shaken from both ends. On one side, the people of Russia and Great Britain were begging for a savior to protect them from the German horde. On the other, the Americans were demanding an immediate and massive response against Japan, revenge for the insult of Pearl Harbor.

But what the people of the United States didn't know was that their president wasn't going to avenge them. Roosevelt was committed to a strategy of "Germany First." Controversial, perilous, and getting more so every day, the doctrine of Germany First was as much a danger politically as it was a military risk.

General Marshall was very familiar with the doctrine. Indeed, he'd been one of those who had developed it. And the planning had taken place many months before.

Beginning in late 1938, when it had become apparent that a two-pronged war in Europe and the Pacific was not only possible but perhaps inevitable, military strategists had started planning the best way to win both wars. After a thousand hours of "gaming" they had reached a final conclusion. The U.S. had to place their priority in defeating Germany first. Following his reelection in 1940, President Roosevelt had been persuaded that the United States had no choice but to seek the defeat of Germany before they could defeat Japan.

Plan D, as it came to be known, called for the creation of a line of defense from Alaska to Hawaii and east to the Panama Canal. That meant that everything west of that line was expendable, including Australia and the American military forces in the Philippines and other Western Pacific locations. Thinking of this, the general lowered his eyes. He knew, perhaps in a more painful way than even the president, what was happening in the Western Pacific at that moment—the men they'd lost already, the men they would yet lose. Thousands of them. Tens of thousands. Most of them were going to die.

Now, as they had feared, both the public and Congress were demanding that the American military focus on Japan. Some of Marshall's own staff wanted to fight in the Pacific, seeing the rising tide of anger, nearly impossible to hold back.

The clock ticked and then chimed once. Fifteen minutes after midnight. The night was dark outside.

Across the partially lit desk, Roosevelt searched the general's face for any hint of hesitation, then nodded toward a manila folder. "Churchill is becoming nervous."

The general didn't answer. He knew that, following the attack at Pearl Harbor, when the Americans had started screaming for revenge, British Prime Minister Winston Churchill had feared that Roosevelt would abandon Plan D. So concerned had he become that he had crossed the Atlantic aboard the British battleship HMS *Duke of York* to rally his needed friend. "We've got to stand firm!" he had pleaded with the president. "Don't abandon the only thing that's going to save us."

Remembering the meeting between Roosevelt and Churchill, the general frowned. He knew Roosevelt as well as anyone and understood that, in the very depths of his soul, the president was a politician, not a warrior. Because of this, the president thought differently than the general did. He perceived things differently. He acted differently. It took a different set of values, a different set of skills, a different way of thinking to become president of the United States. It was a set of skills that Marshall respected, but it was different from his, and when it came to matters of policy, the general was careful in what he said.

"We've made a commitment to Churchill," he finally answered. "And, sir, it's important to remember, we didn't make this commitment to be generous. We committed to make the war in Europe our first priority because it's the right thing to do. It's the only way we win this. We've got to cut down Germany. And we don't have much time."

Roosevelt shook his head. "But our people, those everyday people who live in your hometown in Pennsylvania or out in Wisconsin or Texas or Idaho, are clamoring for a victory against the Japanese. Revenge can be a very powerful emotion, General Marshall, and it's not one we want to waste. We need to harness that emotion and funnel it into the war. But it's a difficult thing to do, to turn that anger and refocus it on Europe. We've fought a war over there already, not that long ago. Most of our people remember the mud and death and stench that was the First World War. Most of them remember the frustration of unbroken lines of battle that didn't move in years, trenches across France and Germany filled with bodies and blood and nothing more. Little wonder few are excited about fighting in Europe once again."

Marshall nodded slowly. His lips were cracked and dry. "Do you have any tea, Mr. President?" he asked politely.

Roosevelt nodded to a serving tray. "It'll be cold by now."

The general walked toward the mahogany table opposite the president's desk. He lifted the sterling silver server, a beautiful antique piece fashioned after an eagle's claw, and slowly poured. He didn't so much want the tea—his stomach was already filled with acid and the tea would only make it worse—as he wanted something to fiddle with while they talked.

Marshall sipped the warm tea as he thought. He knew that Plan D could never be disclosed to the American public. Not only would it be politically unacceptable, it would make it clear to the Japanese that they had a green light in the Pacific to do whatever they wanted to do.

He swirled the tea and bent forward. "Sir, if I could venture a reminder?" he asked.

The president nodded.

"It's important to stay the course for at least three reasons. First, we now have an army of nearly two million recruits. In a couple of years, we'll have eight million. All of them are full of piss and vinegar and begging for a fight. They are anxious to get into combat, and we need to get them there. Europe is the only place that we can use them. We can't bottle eight million combat soldiers onto ships and send them hopping across the Pacific, looking for a war.

"Second, it is at least possible, if not likely, that the Soviet Union will collapse. Germany has thrust to the very outskirts of Moscow. Stalin is asking—no, he's begging—for us to get into the fight. The Allies need to open up a second front against Hitler somewhere, anywhere! Russia simply can't wait for us to win in the Pacific. They won't make it that long.

"And last, Mr. President, but perhaps most important, if Germany is able to develop some of the new weapons we have talked about, this war is over now. We know Germany is attempting to split the atom to make a nuclear bomb. They're developing an intercontinental rocket, a four-engine jet bomber with a speed of 500 miles per hour. Our intelligence has talked about a German spy plane capable of flying to New York and back to Europe! If Germany proves capable of launching bombing attacks on our mainland, this will be a very different war. If we give them enough time—and it won't take long— German scientists could tip the balance."

The president was silent for a long moment. "I know that," he finally said.

"It's imperative then, sir, that Hitler be defeated now. Despite the pressure you are under, we have to suppress the urge to fight the wrong war. The battle in the Pacific has to take a backseat. It's the only way that we survive."[4]

Japanese Final Battle Plan

Following their unexpectedly easy and overwhelming victory at Pearl Harbor, the Japanese were feeling optimistic. The commander of the carrier task force that had undertaken the surprise attack, Vice Admiral Chuichi Nagumo, had fully expected to lose up to one-third of his task force in the Pearl Harbor attack, but had returned with not one of his ships having been touched by American armaments.

Upon returning to Japan, the task force was met with a jubilant welcome. The highest honor was the invitation for Nagumo and his two air commanders to meet with Emperor Hirohito himself.

After a period of celebration, Japanese military planners began to plan their "second term strategy." The Japanese commanders knew they had a window of opportunity to win not just the next battle but the entire war. The opportunity was short, and it would require daring, but total victory was possible.

The attack against Pearl Harbor was the beginning. If they were successful, the next battle could be their last.

The Japanese commanders were intelligent enough to realize that the U.S. was preparing its people and its forces for a European war. They also knew they had thrown the U.S. Pacific Fleet back on its haunches. Finally, they understood how difficult it would be for the U.S. to extend and maintain its supply, communications, logistic, and combat forces across the wide expanse of the Pacific in the face of an entrenched and hostile Japanese military. If they could destroy American naval forces in the theater, it would take the U.S. many years to rebuild, time the Japanese could then use to consolidate their holdings, making it impossible for the U.S. to rout them out.

With the U.S. fleet destroyed, its strategic positions throughout the Pacific lost, its bases occupied by entrenched and superior forces, the

Americans would have to ask the question: Was it worth the loss of blood and treasure to win the Pacific war?

The Japanese leaders were betting the answer to that question would be no.

After considering their options, the Japanese commander in chief of the Combined Fleet, Admiral Isoroku Yamamoto, agreed to an operation against the pinprick on a Pacific map known as Midway Atoll, a tiny speck of coral consisting of Sand Island and Eastern Island. Combined, the two islands covered only 1,540 acres, an area roughly nine times the size of the Mall in Washington, D.C. Positioned 1,260 nautical miles from Honolulu, about one-third of the way between Hawaii and Tokyo, Midway was small, but it was still a treasure, for it held the only airfield sufficient for military operations in the central Pacific region. If they controlled Midway, the Japanese would control all of the air and sea lanes west of Honolulu. They could trap the U.S. fleet. And Midway's airfield could serve as a staging field for land-based attacks against Hawaii as a precursor to an all-out invasion.

But this wasn't the only reason to go after the Midway atoll. The Japanese commanders also wanted to lure the remaining vessels of the U.S. Pacific Fleet into a confrontation where they could be destroyed.

Their plan was complicated. First, it called for some Japanese forces to be deployed to the north in a sham campaign against the Aleutian Islands. It was hoped this pretended attack would draw some of the remaining U.S. fleet out of the area of Midway. Yamamoto also divided his Midway attack force into three different groups. The first consisted of an invasion force made up of transport ships carrying 5,000 troops, with a powerful escort of warships, including two battleships. The second element was Vice Admiral Nagumo's strike force, consisting of four heavy aircraft carriers, the *Akagi, Kaga, Hiryu,* and *Soryu.* This element was to be accompanied by two battleships and other escort ships. The main battle group, three battlewagons and four battleships accompanied by a large number of lesser escort ships, was held in reserve. It would bring up the rear and move forward once the carriers had cleared a path to Midway.

In total, Admiral Yamamoto commanded a force of more than 129 ships, including 86 fighting ships. Virtually every Japanese warship that wasn't immediately needed in some kind of secondary mission was included in the invasion force, creating one of the greatest armadas of the war.[5]

A New Kind of War

Warfare on the seas had evolved quickly and dramatically between World War I and World War II. In the First World War, heavy battleships had been the kings. With massive guns that could shoot one-ton projectiles up to ten miles, battleships were fearsome weapons.

But there were a few military men—and they were very few—who realized there was a way to extend the range of seaborne weaponry far beyond a ten-mile range. For years, they sought for funding and support from the naval brass. Most of their fellow sailors thought that they were crazy until, in 1922, the USS *Langley* finally took to the sea. Long and boxy, a converted cargo ship, the *Langley* was as ugly a ship as had ever set upon the water. But it was as revolutionary as it was ugly. Its dual funnels moved outboard, its hull flattened and extended, its square deck cluttered with little aircraft, the former trash hauler was designated VC-1, the first aircraft carrier ever built.

With the launching of the *Langley*, the age of modern naval warfare was born.

Both the United States and Japan quickly adopted the strategy that the carrier battle group was the best way of extending a nation's military might in the vast distances of the Pacific Ocean. Japanese victories at Pearl Harbor and the Coral Sea proved this strategy was correct, making it obvious that carrier-based airpower was one of the most powerful weapons a nation could employ.

The twenty years that followed the maiden voyage of the *Langley* brought breathtaking advances in the technology, scope, and size of the carrier fleets. As the tactics and carrier employment theories evolved, one thing became very clear: The element of surprise was critical to the outcome of the battle. Unlike land warfare, where battlefield commanders could take advantage of concealment and terrain, warfare on the open seas often came down to the tremendous advantage of good intelligence about the enemy's location and intentions. If you could somehow surprise the enemy before they could launch their airplanes, victory was almost guaranteed.

Each carrier, both American and Japanese, employed three types of aircraft: fighters, dive bombers, and torpedo planes. Once the enemy fleet was discovered, squadrons of all three types of aircraft were launched as quickly as possible. Some of the fighters would remain with the carriers, circling above the fleet to provide protection in the event of an enemy counterattack, while the remaining fighters, dive bombers, and torpedo planes would turn toward the enemy fleet and attack with all possible speed.

Somewhere before engaging the enemy fleet, the three squadrons of different types of aircraft were to rendezvous and join up as one seamless attacking force. This was extremely important. In order to be successful, there had to be a coordinated attack.

The fighter aircraft would be the first to engage. Their purpose was to destroy as many of the enemy fighters protecting the carriers as possible. Those they couldn't take out, they were to keep preoccupied, making it difficult for them to attack the much slower and more vulnerable dive and torpedo bombers as they started their bombing runs.

After the fighters had engaged, the dive bombers would move in. Although they were expected to have some success in their bombing, everyone knew the Japanese had reinforced their carrier decks with armor, making them almost impossible to severely damage from a top-down attack. This being the case, the dive bombers had accepted a more important and much more deadly mission—to act as decoys for the torpedo planes.

Once the American fighters and dive bombers were drawing fire from the Japanese defenders and antiaircraft guns, the torpedo planes would press their attack. In order to drop their deadly weapons, the torpedo pilots had to fly very "slow and low" for several agonizing minutes, all the while maintaining a straight flight path toward their targets. Under the best of circumstances, this was an extraordinarily dangerous mission. Under combat conditions, it was nearly suicide. But it was also the only way to inflict heavy damage against the Japanese fleets, for torpedoes hitting below the waterline were the only weapons able to sink them.

The torpedo squadrons flew the Devastator, which, despite the intimidating name, was a relatively old and awkward aircraft, slow and underpowered. No wonder, then, that flying such extraordinarily dangerous missions in inferior aircraft, some of the pilots joked about their squadron, calling themselves the *Sitting Ducks.*

The Fighters

To fully appreciate the enormity of the task facing the U.S. forces, it is useful to compare the capabilities of the aircraft involved in the Battle of Midway:

Japanese Zero: At the time of the Midway attack, the Japanese Mitsubishi A6M2 Zero was considered the best carrier-based fighter in the world. With a deadly combination of speed, power, and maneuverability, it was greatly feared, gaining a legendary status as a killer. The 925-horsepower engine drove the aircraft to a top speed of 336 mph and an altitude of 33,000 feet. It had two 7.7-mm guns and a 20-mm cannon mounted on each wing. It also could carry two 132-pound bombs.

American Devastator: When the Douglas TBD Devastator first entered service in 1937, it was touted as the most advanced aircraft flying in the U.S. Navy. Only five years later, it was considered obsolete. After its crushing performance at Midway, the aircraft was pulled from frontline duty. The 900-horsepower engines only drove the aircraft to a max speed of 206 mph, and the Devastator couldn't even top 20,000 feet. It was protected by either a .30- or a .50-caliber forward-firing machine gun as well as a .30-caliber machine gun facing the rear. The aircraft could carry a single 1,000-pound bomb or a 1,200-pound torpedo.

American Vindicator: Also developed and deployed in the 1930s, the Vought SB2U Vindicator was the first dive bomber monoplane ever built. It had an 825-horsepower engine, a top speed of 242 mph, and a ceiling in the mid–twenty-thousand-foot range. It carried forward- and rear-facing machine guns and a single bomb weighing either 500 or 1,000 pounds. Like the Devastator, it was quickly withdrawn from frontline service after Midway.

American Dauntless: The Douglas SBD Dauntless was the most capable of the navy fighter bombers and continued in operation throughout most of the war, though after Midway it was augmented by the newer and more capable Helldiver. Faster, stronger, more maneuverable, and with the capability to carry larger bombs, the Dauntless was perhaps the best dive bomber used against the Japanese fleet. The problem was, the Midway pilots had very little time to train in their new aircraft, some of them having as little as a couple of hours total flight time in the Dauntless. With a 1,000-horsepower engine, it could reach a speed of 250 mph and climb above 25,000 feet. More important, it could carry a massive 2,250-pound bomb, large even by modern standards.

American Wildcat: The Grumman F4F-4 was the newest fighter in the American arsenal, having entered service just a few months before the battle. With folding wings, the F4F-4 was heavy and slow to climb, though the wing configuration did allow for more aircraft to be stowed on a carrier deck. Its 1,200-horsepower engine drove the aircraft to a respectable speed of 320 mph and up to almost 40,000 feet. It carried four guns, an option most pilots didn't particularly appreciate, and two (mostly meaningless) 100-pound bombs. (In fact, in the Pacific it was far more likely to find two 58-gallon drop fuel tanks under the aircraft's wings than bombs.)[6]

The Men and Their Mood

While Japanese morale and confidence were bursting at the seams, the attitude of the American forces in the Pacific was just the opposite. Belief in their military might had been shattered. Many at Pearl Harbor lived in fear that at any moment the Japanese would return and finish the job they had begun on December 7 by blasting the docks, repair shops, and fuel supplies. The navy would then be forced to abandon Hawaii, leaving it open for invasion.

If anyone began to forget what havoc the Japanese were capable of, all they had to do was look at what remained of Battleship Row.

Careers were ending prematurely as finger-pointing for the failure to defend Pearl Harbor became rampant. Investigations were undertaken. Admiral Kimmel, commander in chief of the U.S. Pacific Fleet, was relieved of command.

As the Japanese undertook to conquer the Pacific Islands and Indochina, the complete impotence of the Allied response was telling. There came no counterstrike. No attempt to salvage the crushed reputations of the military leaders or the outposts they had lost throughout the Pacific. Thousands of U.S. marines and army troops were essentially abandoned at Wake Island and the Philippines. The U.S. military—especially the navy—appeared to be a completely incompetent fighting force.

It was into this desperate and critical situation that a new naval commander, Rear Admiral Chester W. Nimitz, had been thrust.

The wrong leader might have shrunk under the weight of the ongoing failure to stem this tsunami. Just the opposite happened in this circumstance. Nimitz was the right leader for the demoralized American military in the Pacific, as the ensuing months and years would prove.[7]

The most important task for Nimitz and his staff was to determine where the next Japanese attack would be and when it would occur. Was Australia to be invaded? Was Hawaii at risk again? Would the Japanese occupy islands in the Aleutians as a step toward invading the west coast? Would there be further attacks on the west coast itself? What was the fate of Samoa and the Fiji Islands?

Despite all that seemed to be going against them, the Americans did have one ace up their sleeve. Under the direction of Commander Joseph Rochefort, the Combat Intelligence Office at Pearl Harbor had been working tirelessly to break the Japanese operational code. This code, JN25, consisted of 45,000 five-digit numbers that represented words and phrases. An even larger pool of numbers was available that could be thrown into a message at random in order to mislead anyone trying to break the code. With only the most rudimentary of machines, and no access to a code book, deciphering this code required men of genius, an aptitude for math, an unlimited attention to detail, immense patience, and genuine enthusiasm for work—work that was little understood and not much appreciated.[8]

Rochefort had a team of such men. Aided by a group of very skilled navy radio operators, by March 1942 the Combat Intelligence Office could locate within a couple of hundred miles where most Japanese ships were. Within weeks, they were able to read every fourth or fifth grouping of any transmission picked up by the radio operators. It was determined that a large force was being organized to invade "AF." Rochefort and his determined crew believed that "AF" was Midway. Sometime in April, Nimitz was given this information.

The navy brass in Washington were not convinced. Many of them thought the next target was Hawaii, or perhaps even the west coast. Against the fervent advice of his subordinates in Hawaii and the hostile reception of his superiors in D.C., Nimitz kept his faith in the conclusions of his Combat Intelligence Office. Following a personal tour of Midway on May 2, Nimitz informed the island's commanding officers to expect an invasion in late May.

The uncertainty was removed on May 10 with the setting of a clever trap. With the permission of Nimitz, a message was sent from Midway to Hawaii in open traffic (most of the communications between Midway and Hawaii were sent through a Pacific cable that the Japanese had no way of intercepting), informing Honolulu that a desalinization facility had broken down and that Midway was running short of water. Soon afterward, a message was intercepted informing all Japanese commanders that "AF" was suffering a water shortage.

Nimitz was convinced and stuck to his guns despite repeated messages from Washington not to put too much faith in the decoders. It speaks to his tenacity and faith in his subordinates that he remained undaunted, even when the Japanese feint at the Aleutians occurred.

A key decision for Nimitz was whom to put in charge of the strike force to defend Midway Atoll. The natural choice was Vice Admiral Bill Halsey, a man already famous for his military successes. But when Halsey docked his Task Force Sixteen (consisting of the heavy carriers *Enterprise* and *Hornet* with their escort ships) on May 26 at Pearl Harbor, he was seriously ill and clearly in no condition to lead the task force against the Japanese. He contributed in a major way, however, by recommending that he be replaced by the commander of his cruiser force, Raymond A. Spruance. As with Admiral Nimitz, history has proven that Spruance was exactly the right man for the job.

During the last week of May, Nimitz began to gather his forces to defend Midway. In contrast to the eighty-six fighting ships available to Admiral Yamamoto, Nimitz only had twenty-seven. Yamamoto commanded four heavy aircraft carriers; Nimitz had three, one of which was the badly damaged *Yorktown* that had limped into Pearl Harbor after suffering serious damage in the Battle of the Coral Sea.

After being told it would take up to three months to repair the *Yorktown*, Nimitz proclaimed that that simply would not do. Under intense pressure, twelve hundred repairmen completed the needed repairs in a miraculous forty-eight hours, allowing Task Force Seventeen, under the command of Rear Admiral Frank Jack Fletcher (and created around the *Yorktown*), to join the *Enterprise* and *Hornet* carrier task force.

Going into the Battle of Midway, the Japanese had 325 total airplanes, all of which were based on carriers. The United States had 348 airplanes—233 carrier-based and 115 based on Midway itself. But comparing just the numbers of airplanes does not really show the true picture. Twenty-three of the U.S. planes were land-based bombers that proved to be virtually worthless as the battle unfolded. And, as already stated, the Japanese Zero fighters were vastly superior to U.S. fighters in their speed and ability to maneuver. American torpedo planes were underpowered death traps, and the torpedoes they carried were famously bad. Far too many times the brave pilots would fly through a barrage of antiaircraft fire and Japanese fighters only to have their torpedoes jam or malfunction. Perhaps most important of all, the Japanese fliers were experienced combat pilots, having been fighting and winning now for years. Most of the American pilots at Midway had never flown in combat. Many had never dropped real torpedoes or bombs before. Some were hardly checked out in the aircraft they were assigned to. All of this against the most experienced and deadly fighting force in the Pacific skies.

The Japanese seemed to have it all. More than three times the number of combat ships. Squadrons of vastly superior fighters. Far more experienced combat pilots. Hardened combat sailors. Momentum. Confidence. Control of the seas. In almost every measurable combat asset, the Japanese forces were vastly superior to what the Americans were able to drag to the fight.

As the three elements of the Japanese armada steamed toward Midway, optimism and confidence were everywhere. In the six months since Pearl Harbor, Nagumo's First Air Fleet had operated at will from Hawaii to the Indian Ocean. It had sunk five battleships, a carrier, two cruisers, and seven destroyers, and had sent tons of Allied shipping to the bottom of the sea. In turn, Nagumo had suffered not so much as a single loss. There was every belief that if the Japanese could just engage what remained of the U. S. Navy Pacific Fleet, an overwhelming victory would be assured.

And there was no reason to doubt it. The Americans had been defeated in every conflict and battle so far. Their supply lines were extended. They were already shifting their resources to the European war. The Pacific Fleet had been decimated. What did the Japanese have to fear?

But not all was well within the Japanese fleet.

One of Nagumo's two air commanders, the highly respected Mitsuo Fuchida, was diagnosed with acute appendicitis the first night at sea. He pled with his physician not to operate but to treat him in some way that would still allow him to lead his men in the upcoming battle. The doctor insisted that an operation be undertaken immediately. Fuchida was not to lead his command in the upcoming Battle of Midway.

A few days later, another of Nagumo's key personnel, Commander Minoru Genda, the genius behind the air attack on Pearl Harbor and one of the commander in chief's two most trusted associates, was laid low by pneumonia.[9]

Many took these unfortunate events as a bad omen. But the Japanese did not know the worst of it. On May 24, Rochefort and his men had intercepted an unusually long message. Laboring through the night, they had translated what was, in effect, the Japanese Order of Battle. With this in hand, Nimitz was able to determine with considerable accuracy the makeup of the invasion force and that it intended to begin its work on Midway around the third of June.

Three significant events, then, had unfolded before the Battle of Midway even began: the breaking of the Japanese code—45,000 ciphered words and phrases broken by sheer work and genius; the sudden illness that took out two of the most brilliant and experienced Japanese commanders; and the magnificent decision to put the quiet and unflappable Admiral Spruance in command of Task Force Sixteen.

During the first week in June, the Japanese armada steamed east while the American fleet steamed to meet it. And though the U.S. fleet had the advantage of knowing more about their enemy than the Japanese knew about them, the entire outcome of the battle still hinged on one thing: *Who would be the first to discover the other fleet?*

Midway Atoll
June 3, 1942

THERE WAS A SUDDEN heavy knock on his door, but the pilot was already awake, having acclimated to the routine. Rise at a completely unnatural hour. Brief. Cram down a little breakfast. Climb into his aircraft and set off into the sky. Hours of tedious droning, looking at miles of empty seas and barren sky. Sometimes, if they were lucky, they'd run into the enemy, but such encounters were rare. In general, the mission of scout pilots could be described as unending hours of boredom interrupted by minutes of sheer terror when the occasional Japanese Zero happened on them and attacked.

Twenty minutes later, freshly shaved but still bleary eyed, his mouth full of the last of the biscuit and heavy gravy, the pilot walked into the briefing room and sat down with his crew. Looking around, he noticed that the two door gunners weren't in their assigned seats. He swore under his breath. Particular about details and meticulous in his own work, he was equally demanding of his crew, which was why there was a chance they might actually survive the war. Two minutes before the doors were closed to begin the morning briefing, his side gunners slipped into the room. He eyed them angrily, but they avoided his deadly stare, keeping their eyes low. At exactly 3:00 A.M., the doors shut and their squadron commander stepped behind the makeshift podium. Looking at his boss, the pilot knew immediately that something was up. His stomach muscles tightened. They had known it was coming. Was the moment finally here?

The boss pulled down a chart and started pointing. "The Japanese fleet is somewhere out there," he stated matter-of-factly, as if announcing the coming sunrise. "They've gathered a massive armada and are sending it our way." He looked down and read directly from the message they had intercepted and deciphered from the Japanese fleet. "COMINT confirmed the participation of *Kaga, Akagi, Soryu,* and *Hiryu* in the offensive." He paused and looked up. "The *Kaga, Akagi, Soryu, Hiryu.* I'm sure you recognize those names." Looking down again, he read from a second intercepted message: "Please change the directive of the movements of the AF and AO Occupation Forces and related forces in the following manner. In accordance with (unreadable) Operation Orders. The position in which submarines must be prior—will be 150 miles more or less eastward of A1."

The squadron commander looked up. "Unless all of you are stupid, I don't need to explain to you what this means."

The room fell into a deadly silence.

No, he didn't need to explain.

• • •

Ensign Jack Reid stood in the dark, his outline framed by the starlit sky. The moon was low now, reflecting a shimmering yellow line against the choppy ocean, and the waves crashed against the beach in a constant roll, their drumbeats so predictable he could have used them to count time. It was early, closer to midnight than to sunrise, and the pilot felt a little out of whack being up at this time of day. He glanced at his watch and shivered, the adrenaline seeping through his veins. Behind him, the seven other members of his crew were busy pre-flighting the aircraft and loading their gear, all of them working in the dark. The copilot, a young man named Swan (the entire crew was so young!), was throwing a bundle of parachutes through the main hatch, his silhouette illuminated only by the moon.

The aircraft commander turned and walked toward his crew. R.J., the plane captain, turned and reported, "She's good to go."

The pilot stood back, taking in the large aircraft. High-winged, silver, with a canted nose and sealed belly to land on the water, two massive engines set above the cockpit, and dual blisters just behind the wings, the aircraft was a workhorse and very reliable. But it was a utility aircraft, not a fighter, and he hated taking it to war. Worst case, if the Japs were to get him, he knew he could always set the Catalina down upon the water, but it was impossible to kill the enemy while bobbing in a wounded aircraft on the ocean, and he prayed he wouldn't have to do that.

Lowering his gaze from the high-winged aircraft, he saw his co-pilot walking toward him. "I had them load up a little extra fuel," the young man told the mission commander.

The pilot eyed him in the darkness. "How much extra?"

"Fifty for the wife and each of the kiddies."

The pilot almost frowned. "That's a lot of extra weight. We gonna crash at the end of the runway when we take off?"

"Might. And if we do, it'll be a real crowd pleaser with all that gas."

The mission commander frowned again. "Might not be such a good idea, Bob."

"Maybe not. But we think we're going to need it."

The pilot took a breath. "I didn't sign up for this war to die in a fireball on the end of my own runway, you understand that? If we're going to go down, I want some enemy skin underneath my finger-nails."

The copilot slapped him on the shoulder. "Trust me," he said.

Thirty minutes later, with sunrise still hours away, the heavy PBY lumbered into the dark sky. It accelerated slowly, barely clearing the low brush at the end of the runway, then continued straight ahead for an excruciating distance before it finally started climbing into the star-lit sky. Turning slowly, its wings bobbing from the currents circulating over the cooler ocean, it made its way west toward the open sea.

The entire Japanese fleet was out there somewhere. But there was no certainty that they would find it, not with a thousand square miles between Midway and the fleet.

One aircraft. Eight sets of eyeballs. So much open ocean they had to search.

For the next six hours, Jack Reid and his crew patrolled west of Midway on a line that led in the direction of Wake Island. The crew was unusually alert, looking for any sign of the Japanese fleet while keeping a watchful eye for enemy patrol planes flying out of Wake.

"Give me a chance to get one of them!" the right door gunner kept saying over the intercom. Sitting behind the cumbersome wheel of the aircraft, Reid couldn't help but smile. His crew was itching for a fight, hoping to locate one of the Japanese patrol planes. They'd been given a handful of new .50-caliber explosive cartridges that were designed to explode upon impact rather than penetrate the target, and all of them believed if they could get a single hit with one of the blue-tipped cartridges, they could bring an enemy patrol plane down, exacting a bit of revenge for all the PBYs that had been shot up by the Japanese.

Reid glanced nervously at the main fuel panel. The copilot watched him from the right seat. "Time to turn around," he said.

They were flying north now, getting farther and farther from their base.

"If we don't turn back soon, we're going to have to ditch this puppy in the sea," the copilot told his mission commander. "Yeah, I threw on a little extra gas, but Jacky, I didn't add that much!"

The pilot kept on flying. "They've got to be out here somewhere!" He was talking to himself.

The rest of the crew was silent. The mission commander stared through his window. The sea looked black and lonely, stretching a thousand miles in every direction. If they had to put it down out here, they might as well have landed on the moon.

The pilot started to fidget nervously in his seat. He wanted to find the Japs as much as anyone, but he also had a responsibility to his crew. If they were to die, he didn't want it to be because they ran out of gas and had to ditch. He gripped his hands against the yoke and gently started turning, then rolled out once again.

"What do you say, boys?" he asked the others.

All of them were silent a long moment. He listened to them breathing into their masks. They flew a full minute without speaking, each of them lost in their own thoughts, all the while flying farther from their base.

He started another gentle turn.

"Give us another couple minutes!" one of the door gunners urged. Having already accepted that they were probably going to ditch into the sea, he thought they might as well keep on searching and make it worth their sacrifice.

The aircraft commander didn't answer. "Is it unanimous?" he said.

"Roger that, boss," his crew answered one by one.

Jack sat straight up in his pilot seat. He'd never been prouder in his life. "Okay, guys, but you understand the risk we're taking?"

"Boss, I'm trying to concentrate!" the plane crew chief shot back.

Jack hesitated. "We'll go ten more minutes," he said. "Okay, guys. Ten more minutes. Then we're going to turn around!"

Jack kept his eyes moving, concentrating on the sea below. There was a method to his searching, taking in small blocks of ocean, then moving his gaze to take in another patch of sea. His eyes were tired and his neck was sore from always looking to his left. He glanced at his watch. Four minutes had passed. He looked out again. The skies were becoming patchy with growing clouds as moisture evaporated off the sea from the building heat. He skillfully maneuvered the Catalina—it was as easy to fly as to drive a car—and dropped down a couple of hundred feet. He flew north—they had to be here somewhere!—and glanced at his watch again. Two more minutes. Another minute. He looked in fear at his fuel gauge. "We've got to turn around here!" he announced to his crew. He moved the wheel and started turning. "We've gone too far already."

"Ten more minutes!" someone begged.

Jack gritted his teeth and straightened out the aircraft. "Ten more!" he answered into his mask.

Ten minutes later, his stomach in his throat, he finally started turning the aircraft back toward base. Staring across the hazy horizon, he looked in the direction that he was steering when something caught his eye. Specks of dirt on the windscreen? Maybe something on the sea? He squinted and leaned into the turn, looking more closely. His copilot suddenly pointed excitedly.

Five or six miles ahead of them, barely visible upon the horizon, they saw the group of Japanese ships that carried the 5,000 troops intended for the ground assault.

Speechless, Ensign Reid stared in awe, then picked up the aircraft's radio microphone. Glancing at his watch, he noted it was 9:30, then sent a message back to Midway. "Sighting main body," he said.

Reid and his crew began a deadly game of cat and mouse, flying in and out of clouds while skirting around and behind the fleet. Every moment they were out there, they grew lower on fuel. Every moment they were out there, they took the chance of a Japanese fighter or patrol plane flying toward them to attack. For two hours, they sent reports about the size and makeup of the Japanese invasion fleet before finally being given permission to return to Midway.

Flying literally on a wing and a prayer, they arrived back at base after fourteen hours in the air, longer than any PBY had ever flown with the same fuel load before.

A little extra fuel for the wife and kiddies had saved their lives that day.[10]

• • •

At 12:30, nine B17 bombers lifted off from Midway to attack the invasion force. A little more than four hours later, the bombers found their target and dropped their bomb loads from 8,000, 10,000 and 12,000 feet. The Japanese responded with heavy antiaircraft fire. After a few minutes of explosions, noise, and commotion, nobody was hurt—either in the air or onboard the ships—and the B17s returned to Midway.

Although the B17 attack did not result in any damage to the Japanese fleet, it did reveal to the Japanese that their presence was known. However, because the attacking aircraft were heavy bombers out of Midway, the key leaders of the Japanese invasion force did not believe that the American navy was close at hand. At best, they estimated, any carriers were still far to the east and just forming up.

The Final Battle Begins

The Japanese plan called for a massive air strike against Midway early in the morning of June 4. At 4:30 A.M., the carriers having turned into the wind, the first of the Japanese attack aircraft lifted off from the *Akagi*. Within minutes, the entire first-wave attack force of 108 aircraft was in the air. They quickly created a formation and headed toward their target.

Three Japanese reconnaissance planes were among the first planes aloft, and they fanned out to cover different sectors to the east. Four more scout planes were meant to be launched by the Japanese at 4:30 A.M., but for different reasons all of them were late. The last of these reconnaissance planes, having suffered a mechanical malfunction, didn't take off until 5:00. Because of this extremely unlikely coincidence, the scout plane scheduled to search the very sector where the U.S. fleet was hiding gave them an extra half hour to hide.

When it became clear that the reconnaissance aircraft from the *Tone* and *Chikuma* were going to launch significantly later than the Order of

Battle called for, Vice Admiral Nagumo could have ordered replacement aircraft to launch in their place. Inexplicably, he didn't, and to this day, no one knows why. Nagumo understood how critical it was to find the U.S. fleet if it was out there. He knew how important it was to claim the element of surprise. Knowing this, it was an astonishingly poor decision and completely inconsistent with everything the admiral had ever done before.

Indeed, this tardiness proved to be a critical factor in the day's battle. Had the Japanese planes from the *Chikuma* and *Tone* left when scheduled, they likely would have discovered all three of the American aircraft carriers early enough to have altered the fateful battle that lay ahead.

•   •   •

At 5:20 A.M., PBY 4V58, a Midway-based scout plane piloted by Lieutenant Howard P. Ady, sent a message to Midway indicating that he had sighted an unidentified aircraft. In all likelihood, he had spotted one of the late-leaving Japanese scout planes. Ten minutes later, Ady reported the sighting of a single Japanese carrier.

The island of Midway began to come to life. At 5:45, a PBY scouting in the sector next to Ady's messaged Midway that two groups of forty-five planes were headed in their direction.

Meanwhile, Ady, flying in and out of rain squalls, had just turned his plane around, when, through a break in the clouds, he saw a sight that would destine him for fame—the main Japanese carrier force, the target that, if it could be destroyed, could change the outcome of the war! At 5:52, he radioed Midway with the critical message.

Hearing of the sighting of the Japanese carrier fleet, Spruance didn't hesitate. "Launch everything you have at the earliest possible moment!" he cried.

The decision to launch was a critical and decisive one. But it was also a deadly and difficult decision, one that was filled with agony. The Japanese fleet was still 200 miles from the American carriers.

The range of the torpedo planes was only 175 miles. Sending the American aircraft to attack a target that was outside of their combat range condemned many of these pilots to their deaths.

Every commander has contemplated the possibility of sacrificing some fighters for the common good. Spruance understood he was sacrificing some of his best men—and there is no doubt from his words or writings that he loved them all—in order to advance the battle. But he confronted this decision without hesitation. He did what he had to do.

Strapping into their torpedo bombers, all of these pilots knew the deadly situation they were facing. Yet they didn't vacillate.

In anticipation of the coming battle, Lieutenant Commander John C. Waldron, commander of VT-8, one of the *Hornet's* torpedo squadrons, had distributed a message to his men: "My greatest hope is that we encounter a favorable tactical situation, but if we don't and worse comes to worst, I want each one of us to do his utmost to destroy our enemies. If there is only one plane left to make a final run-in, I want that man to go in and get a hit. May God be with us all. Good luck, happy landings, and give 'em hell."[11]

As Spruance watched his aircraft launch, he reviewed the timing in his mind. He knew about how long it would take his pilots to locate and attack the Japanese carriers. He knew that about the time his pilots found the Japanese carriers, the Japanese would be in the middle of landing, refueling, and rearming their own aircraft as they returned from their Midway attack. Almost all of the Japanese aircraft would be exposed on the carrier decks. Hundreds of bombs, thousands of pounds of fuel being pumped through high-pressure hoses, aircraft and ammunition and waiting pilots, all crammed atop less than 1.5 acres of open steel. If they could hit the Japanese carriers with all of it exposed, they would be nothing but floating death traps.

But first, his pilots would have to find the enemy in the vastness of the sea. And some of his bombers and torpedo planes would have to make it through the deadly lines of fighters and antiaircraft fire.

Midway Island

Midway knew the attack was coming—it was just a matter of when. Shortly after the first reports of incoming planes, radar on Sand Island, the smaller of the two islands on the atoll, picked up the images of "many planes" incoming.

When the air-raid sirens erupted, all of the aircraft on the island immediately headed for the sky, the Americans not wanting to get caught as easy targets on the ground the way it had happened at Pearl Harbor.

As the Japanese bombers approached the atoll, navy and marine fighter planes engaged in a valiant defensive stand. And though they were able to shoot some of the bombers down, they did so at a great loss. The American fighters were simply no match for the Japanese Zeros.

The bombers hit the islands first, inflicting massive damage to fuel depots, ammunition dumps, power house, water distillation plant, and antiaircraft emplacements, with minimal loss to their own forces. The dive bombers arrived shortly afterward and delivered their loads almost unscathed.

None of the bombers attacked the runway, however, intent on landing there as victors later in the day.

The Americans on Eastern Island—the larger of the islands as well as the location of the triangle-shaped airfield—were eyewitnesses to an amazing display of bravado. The lead Japanese dive bomber dove to within 100 feet of the ground, turned over on his back, and flew leisurely the length of the island, thumbing his nose at the amazed defenders. After a moment, the American defenders gathered their senses, shot the plane to pieces, and crashed it into the sea.

The Japanese bombers were followed by fighters, who worked to finish off any surviving American aircraft, strafing American defenders at will. In the midst of the battle, they found time to strafe a helpless American pilot who had parachuted from his damaged aircraft, firing at him until his dead body hit the ground.

The bombing attack lasted less than fifteen minutes.

The American fighter pilots had suffered greatly in their inferior planes. Fourteen of the twenty-six fighter pilots had been killed. Only two of the twenty-six planes were fit to fly again.

The Japanese suffered the loss of only nine aircraft: five level bombers, one dive bomber, and three Zeros.

Although the Japanese had inflicted substantial damage to the Midway defenders, the leader of the bombing raid believed the Japanese landing forces would still receive a very hot welcome. Fearing this, he signaled Nagumo that it would be necessary for a second bombing raid on Midway Island.

If any single piece of information was about to change the battle, this was it.[12]

Nagumo understood the implications of what his bombing leader had just told him. The air-raid commander had requested that the Japanese aircraft be loaded up with bombs and sent off to hit Midway again. Planes loaded with bombs were useful only against the land-based targets. In order to attack a carrier, he would need some of his fighters armed with torpedoes.

But Nagumo didn't know yet that the U.S. fleet was out there.

• • •

Just before the Japanese attacked the island, all of the U.S. bombers, scout planes, and torpedo planes at Midway scrambled into the skies. This odd mixture of airplanes, Midway's only offensive weapons against the main Japanese carrier fleet, included four army B-26 bombers equipped with torpedoes, a historic first in that army planes had never attacked with torpedoes before.

The first of this group to discover the Japanese carriers were six TBF torpedo planes and the four B-26s, all of which immediately attacked. The low, slow-flying torpedo planes were easy targets for the Zeros, and only one of the TBFs and two of the B-26s survived. And what did they accomplish? Literally nothing. No damage was done to the Japanese fleet.

However, this attack by land-based bombers from Midway factored into Nagumo's decision to accept his bombing commander's request for a second attack on the island. Still, it was not a decision that came easily. His carriers' second-wave attack planes, those that had been held back from the initial bombing run, had been armed with torpedoes in order to respond to the sighting of any American ships in the area. In order to have those aircraft undertake a second bombing run on Midway, the planes would have to be lowered into the hangars below deck and their torpedoes replaced with bombs. This would take an hour.

Nagumo made the difficult decision to rearm his second-wave airplanes with bombs for four primary reasons: First, he had been told by his mission commander that Midway still needed to be softened up; second, American land-based bombers were still operating out of Midway; third, he had been informed by Tokyo just the day before that there was "no sign" that the Americans perceived their intentions; and finally, his scout planes had not sent any messages indicating the existence of an American fleet in the area.

At 7:15 A.M., he commanded all the carriers to rearm their second-wave planes with bombs for a second attack against the island.

Along the carrier decks, the Japanese seamen went to work, likely wondering if their commanders knew what they were doing. Did the admirals understand how difficult it was to change the munitions loads underneath each aircraft? Did they have any idea how exhausting and dangerous this work could be?

Standing in the tower, Nagumo must have asked himself: Was he doing the right thing?

• • •

The Japanese pilot of the scout plane that launched late from the cruiser *Tone* had experienced an eventful flight, having already sent several messages regarding the sighting of enemy aircraft and submarines. At 7:28, he messaged the main fleet that he had observed ten enemy surface ships some 200 miles east of Nagumo's fleet. But the message did not give any details as to the makeup of the enemy fleet—specifically, it did not mention whether there were any carriers among the ten ships.

Receiving news of the U.S. fleet, Nagumo and his staff huddled. What did the fleet consist of? Were there carriers? They didn't know. The scout pilot didn't answer.

Fearing even the possibility of U.S. carriers being in the area, at 7:45 Nagumo ordered that no more planes be refitted with bombs. Those already fitted were to be sent to Midway. The planes with torpedoes were to be returned to deck and prepared to deal with the American fleet.

Two hundred miles to the east, Admiral Spruance listened to his own discouraging report. A Japanese reconnaissance plane had just been spotted north of the American fleet. The enemy aircraft had ducked and hidden among the cloud banks, but surely the pilot had spotted them and reported their position to his Japanese commanders.

Their secret had been revealed.

After all the deception, planning, and gut-wrenching decisions, it had all come down to this. And there was nothing the American commander could do but wait and hope for the best result.

In the midst of this frantic activity, sixteen Dauntless dive bombers from Midway delivered another attack against the Japanese fleet. These sluggish planes, piloted by green pilots who had no experience in this type of aircraft, made easy targets for the Zeros, and half of the bombers were shot down. The remaining planes managed to drop their bombs, but none of them hit a target. The result? Another brave but futile effort by the Midway defenders against the enemy fleet.

The confusion caused by these seemingly ineffectual efforts, however, caused Nagumo and his staff to miss the importance of a message sent by the *Tone* scout plane just minutes before: The American fleet had changed course and turned into the wind.

Because of their extremely short runways, it is necessary for aircraft carriers to be headed into the wind to give their airplanes the needed relative speed for takeoff. When landing, the airplanes have to be moving into the wind as well. The Japanese scout plane had not yet identified whether there were any carriers among the ten ships he was scouting—but this change in direction should have signaled that planes were being launched.

Back at the command center aboard the Japanese carrier, the scream of the Midway-based dive bombers coming at them, the exploding bombs, the roar of fighters and their machine guns, and the constant blasting of their own antiaircraft fire combined to make it impossible for Nagumo and his staff to communicate. Critical minutes passed. Critical decisions were not made.

At 8:09, the *Tone* scout plane sent a message that the American fleet consisted of five cruisers and five destroyers. No carriers had been sighted. The Japanese commander breathed a sigh of relief. At that exact moment, U.S. bombers from Midway attacked the Japanese fleet once again. B-17s, carrying loads of eight bombs each, dropped their weapons and escaped with little damage from either antiaircraft fire or the Zeros.

At about the same time, the U.S. submarine *Nautilus* began stalking the Japanese fleet, surfacing several times before firing off a torpedo at a Japanese destroyer, the *Arashi*. Detecting the American submarine, the destroyer broke position in order to depth-charge it, a move that caused it to fall behind the fleet. This would prove to be another of those singular events that would be pivotal to the outcome of the Battle of Midway.

At 8:20, the last of the Midway airplanes attacked the Japanese fleet. Facing exhausted Zero pilots who had been combat flying for four hours, they had an advantage that resulted in minimal losses. However, once again, they failed to inflict any damage on the Japanese ships.

At this point, it appeared that Midway was doomed. All of the aircraft that were truly capable of withstanding the approaching invasion force—the fighters, torpedo planes, and dive bombers—were gone. The marines and navy personnel on Midway were exposed to a second air raid and ship bombardment. The 5,000 Japanese ground troops would have made easy work of the remaining defenders.

Unable to make contact with the American fleet, the Midway soldiers hunkered down and awaited their impending doom.

American Carriers Sighted!

At 8:20, the *Tone* scout plane sent a message that shocked Nagumo and his staff. "The enemy is accompanied by what appears to be a carrier in a position to the rear of the others."

This message was received at the same time that the Japanese bombers returning from their attack against Midway started appearing on the horizon. Nagumo had to make a critical decision: Should he use his precious carriers to launch those forces that were then available to attack the American carrier? Or should he allow the returning bombers to land, refuel, and rearm, and then launch a massive strike against the fleet?

At that moment, Nagumo had only thirty-six dive bombers available for an attack. He had no fighters to accompany these attack craft, for they were all in the air responding to the repeated attacks from the Midway-based bombers. Many were damaged and low on fuel. Further, he now had a hundred returning bombers, all of them also low on fuel. The waiting fighters started circling overhead. If they were not allowed to land because the carriers were launching the attack planes, the returning bombers would have to ditch into the sea. And he had to make a decision now!

Nagumo ordered the flight decks cleared so his returning bombers could land. Further, he ordered that all of the attackers have their bombs taken off and be rearmed with torpedoes. For the third time that morning, weapon crews had to arm their aircraft with another type of weapon, replacing the large bombs they had just attached to the Japanese fighters with smaller torpedoes once again.

The last of the Japanese bombers and fighters touched down at 9:18. It was estimated that *Akagi* and *Kaga* would be ready to launch their attack aircraft on the American fleet by 10:30, and the *Soryu* and *Hiryu* a half hour later.

The *Tone* scout plane was ordered to remain in visual contact with the American fleet until he was relieved by scout planes being sent in his direction.

At 8:54, the *Tone* scout sent a message to his admiral acknowledging receipt of the order. He also added, "Ten enemy torpedo planes heading toward you . . ."

Torpedo Squadron Eight, East of the Japanese Fleet

THE AMERICAN PILOT expected it might turn into a gaggle, but he hadn't thought it would get so bad, so quick.

It had taken an hour for the various fighter, torpedo, and dive bombers to take off from the carriers and form up. An hour wasted. An hour of circling the carriers, bobbing through the skies, burning fuel and getting agitated, the pilots growing tired. By the time everyone was airborne and the aircraft had turned toward the last known position of the Japanese fleet, the tropical heat had formed an overcast that covered the sky with a carpet of gray, making it impossible for the pilots to keep each other in sight. Though they struggled to stay in some type of combat formation, it proved impossible. There were too many of them, and visibility was too low. Under strict orders to maintain radio silence, it wasn't long before each of the squadrons was on its own, the various aircraft scattered for a hundred miles across the sky.

The pilot flew the Devastator. Slow. Maneuverable as a soggy piece of bread in a bowl of soup. Lightly armored. There was no love lost between the Devastators and their aircrews. The pilot glanced behind him at the long greenhouse of a cockpit stretching almost half the length of the fuselage, where his gunner/radio operator manned the .30-caliber machine gun that faced the rear. Until he had something he could shoot at, the gunner was an intensely interested passenger and occasional navigator, but not much more.

As they flew west, the pilot's stomach climbed. He glanced around, looking at other aircraft in his formation, fifteen torpedo bombers in all. The Devastators from the USS *Hornet*'s VT-8 were tucked together, the pilots trying desperately to keep each other in sight. A few seconds later, they dropped below the layer of clouds and spread out, the silver-and-black aircraft dotting the sky on both his left and right. His commander, John C. Waldron, was a couple of miles ahead of him, leading the formation of torpedo bombers. Watching his commander, the pilot pulled a deep breath and forced himself to relax. With the heavy torpedo hanging from its belly, the Devastator felt even more sluggish than it usually did, and he moved the control stick gently, feeling the aircraft wallow. This was the first time he'd ever flown with a torpedo, and it amazed him how much slower the aircraft was. He thought back on the takeoff from the carrier—another first—and the sickening feeling he'd experienced as the aircraft had momentarily dipped below the flight deck before finally lumbering into the air.

He checked his heading and position with the formation, then shouted to his gunner, "They should be here, right?"

The man behind him had been checking their heading, speed, wind correction, and altitude, but the open ocean made it pretty much impossible to navigate. He knew within twenty or thirty miles where they were, but that was about all. "Yeah, boss, this should be it," was all he could say.

The pilot looked around and swore. The Japanese fleet should have been here! He checked the open ocean four thousand feet below. There was simply nothing there. He scanned the skies around him. Nothing but fellow Devastators in the air. None of the F4F-4s to escort them. None of the dive bombers. So much for their coordinated attack!

Looking at his squadron mates, he shook his head. If they went in alone, without their fighter escorts or the dive bombers, it would be suicide. Turning in his seat, he looked behind him, then glanced up at the sun where it had broken through the clouds. As they flew west, the clouds got thinner, but though he could see above him now, there were no friendly fighters there.

"Where are our fighter escorts?" he demanded of no one in particular.

The gunner grunted. "We're going to link up with them before we start an attack, right, sir?" His voice was high with fear. He understood what it would mean if they had to attack the Japanese fleet without their fighter escorts and dive bombers to take off at least a little of the heat.

The pilot looked down at the ocean. "If we can't find the carriers, it isn't going to matter."

"This is their last reported position," the gunner answered. "They should be here or somewhere south and west of here."

"If that was the case, we would have passed them already."

"Think we might have missed them?"

"Four carriers. Dozens of support ships. Kinda doubt it."

The pilot looked forward to his leader's aircraft once again. The boss had trained and taught them, beating their combat tactics and procedures into them like an obsessed father trying to protect a child. And that was the only thing they had now: the training and coaching of the boss, Lieutenant Commander John C. Waldron, who, with the exception of his father, was the best man the pilot had ever known.

He looked around him once again, praying he would see some of his own fighters, praying harder he'd see some of the Japanese ships, then instructed his radioman, "Check the emergency channel."

The radioman grunted and looked down. There was static for a few seconds as he changed the channel on their only radio. Two or three minutes of silence, then the radioman came back. "You're not going to believe this, boss."

"What you got?"

"All of the fighters in the first wave have either turned back or landed at Midway because they were running out of gas. None of them found any of the Jap ships. Can you believe that, sir!"

The pilot shook his head, then looked at the open ocean down below. Yeah, he believed it. The plan was always perfect until it encountered the actual war.

The radioman hesitated as he listened. "Get this, boss. VF-8—the whole fighter squadron—had to ditch it in the ocean. Every one of them ran out of gas. Not a bomb or bullet fired between them. All of them are in the drink!"

The pilot frowned in disgust, thinking about his buddies in the water. When they had taken off from the carrier, they had known it might come to this, but still, it was hard to hear about.

The formation continued flying, moving farther and farther from their ships.

He continued searching.

Where were the Japs!

Minutes later, without explanation or warning, Commander Waldron started a gentle turn to the north.

None of the pilots broke radio silence to ask him where he was going. All fourteen of them followed him.

"Where's he going?" the radioman demanded.

"Don't know," the pilot said.

"He's taking us away from the ship!"

The pilot kept his eyes on Waldron's aircraft, knowing if there was anyone in the world he trusted, it was this man.

The two crew members were silent for a few moments. "Do you think he's got any idea where he's going?" the gunner finally asked.

"He's following his instincts," the pilot answered. "It's the only thing we got right now."

"But the Japs must have changed course. They could be anywhere!"

"The boss is going to find them."

"How? He isn't magic!"

"He's not magic, but he's good. And more than that, he's a fighter pilot who's itching for a fight. We're going to trust him. He's going to do it. Now, keep your eyes out. I'll bet my horse and wife that Waldron leads us to the fleet. And it's going to be a bugger when we get there without any of our fighters or dive bombers by our side. So keep a tight one and keep on looking . . ."

Seven minutes later, they saw the Japanese carriers directly off their nose: four huge, beautiful floating tinderboxes, all of them having broken combat formation from the Midway attacks.

"Like he was following a string toward the carriers," the gunner mumbled to himself.

His watch read 9:18. The last of the Japanese fighters involved in the bombing of Midway Island had barely landed to rearm and refuel. The enemy was sitting on enormous flattops of improperly stored ammunition, loaded aircraft, and exposed fuel.

Without waiting either for instructions or for their fighters to escort them, the group of torpedo bombers split up. Enemy Zeros started swarming from the carriers to meet them.

"Going to get hairy!" the gunner cried.

"Roger that!" the pilot shot back.

The pilot rolled the aircraft and dipped toward the sea. A line of smoke screens started spewing from the carriers, filling the sky with trails of white and gray. It seemed there were a thousand Zero fighters coming at them, most of them screaming down from a higher altitude. Antiaircraft fire erupted from the escort ships, carriers, and destroyers, spewing black smoke and razor-sharp shrapnel. Waldron went after the first carrier. The other torpedo bombers scattered behind him. All of them went after the carriers, ignoring the other ships. Unimaginable chaos followed. Aircraft crashing into the sea. Huge towers of spouting water blowing into the sky from the impact of the Devastators. The whistle of passing Zeros as they swooped down from twenty thousand feet. Bursting, smoke-filled rounds of antiaircraft fire seemed to fill every foot of sky.

The pilot leveled off just above the water, then lined up on the second carrier. He thought it was the *Soryu,* but he wasn't sure. Slowing to a painful airspeed, and barely a few feet above the water, he flew straight and level toward his target, nervous sweat dripping in his eyes. A Japanese destroyer, smoke and antiaircraft fire spitting from its bow and stern, suddenly turned to port, moving between the Devastator and the carrier, and the pilot had to jerk back on his stick to keep from crashing into it. Clearing the destroyer's tower by only a couple of feet, he was low enough that he could see the Japanese commander dive onto the deck. Ahead of him, he saw his squadron mates pressing the attack against the carriers. Zeros all around them. Bursts of black smoke and red fire. One Devastator down. Then two, then three, then four. Too many now to count them. His buddies were dying all around him. He felt a sudden burst of rage and fear. He wanted to kill a carrier! He wanted some revenge! Flying over the destroyer's bridge, he dropped back toward the water, adjusted his aim, and flew toward the carrier once again. His gunner was screaming something at him that he couldn't understand. Another Devastator went flying by him, its cockpit on fire. He saw the pilot—it looked like Commander Waldron!—push his canopy back and start to pull himself out of the cockpit, but his aircraft crashed into the sea before he could escape.

The pilot cried with rage and started jinking left and right. There were more Zeros behind him than he could count. With no American fighters to keep them off him, the torpedo bomber was a sitting duck. So many had been killed already! He wondered if he was alone. His heart slammed against his chest. The gunner kept up a constant line of fire, the .30-caliber gun jarring the aircraft and filling the cockpit with acidic smoke.

The target lay before them, less than four thousand feet away. A rip of bullets passed through his left wing and the fuel tank burst into flames. The aircraft shuddered underneath him. He thought it was going to blow apart. The gunner let loose another burst of machine gun fire. Another round of bullets shattered through his plane.

"SLOW DOWN!" the gunner screamed in panic. "YOU'VE GOT TO GET BELOW A HUNDRED KNOTS TO DROP THE TORPEDO!"

The pilot struggled to keep the wounded aircraft in the air. It wobbled and fell toward the ocean. It took everything he had to hold it back.

"SLOW DOWN OR THE TORPEDO WILL MALFUNCTION!"

The pilot jerked the throttle back, and the engine sputtered and backfired as the aircraft slowed.

A hundred knots! A hundred knots! It was worse than suicide! Less than half a mile from the target now.

"BOMB AWAY!" the pilot cried.

Nothing happened. No jolt or lifting of the aircraft as the weapon separated from its belly. No whoosh of air. No splash in the water from the torpedo dropping into the sea. Nothing! It had malfunctioned.

All of this for nothing.

The pilot screamed again.

Hunkering in his seat, he aimed his broken aircraft at the carrier directly off his nose. The torpedo still strapped to the Devastator's belly, he aimed directly at the bridge. If the torpedo wouldn't drop, he'd hit the carrier himself. He jammed the throttle forward, and the Devastator seemed to lurch. The fire on his left wing billowed smoke. The flight controls were heavy. It took every ounce of strength that he could muster to keep the fighter from rolling on its back and dropping into the sea. To his right, another Zero screamed toward him. He saw the burst of white smoke from the fighter's cannon. He saw the tracers move toward him. He turned back toward the target. Less than seven hundred feet to go. He needed five seconds. Just five seconds! He held the aircraft steady. The gunner started crying. He was crying too.

The aircraft shuddered from another round of exploding bullets passing through his cockpit and wings. He couldn't control it any longer. His flight controls were gone. Blood seemed to splatter everywhere, blown forward by the wind that was howling through the shattered cockpit. The rear gun had fallen silent. The pilot didn't turn around. He knew his friend was dead.

The carrier's enormous bridge passed underneath him as the aircraft rolled and crashed into the sea.

• • •

Fifteen Devastators from VT-8 had taken off from the USS *Hornet* two hours before. Every one of them was gone now. Thirty Americans inside the Devastators, twenty-nine of them dead. Beyond VT-8, twenty-six Devastators from two other squadrons had attacked the carriers. Only four of them had survived.

Not a single Devastator hit a target.

But their sacrifice was not in vain.

Bomb Squadron Six, South-Southeast of the Japanese Carrier Fleet

A FEW MINUTES BEHIND the flight of Devastator torpedo bombers, and in a different piece of the sky, Lieutenant Commander Wade McCluskey, air-group commander from the USS *Enterprise,* led thirty-two Dauntless dive bombers toward the last reported location of the Japanese fleet. Getting there, he too found nothing but open ocean and empty skies. No carriers. No wakes. No escort ships or Japanese defenders. Like every one of the pilots who'd gone before him, he swore in bitter disappointment.

He knew he had to find them.

But unlike the commander of the torpedo planes, he didn't use his gut to find the Japanese fleet. Providence was going to provide another way.

"Look at that!" he almost shouted to his gunner.

Twenty thousand feet below him, and at the very edge of the distance he could have seen it in the haze, he saw a single wake.

The Japanese destroyer *Arashi,* having abandoned its efforts to find and kill the U.S. submarine that had been hassling the Japanese fleet, had reversed course and was steaming at top speed back toward the Japanese task force. Heading northwest, the *Arashi* was acting like a homing beacon, leading the American attackers toward their targets as if it were a guide.

The dive bombers followed it and, after anxious miles, the Japanese carrier fleet came into view.

From their perch at 20,000 feet, the Dauntless pilots witnessed the devastating torpedo bomber attacks. One by one, McCluskey watched his navy brothers get shot down and crash into the sea. It was a horrible thing to witness and it made his blood grow hot.

Thinking quickly, he split up his formation, commanding Lieutenant Best of VB-6 to attack the right-hand carrier while he led his men toward the target on the left.

As they approached the aircraft carriers, the commander almost cried out in surprise. *All* of the Zero fighters had been ordered to descend from altitude to stop the American Devastator attacks. Between his dive bombers and the carriers, there was nothing but clear sky. He couldn't believe the Japanese commander could make such a horrible mistake, but it was right before him: All of the Zeros had descended and taken after the Devastators, leaving the carriers exposed to an attack from altitude.

He shook his head in disbelief. "Do you see that?" he demanded of his gunner.

His gunner turned in his seat, studied the clear skies, and swore.

The commander rolled the aircraft and set up the formation for a coordinated attack. As they descended, the chaos aboard the carrier became clear: dozens of aircraft crammed on the deck, multiple fuel lines stretched between them, hundreds of exposed bombs thrown around the deck.

It was a tinderbox! A death trap!

He couldn't believe his eyes.

The commander rolled level, flew another half a mile toward the target, rolled his aircraft over again, laying it on its back, then pulled the nose down and started screaming vertically toward the carrier in a Helldiver maneuver.

It was a nearly perfect attack.

The first bomb hit among the refueling fighters, exploding in a fury of black smoke and red flame. Another bomb penetrated the forward elevator and exploded among more refueling aircraft, torpedoes, and bombs. A third bomb hit a fuel truck sitting directly underneath the captain's bridge, instantly incinerating the captain and his senior officers in a yellow fireball. The elevator collapsed, sending fire into the waiting aircraft below the deck, all of them fueled and loaded with torpedoes and bombs. By themselves, the three bombs wouldn't have been enough to sink the carrier, but they set off a conflagration of fuel tanks and aircraft and torpedoes and bullets and fragmentation bombs.

In minutes, the fires on the *Kaga* were completely out of control.

A thousand meters to the south, the Japanese carrier *Akagi* was experiencing almost exactly the same thing. The first bomb hit the midship elevator, detonating improperly stored ammunition, fuel, and bombs. The second bomb hit among the waiting aircraft. Two bombs were all it took to take her down. Farther east, the *Soryu* had also been hit by three bombs neatly placed from fore to aft. Five minutes after the attack, the *Soryu* captain gave the devastating order to abandon ship, then committed suicide by rushing into the towering fires that had spread across his deck.

Three minutes after starting their attack, the dive bombers left most of the Japanese carrier fleet in flames.

Within hours, three carriers slipped into their watery graves.

The Battle Not Yet Complete

The dive bombers had destroyed the *Akagi,* the *Kaga,* and the *Soryu.* But they had left the *Hiryu* untouched. The Battle of Midway was not quite over yet.

The Japanese launched all of the planes they had available from the *Hiryu:* eighteen dive bombers and six fighters, their pilots driven by revenge. Despite being detected in time for American fighters to intercept them, not to mention the deadly antiaircraft fire, the *Yorktown* took three hits. Although the Japanese pilots returning to the *Hiryu* believed that they had sunk the American carrier, the damage was quickly repaired, and within two hours the *Yorktown* was back in operation.

That afternoon, ten torpedo bombers and six fighters from the *Hiryu* made a second assault on the American fleet. Taking two more torpedo hits, the *Yorktown* was doomed. An orderly evacuation of the 3,000 crew members ensued, including all those wounded from the earlier assault. The *Yorktown's* commander, Captain Elliott Buckmaster, was the last to leave his dying ship.

Because the repairs to the *Yorktown* had been made so quickly (again!), the Japanese pilots thought that they had attacked and destroyed a second carrier. An earlier decision by Fletcher to keep the two task forces separated instead of bunched, as the Japanese carriers had been, misled the Japanese into attacking the *Yorktown* a second time instead of looking for either the *Hornet* or the *Enterprise.*

Shortly before the "Abandoning Ship" signal was given by the *Yorktown,* a scout plane from one of the other American carriers located the *Hiryu.* At 4:45, the aircraft from the *Enterprise* and *Yorktown* attacked the last of the Japanese carriers, hitting it with four bombs in rapid succession. Within minutes, fire spread over the entire ship. As with the Japanese carriers destroyed earlier in the day, the *Hiryu* was doomed because its planes were sitting with full fuel while bombs were being loaded.

When the reality of what had occurred that day hit Admiral Yamamoto, he tried to lure the American fleet into a night battle against his seven massive battleships, a force that had not yet become known to the Americans. But Spruance, now in command of both task forces, refused to take the bait. Retreating to the east, he moved out of range of the Japanese fleet.

The Battle of Midway had finally come to an end.

Despite the fact that the Japanese outnumbered and outgunned the U.S. fleet, they suffered a devastating defeat. The total casualties suffered by the Japanese included 2,500 men, four aircraft carriers, and 332 airplanes. The United States, in turn, lost 307 men, one carrier, and 147 airplanes.

The Japanese military would never quite recover. Their finest and most experienced pilots were gone. From this point forward, the United States would be on the offense throughout the Pacific campaign.[13]

A Miraculous Event?

By every estimation, the U.S. should have lost the Battle of Midway. Consider the list of seemingly impossible occurrences that led to U.S. victory:

- There was one chance in a million the U.S. could have broken the Japanese code that revealed the time and place of their next attack.

- Workers at the Honolulu shipyards were able to complete three months' worth of repairs on the damaged *Yorktown* in just two days.

- Against all odds, and while running out of fuel, Ensign Jack Reid was able to locate the Japanese fleet, removing any doubt that they were headed for Midway.

- Scout aircraft from the *Tone* launched half an hour late, allowing U.S. reconnaissance aircraft to discover the Japanese fleet first.

- In the midst of the battle, Vice Admiral Nagumo ordered his fighters to change their ordnance from torpedoes to bombs then back to torpedoes, allowing the U.S. to catch the Japanese aircraft on the carrier decks before they could be launched.

- Nagumo got word from his scout plane that the U.S. fleet was turning into the wind in the middle of an attack from Midway aircraft, wasting precious minutes before he realized the U.S. fleet included aircraft carriers.

- Lieutenant Commander Waldron somehow, instinctively, selected the right course to fly.

- The Japanese destroyer *Arashi* chased after the U.S. submarine *Nautilus,* then turned back, leading U.S. dive bombers directly to the Japanese carrier fleet.

- Despite the fact that the U.S. attacking squadrons got separated while searching for the Japanese fleet, all of them arrived at the exact location and at the exact time they needed to in order to mount a devastating attack.

- Nagumo made the mistake of ordering all of his Zero fighters to descend from high altitude and attack the low-flying torpedo planes, leaving the American dive bombers able to press their attack without interference from the Japanese fighters.

- The dive bombers were able to hit the enemy carriers at the exact moment when they had their aircraft, ammunition, bombs, fuel, and aircrews exposed atop the carrier decks.

The attack against the Japanese carriers took place in a manner exactly opposite to how the Americans had planned, trained, and expected it to happen. There weren't any U.S. fighters available to draw off the Zeros. The torpedo pilots, with their slow aircraft and extraordinarily dangerous mission, were the first to attack, taking withering losses. None of them were able to hit the targets. The dive bombers, intended primarily as decoys, were the last to go in and the only aircraft to score a hit. Yet the outcome was devastating for the Japanese fleet.

What If?

If the United States had lost the Battle of Midway, the history of the Second World War would have been different—and it might have been very different.

It appears that Yamamoto's next target would have been Australia. With no naval force to oppose it, Australia would have been lost. Japan would have then controlled the South Pacific and Indian Oceans. It would have had control of Southeast Asia and access to all of its natural resources. The Pacific would have become a Japanese sea.

Midway would have served as a launching point for Japanese bombers to attack Hawaii. Once the fuel and docks of Pearl Harbor had been destroyed, the remaining naval forces would have had to retreat to the west coast, leaving Hawaii open to invasion.

Hawaii would then have been a base for further attacks on the west coast. Roosevelt would have been forced to abandon his "Germany First" doctrine. Prior to the victory at Midway, the United States was already moving troops to the west coast, reinforcements that had been intended for the planned invasion of Europe. When Midway turned out as it did, Roosevelt was able to divert those troops back to operation "Bolero," which ultimately became known as operation "Overlord," the invasion of France. Had the United States fleet been destroyed at Midway, these troops, and many more, would have been needed to defend the west coast.

If "Plan D" had been abandoned, how would the war in Europe have evolved?

Might Russia have been lost to the Germans if there had been no western front to divert a major portion of the German army? If Russia had been lost, Britain would have fallen. Next would have been the Middle East, and then India.

If Germany had been given time to perfect its weapons of mass destruction and the capability of delivering them, might even the United States have been forced to capitulate?

How might the United States have lost the Battle of Midway? The battle might have turned out very badly if any one of many critical decisions had been made differently. What if Nimitz had failed to accept the intelligence provided by Rochefort's Combat Intelligence Office? What if he had succumbed to the pressure from Washington and failed to focus his attention on Midway, when the brass in D.C. were telling him to focus on Hawaii or the west coast? What if he had fallen for the Japanese feint at the Aleutian Islands and spread his forces too thin by sending one of his three carriers to the north? What if Spruance had failed to send his planes immediately upon the Japanese force once they were sighted? What if the Japanese scout planes had left on time? What if either Reid or Ady had turned back minutes earlier? What if Waldron had not been led to the carrier fleet as he was?

Most important, what if the men of the three torpedo squadrons, upon finding the Japanese fleet, had circled and waited for fighter support or dive bomber distraction, or had simply turned around? What if they had not been led by men of courage and self-sacrifice?

Any of these decisions made differently might have changed the outcome of the war.

Many books have been written about the Battle of Midway. Indeed, the fact that the U.S. won, under a set of circumstances and after a chain of events so unlikely, has been called a miracle by those who have studied the battle more than anyone.[14] On the other side of the Pacific, some of the more spiritually oriented of the Japanese commanders expressed their opinion that Midway was God's punishment for their sins of pride.

However it might be explained, this much is true: Despite overwhelming odds, three minutes of combat led to a miraculous U.S. victory that changed the outcome of the war.

Notes

1. An account of this episode can be found at the California State Military Museum, online at July 10, 2009, www.militarymuseum.org/Ellwood.html. See also Schweikart and Allen, *Patriot's History*, 608.
2. *New York World-Telegram,* March 5, 1942, as quoted by William F. Warde in *Fourth International,* Vol. 3, No. 3 (March 1942), 73–76.
3. Information on the success of the Axis Powers comes from Dear, *Oxford Companion to World War II;* Morison, *Growth of the American Republic,* 2:564–66; Prange, *Miracle at Midway,* 2–9, 40–48, 95; Schweikart and Allen, *Patriot's History,* 589, 607–12.
4. For information about the "Germany First" strategy, see Dear, *Oxford Companion to World War II,* 493–500, 928; Prange, *Miracle at Midway,* 365, 396; Schweikart and Allen, *Patriot's History,* 605; Ward and Burns, *The War,* 24. For details of the German advances in weaponry and weapons of mass destruction, see Schweikart and Allen, *Patriot's History,* 605.
5. Background on Japan's "second-term strategy" can be found in Prange, *Miracle at Midway,* 13–39; Department of the Navy, *Battle of Midway: 4–7 June 1942.*
6. Information on aircraft carriers, carrier tactics, and the various aircraft involved in the Battle of Midway comes from Dear, *Oxford Companion to World War II;* Prange, *Miracle at Midway;* Schweikart and Allen, *Patriot's History,* 576; July 11, 2009, http://www.chinfo.navy.mil/navpalib/ships/carriers/histories/cv01-langley/cv01-langley.html; http://www.history.navy.mil; http://www.aviastar.org; http://www.militaryfactory.com/aircraft/detail.asp?aircraft_id=297. (It should be noted that different models of the same aircraft, follow-on modifications, upgrades, etc., may lead to variations in reported performance data.)
7. See Dear, *Oxford Companion to World War II,* 802–3; Prange, *Miracle at Midway,* 385.
8. Information on Commander Rochefort and his code-breaking team can be found in Prange, *Miracle at Midway,* 16–20, 45–46, 72–73, 104, 126; Department of the Navy, *Battle of Midway: 4–7 June 1942.*
9. See Prange, *Miracle at Midway,* 95–96.
10. Background for the story of Ensign Jack Reid's discovery of the Japanese fleet comes from Prange, *Miracle at Midway,* 160–74.

11. Prange, *Miracle at Midway*, 240.
12. For an account of the Japanese strike on Midway and the Japanese commander's request for a second air attack on Midway, see Prange, *Miracle at Midway*, 187–206.
13. Detailed information about the Battle of Midway comes from Dear, *Oxford Companion to World War II*, 748–49; Morison, *Growth of the American Republic*, 2:569–70; Prange, *Miracle at Midway;* Schweikart and Allen, *Patriot's History*, 610–11; Ward and Burns, *The War*, 46–47.
14. Prange, *Miracle at Midway*. This carefully researched and written book is considered by many to be the "bible" on the Battle of Midway.

Chapter 7

The Miracle of a Fraction of an Inch

East Berlin, German Democratic Republic
December 21, 1980

THE RULES WERE VERY SIMPLE.

Everyone knew something. Everyone had some kind of secret they could tell. A whisper heard about a neighbor. An old man walking in the evening without his spouse. A child talking too much about her parents and what they had said to each other over dinner. Rumor and innuendo hung like the coal smoke in the air.

Remaining silent wasn't an option. In fact, it was a crime.

The prisoner knew the rules—every citizen of the republic understood them, even the youngest child—and now that he was taken, he knew that the best he could hope for was a painless way to die.

But he wasn't feeling lucky.

There were many things he was: a young father, a high-school teacher, a husband, a former sergeant in the army, a diabetic, sometimes an atheist, sometimes a man of faith, but he was not a spy or traitor. He was not an enemy of the State. There was no reason for his arrest.

He replayed the scene again and again in his mind: the early morning knock, the apartment door blowing off its hinges, shouting and calling from the suited men, so many guns it looked like war, the cries of his wife and children, the cold steel of the handcuffs, the first blow about the head. Less than sixty seconds after his front door had been shattered from its hinges, he was shoved into the backseat of the German Trabant, a cheap, smoking, rusted automobile that blended perfectly with the traffic. As the Trabant pulled away, he glanced through the back window at his apartment building, then lowered his eyes and hoped he would not cry.

Why are you doing this? he wanted to scream. *What has someone told you? I haven't done anything!*

His mind shot back to what his kindergarten teacher used to tell them: "Better a hundred innocent men are punished than a single traitor against the State go free."

His mind racing, Dierk Schmidt reviewed every conversation, every look, every person he had talked to. Anything could be used against him—a simple joke, a sarcastic remark about his labor leader, a single reference to the news that was coming out of Poland.

Fifteen minutes later, the headquarters of the *Ministerium für Staatssicherheit,* or Ministry for State Security, as the Stasi was formerly called, came into view. Approaching one of the many guarded gates, the driver flashed his card and was waved through. As the metal rail that blocked the entry lifted, Dierk caught the logo imprinted across the gate: *Schild und Schwert der Partei*—Shield and Sword of the Party.

The Party. The State. One was both and both were one and both were everywhere.

He looked up at the menacing buildings that lay before him and swallowed against a throat so dry he could hardly get down spit.

The Stasi headquarters was a huge labyrinth of seemingly separate but interconnected buildings, some dark gray, some smoky white, all of them stark and ugly, concrete, rough brick, dark glass windows, the architecture dull and menacing. Some of the buildings were only five floors; some towered much higher over the lifeless city. Tinted windows looked down like dark and lifeless eyes, every floor reeking of intimidation and humiliation. And, like the agency itself, the web of interconnecting walkways and corridors between the buildings was impossible to trace.

Dierk knew what took place inside Stasi headquarters. The interrogations. The accusations. The chambers. Torture rooms in the basements. The reeducation camps and executions. Everyone knew someone who'd been arrested by the Stasi and never seen again. The *Ministerium für Staatssicherheit* employed almost a hundred thousand agents, with another three hundred thousand of his fellow East Germans acting as unpaid informers, a few out of a sense of duty, a few for favors, a few for fun. One in seven of his fellow East Germans had shared information with the Stasi at one time or another, leaving no one safe.

As the automobile headed down the sloping driveway to the underground parking lot, the prisoner wondered if he'd ever see the sun again.

• • •

Deep in the bowels of the Stasi headquarters, the prisoner stood in a cement vat built into the brick floor. Ice water to his knees circulated through the vat, and he shivered uncontrollably. The pain was dull and constant—up his legs, down his back, across his chest. Sharp stones lined the vat, and the bottoms of his feet had sloughed off, coloring the water a rusty red with blood. For two days, he'd been forced to stand there. No sleep. No food. No rest. He couldn't count the number of times he'd vomited from cold and pain. He was dangerously dehydrated and hypothermic nearly to the point of losing consciousness. His left ear had been split open and his eyes were swollen, leaving his world spinning and unfocused. And the interrogation hadn't even started. It would only get worse from here.

Hearing a sudden clang of metal, Dierk slowly looked up.

The Stasi officer walked into the room, his face hidden beneath the brim of his hat. He nodded to the guard, who lowered a chain, hooked it around the leather straps that held Dierk's hands behind his back, lifted him with the help of a powered pulley, and dropped him on the cold cement floor.

"Get him ready!" the officer commanded.

The leather handcuffs were removed, a dark hospital gown thrown over his head. Dragged into the interrogation room, Dierk barely had the strength to curl into a ball upon the floor.

The Stasi officer glared at him. "Is it your custom to show such disrespect to a government officer?" he sneered.

Dierk struggled, pulling himself first into a sitting position, then to his knees. It took ten minutes before he was able to actually force himself to stand. The Stasi agent waited patiently, smoking a cigarette. Two guards stood behind the prisoner. Half a dozen high-watt light bulbs hung from the ceiling, making the room painfully bright. A hole was cut into the ceiling, a meat hook connected to a rusted chain suspended through the hole. The walls were white and sterile. The floor was bare concrete. Multiple drains were built into the floor, a garden hose to clean up the messes that took place here rolled up against the wall.

The prisoner's eyes darted about. No desk. No chairs. A chrome table against the corner, a white cloth concealing the tools that lay underneath.

The interrogator looked at his fellow German with contempt, then opened a leather binder and started writing. "Tell me about the incident on the subway," he said.

Dierk wobbled, his mind tumbling with fear and pain and exhaustion. "Sir, I don't know what you mean."

"The subway," the interrogator demanded.

Dierk slowly shook his head.

The Stasi officer was young and cool, with short hair and yellow teeth. The tips of his fingertips were stained with nicotine; his arms were long and lanky and his shoulders weak and thin. But there was something about him that was powerful. He had ambitions. He had a goal. And in a society where every man was willing to knife his neighbor, he'd shown an even greater commitment to the Party than most. Already, he'd been rewarded—he had an apartment, privileges at the State store, coupons for Soviet vodka, women who recognized his stature and were impressed. But he was married only to his job. It was all he had ever wanted and all he ever thought about. He hadn't taken a sick day in almost five years, regularly working more than sixty hours a week. His tiny cubicle was plastered with the latest propaganda from the State; he studied the words of Lenin every morning, the words of Stalin every night. But that didn't mean he was above suspicion. Quite the contrary: His own file inside the ministry was adequately thick, with enough evidence to convict him of many crimes against the State. But that was true of virtually everyone, and so far his hard work had kept him safe.

"Tell me about the woman on the subway, Herr Schmidt?" he said again.

"A woman? On the subway? I don't know what you mean," the prisoner pleaded.

"Are you suggesting you've never been on the subway with a woman?" the officer sneered in an accusing tone. As he spoke, he wrote on his pad: PRISONER EVASIVE. UNWILLING TO ANSWER SIMPLE QUESTIONS.

Dierk watched him write and shuddered. He'd seen black investigation binders like this before. Looking down, he saw that his feet were still bleeding, small pools of dark blood forming underneath the soles. The circulation was beginning to return to his dead legs and feet, and the pain was becoming unbearable. "Please, sir," he begged, "you must have mistaken me for someone else."

The officer wrote again: PRISONER ACCUSATORY TO INTER-ROGATING OFFICER. DISPLAYS DEFENSIVE PATTERNS.

Watching him write, Dierk thought desperately through the pain and then remembered. "There was a woman on the subway. Two, three nights ago. A young woman. She started choking. She actually passed out. No one was able to help her. I've been trained . . ." He stopped and emphasized this point, "I was trained in first aid when I was in the army. In the army, Comrade. So I helped her. She had a piece of bread lodged in her throat. She recovered quickly, thanked me and walked away. I think . . . I think I might have saved her."

"That you did, Comrade Schmidt. Which is a coincidence, we think, for she was under surveillance at the time. In fact, she was executed yesterday for crimes against the State. We have a signed confession, all the evidence we need. But before the execution, she implicated . . ." he hesitated as he smiled . . . "others with whom she worked."

No longer feeling the pain that shot up and down his legs, Dierk watched the Stasi officer, afraid to even breathe.

The forms the Stasi used in their confessionals had five blanks where the prisoners were allowed to reveal their fellow traitors. All of the blanks had to be filled in before the interrogations would end, and everyone eventually reached a point where they would accuse someone else of treason: their mothers, their fathers, their own children, anyone and anything to make the pain stop. Sometimes, to protect their loved ones, those being interrogated would accuse people they hardly knew, describing strangers they'd seen on the streets, distant relatives, people with whom they worked but whose names they hardly remembered, anyone to make their confessions complete.

"When people are under duress, they'll say anything, you surely know that, sir," Dierk softly begged. "I don't know her. I've never seen or talked to her before that night. All I did was help . . ."

"You proclaim your innocence," the officer replied, "and yet you've been arrested. Do you know what the acquittal rate is for those who have been arrested? Less than five percent. Think about that, Comrade. Less than five percent! We don't make a habit of arresting innocent people. If we have enough evidence to arrest you, then you are guilty. It's as simple as that. "

"And the evidence you have against me?"

The officer looked at the prisoner as if the question were so irrelevant it was hardly worth an answer, then pulled out a slip of paper and read, "You were seen conspiring with a traitor—"

"I did nothing but save her life!" the prisoner shouted in defense.

He was angry now, his voice rising. He took a step toward the officer, and the nearest guard struck him with his club and jerked him back.

The Stasi watched the prisoner, then wrote BELLIGERENT in his file.

"I don't know her. I've never seen her before or since!"

"You've never seen her?"

"Never in my life!"

The officer smiled. That was all he needed. Pulling out a blurry black-and-white photograph, he lifted it to show the prisoner. A crowded train. People packed together. Winter hats, heavy overcoats, vacant stares. Some people looking down, others staring out the darkened windows. The prisoner stood in the crowd, his left arm grasping the rail overhead. A woman stood behind him, looking down at a little girl. "You've never seen her before?" the officer taunted. "The evidence suggests that that's a lie."

The prisoner stared blankly at the photograph. "Are you saying that because at some point we rode the public train together, we were . . ."

"I'm saying you just lied to me. I'm saying you're probably going to die here. I'm saying it's time for honesty. Time we had a long and fruitful talk."

The prisoner lowered his head. His body seemed to deflate, his shoulders sagging as his breath came leaking out. "There is nothing I can tell you," he mumbled.

"Everyone has something they can tell."

"But what? What could I tell you?"

"Let's start here," the officer said.

Another photograph was produced. An angry mob along a crowded street. Polish street signs. Handmade placards carried by the protesters. Lines of riot police. The prisoner studied the photograph and then leaned forward. His brother's face was clearly visible on the second row.

He took a breath and held it, then slowly closed his eyes.

Ironically, part of him was relieved. At least he knew now why he'd been arrested. At least he had some idea what he was going to suffer for.

"Where does your brother work?" the Stasi asked him.

The prisoner only shook his head.

"Your brother moved to Poland! He went there to sow rebellion and dissension. He went there to tear down our brother state."

Dierk looked away and started praying.

"WHERE DOES YOUR BROTHER WORK?" the Stasi screamed, spit spraying across the prisoner's face.

Dierk looked away but kept his mouth shut.

Yes, his brother had married a Pole and moved to Poland. Yes, he now worked at the Gdansk shipyard with Lech Walesa. Yes, he had helped to organize his fellow workers . . .

And because of his brother's actions, he knew he would never be a free man again.

Four weeks after he'd been arrested, Comrade Dierk Schmidt, now an enemy of the State, was sent to Special Prison Number Seven.

On the day he was carried into the rehabilitation prison, halfway around the world, the man who was going to save him lifted his hand from a family Bible, turned to the massive crowd gathered in Washington, D.C., and began to change the world.

Less Than One Inch

A little more than two months after his inauguration, having finished speaking to an unfriendly audience at Washington's Hilton Hotel, President Ronald Reagan was moving toward his limousine past a line of press photographers. Waiting just a few feet away, John Hinckley Jr. raised a pistol, aimed, and fired six bullets in three seconds. One of the bullets struck the car, ricocheted, and entered Reagan's body under his left arm. Tearing through skin and muscle, the bullet tumbled, tore a rib, traveled through his lung, and lodged less than one inch from his heart.

Another inch—the length of an infant's finger—and Ronald Reagan would have died.

A Secret Service agent instantly shoved the seventy-year-old president into the backseat of the waiting limousine. Reagan gasped with pain as the agent's weight forced him against the armrest, and he immediately started coughing blood. Realizing for the first time that the president had been hit, the agent ordered the driver to the George Washington University Hospital, which was mercifully close.

Amazingly, a meeting of almost the entire medical staff was being held at that hour. As the presidential limousine screeched to a stop in front of the emergency room, every doctor that was needed to save the president's life was just a few steps away.

A three-hour operation ensued. The hemorrhaging was serious. For a time, the doctors wondered if the patient was going to make it. Reagan lost one-half of his blood before the bleeding could be stopped.

Less than two weeks later, the oldest man ever elected to the presidency left the hospital and went back to work, turning his attention toward one of the greatest threats the nation had ever faced.

Looking back, we have to wonder: What would the world be like if that bullet had traveled another inch and pierced his heart?

A Lost Decade

When President Ronald Reagan took office, the challenges the nation faced were staggering. The power and prestige of the United States had ebbed to its lowest point since the Civil War. A runaway inflation rate of 13 percent was eating at the heart of the American psyche. Pay raises could not keep up. The value of savings accounts was disappearing. Those who were on fixed incomes, especially the elderly, were suffering the most.

Interest rates were at historic levels. The prime interest rate was over 20 percent. Home mortgage interest rates were in the upper teens. The housing industry was in collapse, and it was not alone—every major business and industry was suffering under the burden of the crushing interest rates. And the list of problems didn't stop there. Energy shortages. Cars lined up to purchase fuel. Skyrocketing heating costs. An exploding federal deficit. Extraordinarily high tax rates. Unsustainable unemployment. The list of economic woes was frightening.

Many times since then, politicians have claimed, "We are facing the worst economic crisis since the Great Depression." Bill Clinton said it during the campaign in 1992. It was repeated again in 2008. But there is no question that the worst economic conditions the nation has ever faced outside of the Great Depression were during the last few years of the Carter administration. When President Jimmy Carter (now famously) told Americans that we suffered from a "malaise," the message was clear: Our best days were behind us. We had to get used to having less. Little wonder the nation faced a crisis of confidence in the American dream.

These daunting domestic trials, by themselves, would have severely tested any new president.

But the greatest test Reagan faced was in the area of national security, for the conflict between the United States and the Union of Soviet Socialist Republics (USSR) had taken a pronounced turn for the worse.

Freedom on the Decline

As with the economy, the 1970s had proven to be a disaster for our national security, leaving three enormous threats:

1. *The Ascendancy of Communism and Islamic Fundamentalism.* After becoming president upon Richard Nixon's resignation, Gerald Ford had to watch in frustration as Congress cut off all military and domestic aid to our former allies in South Vietnam, leading to the fall of their democratic government to the communist army of the North. A hundred thousand Vietnamese fled by boat, leaving behind a million to be killed by the victorious communists.

Emboldened by the lack of response from the United States, other communist governments throughout Indochina began a murderous rampage. More than a million Cambodians fell victim to the Khmer Rouge. A comparable number of Laotians were killed by the communist government there.

In Africa, the Soviet Union used Cuban troops as surrogates to impose its "protection" over ten African nations. Soon, the Soviet Union was supporting terrorist regimes in Libya, Syria, Palestine, Eastern Europe, South Yemen, and Cuba. Believing an unsettled world was the best environment for its internationalist agenda, the USSR encouraged acts of terrorism against Israeli and other Western targets. Five years after the abandonment of Vietnam, thirteen other nations fell to Communist aggression.

Jimmy Carter's presidency was based on the belief that the most important foreign policy objective the United States could pursue was the encouragement of "human rights." Focusing almost exclusively on this noble but sometimes impractical goal resulted in the United States abandoning support for a number of governments simply because State Department activists found those governments' human rights records to be less than stellar. The result was the establishing of brutal communist dictatorships throughout the world, especially in Central America, all of which proved to be far more abusive than the regimes they had replaced.

The most far-reaching consequence of Carter's human rights policy was the jettisoning of U.S. support for its longtime ally the Shah of Iran. Weakened by the loss of U.S. support, in 1979 the Shah was replaced by a fundamentalist Islamic regime, a regime that would soon become a major source of terror, military adventurism, and strife throughout the world. In November, fifty-two Americans were taken hostage at the American Embassy in Tehran. For 444 days, they were held prisoner—casting a bright light on the inability of the American military or diplomacy to end the crisis.

In December 1979, the Soviet Union invaded Afghanistan. The response from the United States was feeble: an embargo on grain shipments (which hurt American farmers more than the Russians), a boycott of the 1980 Olympics to be held in Moscow, and the canceling of educational and cultural exchanges. In addition, the Senate refused to ratify SALT II, a treaty with the Soviet Union that would have put some upper limits on nuclear weapons.

By 1980, the United States had apparently abdicated its role as the leader of the free world, seeming to conclude that we would not, or could not, compete with the rise of communist tyranny. While this period of "détente"—where the emphasis was placed solely upon easing tensions between the free world and brutal communist regimes—did result in marginal gains in strategic initiatives and cultural exchange programs, there is no question that the United States had surrendered any thought of actually defeating communism. Our weakness was seized upon by both communists and terrorists, the vacuum of our retreat quickly filled by our enemies.

2. *Proliferation of Nuclear Weapons.* When Ronald Reagan took office, the United States and the USSR were engaged in a feverish arms race. Over the years, terrible advances had been made in the size and accuracy of nuclear weapons, as well as in the means of delivering those weapons. By the late 1970s, tactical and strategic nuclear weapons were capable of being launched from the air, land, or sea. Every year, the United States and Russia were spending tens of billions of dollars building more—and more deadly—nuclear weapon systems.

Strange as it may seem today, both the United States and its communist foe operated pursuant to the military strategy known as "Mutually Assured Destruction," or MAD. This military doctrine was as straightforward as it was insane: Both sides must stockpile enough nuclear weapons such that if the other side were ever crazy enough to launch a first strike against its enemy, the rival would be able to respond with sufficient weapons to destroy it as well. As long as this relative "balance" was in place, neither side would be motivated to attack the other, since it would mean mutual suicide.

The constant challenge was to make certain that neither side in this Cold War ever managed to obtain an advantage that would allow it to launch its nuclear arsenal first and still survive a counterattack. It was assumed that if either side ever gained such an advantage (either real or perceived), it might be tempted to start a nuclear holocaust.

Ronald Reagan once described the situation as two Old West gunslingers "standing in a saloon aiming their guns to each other's head—permanently."[1]

One of the worst outcomes of MAD was the ever-escalating cost of maintaining equilibrium. For example, in the mid-1970s, the Russians brought into operation two new land-based missile systems with warheads powerful enough to take out U.S. missiles in their silos. Soon after, Soviet military leaders began talking about having true "first strike capability," some even believing they could surprise the United States and destroy our missiles, rearm their own (something the U.S. could not do), and then demand some type of political blackmail, maybe even the surrender of the United States. About the same time, Russia deployed new multiple-warhead missiles (one missile that carried several nuclear-tipped warheads, each capable of hitting a separate target), which would also allow them to destroy our missiles in a "first strike."

Because of these new "first-strike" weapons, American military planners were forced to devise a scheme for avoiding the use of missile silos for launching ballistic missiles. The game plan they conjured up was to build thousands of miles of roads, railroad lines, and bunkers in the deserts of Utah and Nevada. Large trucks or rail cars, carrying a new type of ballistic missile known as the MX, would scurry around the desert, going in and out of the bunkers.

This scheme of deception was going to be incredibly expensive and have staggering impacts on the environment. However, it was deemed necessary so that the Russians could not destroy all of our land-based missiles.

Though the madness of the nuclear-arms race was apparent to all, it seemed unstoppable. Because of this, an entire generation of post–World War II youth assumed that they were likely to die in a nuclear holocaust. During this time, demands for an end to the arms race were widespread. But most of those peace movements (some of which, it was later discovered. were secretly funded by communist states) would have left the United States in a much weaker position than the USSR.

3. Decline in American Conventional Military Prowess. By the late 1970s, Russia was spending three times more for its military than was the United States (this from an economy that was only about one-sixth the size), eventually achieving military superiority in both conventional (non-nuclear) and nuclear forces.

During that same period, the United States had quit investing in its military. Fighter planes could not fly and ships could not sail because of a lack of spare parts and adequate maintenance. There had been no major upgrades in bombers or missiles for many years. Planned upgrades such as the MX missile described above met with major public and congressional opposition because of their financial and environmental costs.

The navy had shrunk so much that it was questionable whether it had the ability to protect critical shipping lanes, the source of much of our oil and other essential minerals and ores. And while the United States Navy was dwindling, the navy of the Soviet Union was expanding. Following the Cuban missile crisis of 1962, the Soviet Union built 1,323 new ships, while the United States built only 302. Russia had taken up a permanent naval presence in the northern Atlantic and Pacific Oceans, and was moving into the South Atlantic, the Indian Ocean, and the Mediterranean.

The morale of America's military fighting men and women was at an all-time low. The very best were leaving military service. Pay was so low that many enlisted men qualified for food stamps and other welfare services. The antimilitary feelings generated by the Vietnam War were prevalent throughout society, and there was little pride in military service.

By 1980, the question of whether the Soviet Union would bring most of the Third World, perhaps even Europe itself, under its influence was real. The question of whether it would be tempted to use its superiority to blackmail the United States hung very heavy over the presidency of the United States.

Many wondered how America would survive, alone in the world.[2]

A New Decade, a New President, a New Start

When Ronald Reagan assumed office, many people, both in and out of the United States, were shocked that a man who was "nothing but an actor" could be elected president. Over the next eight years, this "actor" proved to possess the vision, leadership skills, and courage not only to reverse the ailing American economy but, more important, to become the catalyst that altered the relationship between the United States and the Soviet Union, bringing the Soviet Union to its knees and ending communism as a threat to the free world.

Ronald Wilson Reagan was undoubtedly one of those men described by Ralph Waldo Emerson: "There is a serene Providence which rules the fate of nations. . . . It makes its own instruments, creates the man for the time, trains him in poverty, inspires his genius, and arms him for the task."[3]

Ronald Reagan campaigned for the presidency on a broad platform for economic recovery: Reduce income taxes, decrease government spending, remove unnecessary government regulation. Immediately after his election, he and his advisers began to put a specific economic recovery plan together.

Though it was a long and difficult battle, eventually Reagan got most of what he asked for from the Congress. The effect was not immediate, but one year after the first phase of his tax cuts had been implemented, an economic recovery began. By the time he left office in 1989, eighteen million new jobs had been created. Taxes had been cut significantly. The unemployment rate had been reduced to one-half of what it was at the height of the recession. Interest rates had been cut in half. Inflation had been cut to 4 percent. The number of pages in the publication containing federal regulation had been reduced by half. The United States was to enjoy one of the longest eras of economic expansion in our nation's history.[4]

"Morning Again in America," the theme of Reagan's 1984 reelection campaign, had become not just a political slogan but a statement of fact.

• • •

While the remarkable resurrection of the American economy was an admirable achievement, it pales in comparison to the way that Ronald Reagan went on to change the world.

When he took office, Reagan possessed an attitude that was different from that of any of his predecessors as well as the current ruling class and media elite. He had no intention of "containing" communism or engaging it in "détente." Quite the opposite, he believed that freedom and democracy would prevail, that communism *could* be defeated throughout the world. In his mind, communism was doomed as a system of governance.

In a speech at Notre Dame University in May 1981, a short six weeks after the attempt on his life, the president prophesied "that the years ahead are great ones for this country, for the cause of freedom and the spread of civilization. The West won't contain communism, it will transcend communism. It won't bother to . . . denounce it, it will dismiss it as some bizarre chapter in human history whose last pages are even now being written."[5]

In June 1982, addressing the British Parliament, he talked of Poland's courage, "by being magnificently unreconciled to oppression." He noted that "regimes planted by bayonets do not take root." He then threw down a challenge to the free peoples of the earth:

> What I am describing now is a plan and a hope for the long term—the march of freedom and democracy which will leave Marxism-Leninism on the ash heap of history as it has left other tyrannies which stifle the freedom and muzzle the self-expression of the people. . . .
>
> I have often wondered about the shyness of some of us in the West about standing for these ideals that have done so much to ease the plight of man and the hardships of our imperfect world. . . .
>
> Let us now begin a major effort to secure the best—a crusade for freedom that will engage the faith and fortitude of the next generation. . . . [L]et us move toward a world in which all people are at last free to determine their own destiny.[6]

In 1983, he called the Soviet Union an "evil empire."[7] But perhaps the most famous of Reagan's verbal assaults on the Soviet Union occurred in June 1987, when he spoke in front of the Berlin Wall and challenged General Secretary Mikhail Gorbachev to "tear down this wall!" Then, looking at the graffiti-scribbled cement barrier that had been erected between East and West, he prophesied, "This wall will fall."[8]

It cannot be overstated how different this attitude was from the prevailing opinion of the political, academic, and media elites of the time. Most of them mocked Reagan while accusing him of being a warmonger. Many expressed their outrage. Some characterized his ideas as "delusional." The predominant media were willing to ignore the fact that it was the Soviet Union that had invaded Afghanistan and engaged in a staggeringly aggressive military buildup all through the 1970s, instead blaming Ronald Reagan for a renewal of the Cold War.

And they were not alone. With only a few exceptions (including Margaret Thatcher, prime minister of Great Britain), other leaders of the world were skeptical about the ideas expressed by Ronald Reagan. Even some within his own party believed that he was abandoning conservative principles by negotiating with the "evil empire."

His belief was certainly at odds with the prevailing liberal philosophy of the time, which assumed that we were all moving inexorably toward socialism and beyond.

For example, Nobel Prize winner Paul Samuelson asserted that it was a "vulgar mistake to think that most people in Eastern Europe are miserable" and that "the Soviet economy is proof that . . . a socialist command economy can function and even thrive."[9] After visiting Moscow in 1982, former Kennedy adviser Arthur M. Schlesinger reported, "Those in the U.S. who think the Soviet Union is on the verge of economic and social collapse . . . are . . . only kidding themselves."[10]

Ronald Reagan was convinced that such popular and widely accepted viewpoints were simply wrong. Communism as an economic model was a basket case. More, he believed that the Marxist view that men cared about material well-being more than they cared about freedom was contrary to the human condition.

Peace through Strength

Reagan understood that the Soviets' military superiority gave them an undeniable advantage in any negotiations. Because he wanted "peace through strength," he knew that he had to invest in the American war machine if he was going to achieve peace. Because of this, he called on Congress to increase military spending, almost doubling the Pentagon budget from 1980 to 1985.

Ronald Reagan also rejected the nuclear strategy of MAD, refusing to believe that the world should have to live under the interminable threat of nuclear annihilation. He believed that the goal of negotiations ought not to be *limiting* nuclear weapons but *eliminating* them. In 1981, he called for the removal of all intermediate-range missiles in Europe and the commencement of negotiations to reduce the number of nuclear warheads overall. In 1983, he proposed that the United States undertake a major investment in a Strategic Defense Initiative (SDI), an actual defense against incoming nuclear weapons. He also stated ideas that would remain bedrock principles during his time in office, that any agreements with the Soviets had to be verifiable—no more trust without verifying.

Ronald Reagan believed in the power of personal relationships. He sincerely believed that, if given the opportunity, he could convince Soviet leadership that the United States could be trusted as a negotiating power. His desire to develop a personal relationship with Kremlin leaders, however, was complicated by the fact that they kept dying: Leonid Brezhnev in 1982, Yuri Andropov in 1984, and Konstantin Chernenko in 1985. At one point, Reagan quipped, "How am I supposed to get anyplace with the Russians, if they keep dying on me?"[11]

Finally, in 1985, Mikhail Gorbachev emerged as a youthful and urbane Soviet leader. Unlike with his predecessors, the possibility of a true personal relationship was finally realistic.

When Reagan finally began to negotiate seriously with Gorbachev in 1985, the Russian leader understood that his nation's military expenditures were destroying its economy. He also recognized that the United States was committed to spending whatever was necessary to maintain and even widen its technological superiority. Gorbachev realized that he had to negotiate with Ronald Reagan in good faith, something no previous leader of the Kremlin had done.

By this point, Reagan comprehended what most did not: to hasten the decline of communism was not only possible, but the *moral* thing to do.

Special Prison Number Seven, German Democratic Republic January 1986

THEY DIDN'T CALL THEM prisoners, they called them *Wards des Staates,* or Wards of the State. And that was exactly what they were. They were told when to eat, when to sleep, when to wash, where to stand, what to wear. More important, they were told what to do, where to go, what to say, and what to think. They were literally puppets, their faces bland and expressionless, their movements and emotions controlled by the guards who lorded over their daily lives.

Ward #35b789, Dierk Schmidt, had eventually learned the ropes. It didn't matter if he meant it as long as he said what they wanted him to say. It didn't matter if he believed it so long as he went through the routine.

His existence was numbing and meaningless, and he was convinced that most of his fellow prisoners had actually lost their minds. But, on the good side, he hadn't had electrical sockets attached to his tongue or fingers in almost a year. And it had been a couple of months since he'd found a rat head in his soup bowl. Best of all, the indoctrination lessons were a little shorter and didn't involve quite as much shame and humiliation anymore.

Life was good and he was grateful. He was thankful every day.

But sometimes he wondered. Would they ever let them out? Were he and all his fellow prisoners destined to wander through their wretched lives and die here?

After years of broken hopes and fading optimism, he'd become certain that was going to be the case.

He didn't know how long it had been since he'd been dragged, bound and chained, into Special Prison Number Seven. During that endless time, Dierk had never seen a newspaper or television. The only information he'd been able to glean was from the new prisoners, but talking about the outside world was strictly against the rules. None of the prisoners ever had outside visitors; reliable citizens didn't express their love or sympathy for those who had betrayed their own country, after all. It simply was too risky.

No, once a prisoner entered Special Prison Number Seven, that person had no contact with the outside world.

So it was, as Reagan set out to destroy the communist regime, the prisoners inside Seven were completely unaware.

At exactly 8:55 P.M., a horn sounded throughout the compound. Five minutes until lights out. The guards, with German shepherds straining at their leashes, made their final rounds.

The prisoners were housed in large sheet-metal buildings, similar to what Western farmers kept their cattle in. The summer heat was tolerable, but the winters were deadly cold. On this bitter January evening, Dierk settled atop his bunk. The metal wall was cold against him, and the thin blanket he pulled around his body barely kept him warm.

Below him, his friend Jonas rolled onto his wooden bed and pulled his blanket tight. An old man by prison standards, Jonas had been inside Seven for almost twenty years. He was only forty-two, but he looked more like eighty and was in the last stages of tuberculosis. All of the prisoners inside Seven suffered from one or another contagious or chronic disease, and they made little effort to protect themselves from each other any longer.

The two lay awake until the guards and their dogs had passed. Outside, it was sleeting, and the winds blew through the cracks in the walls. An hour passed in silence, Jonas hacking constantly from below, and then Dierk rolled over and whispered to his friend, "The men in Building Four have an orange."

Jonas didn't answer at first. "I don't believe it," he finally said.

Dierk leaned closer, positioning his head over the side of the bunk. "No, it's true. I saw it."

Jonas moved, the flea-ridden bunks creaking from his weight. "You really saw it?"

"I did. They showed it to me this afternoon."

A moment of lustful silence. "What are they going to do with it?" Jonas asked.

"Going to divide it up tonight."

"Hmmm . . ." was all the old man could mutter jealously. Then he asked, "Where did they get it?"

"One of the guards smuggled it in."

"I don't believe it." Jonas's voice was skeptical.

Dierk didn't argue. He didn't believe it either. But where *had* the orange come from? Like the foundation of the universe, it was a question worth pondering but one he would probably never know the answer to.

"The State is good," Jonas whispered in a sarcastic tone. "And because the State is good and men are evil, the State has enemies. It is our obligation to identify them. If we're not willing to identify the enemies that live among us, then we too are enemies of the State."

"Are you going to report them?"

"Of course not, my friendly fool. I'm only going through the reasons why I am certain someone will."

Both of them lay there thinking. They knew that reporting the illegal contraband would buy them favors: an extra helping for dinner, a work assignment indoors instead of in the winter fields, maybe an extra blanket (which might save their lives one night) or a visit to the infirmary when they were sick. A simple word to one of the guards, and they were golden. But neither of them even considered ratting on the other inmates, regardless of the reward.

"The State is good," Dierk whispered tartly from the top bunk.

"The State exists to fight for the common man."

"Man is the natural enemy of the Party."

"The Party exists to defend the State."

The two men were silent for a moment.

"Do you remember what an orange tastes like?" Jonas finally asked in a wondering tone.

Dierk thought for a long time. "No, I don't."

Dierk listened to the man's labored breathing from the bunk below him, knowing he was awake, then leaned over and whispered, "I heard from my brother."

Jonas coughed violently for a full minute before he was able to catch his breath. "The one in Gdansk?" he asked quietly.

Dierk nodded in the darkness. The things they were talking about now could cost both of them their lives, and he kept his voice very low. "He came back to Berlin a couple of months ago. He tried to take my wife and children with him back to Poland."

Jonas coughed, then lay back. Both of them listened carefully for any sound from outside. "How did you hear this?" Jonas asked carefully, part of him not wanting to know. In Seven, the more one knew, the more dangerous and complicated everything became.

Dierk understood this too and didn't answer.

Jonas waited, then changed the question. "Why does he want to take them back to Poland?"

"He thinks the winds of change are blowing. He thinks there is opportunity there, or at least the potential of opportunity. He thinks . . . he thinks . . . there is reason to have hope. Maybe a chance of freedom . . ."

Jonas scoffed. "Freedom! I don't think so. The Iron Curtain is as permanent as the sun or the moon. Nothing's going to change. Not in our lifetimes. Not in the lifetimes of our children. The Party is going to outlive us both."

Dierk settled onto his back, stared at the ceiling, then rolled to his side again. "Have you ever heard of Ronald Reagan?"

"Ronald Reagan!" The foreign name slid with difficulty off Jonas's tongue and he snorted in disbelief. "No American is going to save us! Don't go chasing after dreams!"

A Long and Dangerous Ambition

The path Reagan walked to achieve his dreams of a safer and freer world was littered with obstacles, uncertainty, and great danger. A hostile media and an unfriendly Congress; vacillating allies who, with the exception of Margaret Thatcher, refused to support him; hard-liners within his own administration; a possible Soviet invasion of Poland; the downing of a Korean airliner followed by the shooting of an American army officer in East Berlin; the realization that the USSR had been cheating on the 1972 Anti-Ballistic Missile Treaty; and the discovery of hundreds of listening devices planted in the walls of the new U.S. embassy in Moscow—all of these events made his journey much more difficult. But far and away the greatest obstacle Reagan had to overcome was a hostile Kremlin leadership who believed the United States was the aggressor. Making serious negotiations even more complicated, the Soviet leaders were convinced that the U.S. was weak, one of them stating: "We will always be able to turn out more missiles than you. The reason is that our people are willing to sacrifice for these things, and yours are not. Our people don't require a dozen colors of toilet paper in six different scents to be happy. Americans do now; for that reason you will never be able to sustain public support for military expenditures."12

Even the college-educated and much more modern Mikhail Gorbachev believed some of his own nation's propaganda, expecting the U.S. to be a place where munitions makers ruled, African-Americans were treated like slaves, illegal drug use was rampant, and half the population slept in the streets.

Through all of these challenges, Ronald Reagan pushed on.

A Cold Wind Turns Warm

There is great dispute about how the Cold War ended. Much of that dispute has been generated by Ronald Reagan's political opponents, who never believed him to be anything but a dunce, a figurehead president. Increasingly, however, the following scenario is being recognized as what actually transpired.

Reagan's rhetorical onslaught, incessant through the first years of his presidency, had a dramatic impact in America, around the world, and in the Soviet Union. His assertion that communism was a failed system, economically and morally, focused the American public in a way that had been lost during the years of détente. Citizens of the world began to see that America was willing to stand for something, that communist revolution and domination were not inevitable, that there really was an option for our future. As a result, communism began to lose its appeal as an ideology, particularly to Third World nations.

Reagan's success in lifting America from the economic doldrums permitted a major reinvestment in the military. This not only permitted him to negotiate with the Kremlin from a position of strength but also raised the possibility that the U.S. could bankrupt the Soviet Union by forcing it into an unwinnable arms race.

It soon became clear that Reagan's strategy to bankrupt the Soviet economy included a second element: Work to cut off trade and technology to the Soviet Union in order to limit cash flow to their treasury.

After a major diplomatic effort, Reagan convinced the European allies to resist the construction of two 3,600-mile natural gas pipelines from Siberia to western Europe. The original proposal called for two pipelines, which would have made the Western allies dependent on the Soviet Union for energy as well as generated immense sums of hard cash for the Russian military machine. After a hard-fought battle, in 1983, he got the allies to agree to the construction of just one pipeline.

The loss of the second pipeline deprived the Soviet Union of $10 to $15 billion in annual revenue. Considering that oil and natural gas exports accounted for as much as 80 percent of its hard currency earnings, and that its annual actual cash revenue was only $32 billion, the loss of the second pipeline proved to be a huge, and unrecoverable, hit to the Soviet economy.

Then, in 1985, Reagan convinced Saudi Arabia to open its oil spigot, increasing production from less than two million barrels to nine million barrels a day. The price of crude oil dropped from $30 a barrel in the fall of 1985 to $10 a barrel in April 1986. The decrease in revenue to the Soviet Union was devastating.

Reagan's insistence on countering Soviet moves throughout the rest of the world also kept the Kremlin off guard. This included helping rebels in Afghanistan and Central America and providing support to Poland in an effort to end the communist regime. All of this resulted in the USSR being forced to invest more in military efforts than its economy could afford. That was particularly true in Afghanistan, where the United States poured over $2 billion in support to the Afghan rebels, which in turn forced the Russians to spend between $3 and $8 billion annually, trying to find victory there.

Of major import was Reagan's 1983 call for development of a defense to nuclear missiles. Even though the United States was years away from deployment of a missile shield, the Soviet leadership did not know that. They had seen the impressive military progress by the Americans in just a few years, with no negative impact on the U.S. economy at the same time Russian resources were being exhausted. They had also seen the tremendous technological strides made by the Americans, particularly in the area of computers, and they knew that they could not compete.

The Russians became convinced that the United States had the ability to create a missile shield and that they did not, generating genuine fear in the minds of the Kremlin. At the time, the communist leaders actually believed that the United States was an imperialist nation and that Ronald Reagan was an unstable man. For two years after the 1983 Strategic Defense Initiative speech, a surprise attack by the Americans was anticipated and an intelligence alert was in place.

In the Soviet Union, Reagan's success in shining light on the failures of communism led to the rise of a new kind of leader. When Konstantin Chernenko died in March 1985, he was succeeded by Mikhail Gorbachev as general secretary of the Communist Party. College educated and well versed in the value of personality, Gorbachev was a relative youngster at age fifty-four. He was also viewed as a public-relations counterweight to the U.S. president and the only communist leader capable of dealing with the determined Reagan. Most important, unlike all of his predecessors, he was not perceived by American officials as being dangerous.

When Gorbachev became general secretary, he was astounded to learn that the military portion of the USSR budget was 40 percent, five times the percentage of the GDP that the United States was spending. Seeing this astounding figure, Gorbachev realized his nation was being sucked dry by its militarization. It simply had no more to give.

Gorbachev was also unique in that he recognized his country's shortcomings as well as the failures of communist ideology. However, it would be wrong to peg him with any grand plan for abandoning socialism. He spoke admiringly of Lenin and the communist regime he had created, and it is clear from Gorbachev's words and writings that he fully intended to keep the USSR intact, under communism, and with Eastern Europe under its dominion. In the early years of his reign, he ramped up the military efforts to subdue Afghanistan for communism, scoffed at the notion that the United States was a model for the world to follow, and mocked the idea that the USSR was headed for the "ash heap" of history.

Still, he did acknowledge that the Soviet Union had to make some changes. But what those changes were to be, he didn't know.

In Gorbachev, however, Ronald Reagan felt like he finally had someone he could negotiate with.

The two men first met in Geneva in November 1985. Certain minor agreements emerged from this Geneva summit, but the most important consequence was that Gorbachev developed a trust in Ronald Reagan, a trust that allowed him to propose just two months later the elimination of all nuclear weapons by the year 2000, an amazing turnaround from two years before, when his predecessor had thought Reagan was planning a nuclear attack.

Before the next summit, an event in Russia forced Gorbachev to begin internal reforms. The Chernobyl nuclear power plant explosion and the traditional Soviet reaction to it—denial and concealment— prompted Gorbachev to demand *glasnost* (publicity) and *perestroika* (restructuring) in the Soviet political system. Gorbachev said that Chernobyl revealed the "sicknesses of our system," which demanded fundamental changes.[13]

In the summits that followed, Gorbachev accepted Reagan's proposal to eliminate all intermediate-range nuclear missiles in Europe as well as to reduce all nuclear weaponry by 50 percent. Soon after, the world witnessed the destruction of Soviet SS-20, Pershing II, and cruise missiles.

In May 1988, Ronald Reagan visited Moscow and wowed the Russian people. His address to the students at Moscow University was met with a thunderous standing ovation. Other rousing public appearances and speeches followed. At one event, when asked if the Soviet Union was still the "evil empire," Reagan quickly answered, "No. That was another time, another era."[14] Asked who was to be given credit for the changes in the Soviet Union, Reagan replied that Mr. Gorbachev was—much to the delight of his host.

This visit by the American president laid the foundation for a growing sense of trust and friendship between the two countries. In fact, Reagan was so loved by the Russian people that the American ambassador to Russia estimated that when he left office in 1989, Reagan's popularity in the Soviet Union was greater than in any nation on earth, the United States included.[15]

Reagan's visit also proved to be critical to Secretary General Gorbachev's next move—the passage of essential internal reforms. Basking in the glow of the presidential visit, with the world press acclaiming Gorbachev's leadership and the return of the Soviet Union as a world leader, Gorbachev went into the June 1988 communist party conference with unstoppable momentum.

America, as reflected in its president, was a friend, not an enemy. With no foreign enemy to fear, there was no reason for the Soviet Union to resist fundamental change in its political system.

The communist party accepted Gorbachev's reform package, including contested elections, which doomed the communist party's control of the nation. The reforms also called for an end to party control of government institutions, an independent judiciary, and a presumption of innocence in criminal proceedings.

This was then followed by a major speech to the United Nations in December 1988 in which Gorbachev announced an end to the decades-old "Brezhnev Doctrine," which dictated that socialist states were to stay socialist or risk invasion. From that time forward, nations were free to choose their system of government. In the same speech, Gorbachev announced the unilateral reduction in Russia's armed forces by at least half a million men, thus sending the message that the military was no longer available to enforce socialist hegemony.

During the next two years, all of the nations of Eastern Europe freed themselves of Russian domination. This was followed by the breakup of the Soviet Union itself.[16]

Special Prison Number Seven, German Democratic Republic Winter 1990

ONE MORNING THEY woke up and the sentries were simply gone. There had been no explanation, no instructions, no hint that it was coming, not a whisper from the warden or the guards. The night before, they had gone to sleep inside their barracks, same as they had done for years. In the morning they woke up to eerie silence and a low smoke that curled over the back fence. The prison gates had been thrown open, the watchtowers emptied, the electrified fence powered down. What had been an enormous fire was still smoldering in a freshly dug pit behind the commander's office, where all of Special Prison Number Seven's official records had been destroyed, a million pages of tortured history burned.

The prisoners stared at each other for long and frightened moments. No one dared to move. Some of them mumbled in frightened voices. Had the world outside the prison come to an end? Had all of them gone mad? No one had the courage to move toward the open gates until the sun was halfway above the tree line. Then Dierk Schmidt walked into his barracks, wrapped his few possessions inside his blanket, turned his back on the prison that had stolen almost a decade of his life, and walked away.

Stumbling through the main gates, he went searching for his family, hoping, like his shattered nation, that he could rebuild his life again.

• • •

On Christmas Day 1991, Mikhail Gorbachev signed a decree ending the Soviet Union. On the same day, he bid his countrymen farewell. In this final address to his nation he stated: "An end has been put to the 'Cold War,' the arms race, and the insane militarization of our country, which crippled our economy, distorted our thinking and undermined our morals. The threat of a world war is no more."[17]

What If ?

What if John Hinckley's bullet had traveled one inch more? What if Ronald Reagan had died in March 1981?

Would George H.W. Bush have tried to carry out the Reagan economic recovery program?

Perhaps.

Would it have passed the Democratic House of Representatives?

Probably not.

Without Reagan's communication skills and extraordinary ability to generate public support, it's far more likely that the economic reforms would have been crushed by Democrat opposition. A watered-down version might have passed, but weakened measures wouldn't have reignited the U.S. economy.

Without the economic recovery, we wouldn't have had the ability to reinvest in our military. Without this reinvestment, there wouldn't have been the military superiority that frightened the Kremlin. No SDI. No actions taken to bankrupt the failing Soviet economy.

Bush was a product of the traditional Cold War mentality. Without much doubt, he would have pursued the policy of détente, stability, equilibrium. Relationships would have continued as they had since the end of World War II. There might have been additional SALT Treaties—negotiated limits on the increases in nuclear warheads, perhaps—but a vision of a world without nuclear weapons was never part of George H.W. Bush's world view.

And a sincere belief that the West could actually win the Cold War couldn't have been further from his mind.

Evidence of this fact is found when, upon his own election to the presidency in 1989, Bush called for a pause in negotiations with the Russians to give his national security team time to do a "reassessment."[18] This took several months. By the time he had "assessed the situation," the Cold War was over and the former Soviet Union was well on its way to oblivion.

Even if President Bush *had* adopted Reagan's view of the world, would he have been able to successfully carry out the crusade that Reagan initiated?

It is unlikely.

Bush came from the moderate wing of the Republican Party. He was not a conservative, and it is important to remember that the conservatives had taken control of the Republican Party in 1980. Yet the negotiations Reagan undertook generated intense criticism from the right wing of the GOP. He was able to withstand this criticism only because he was recognized as a conservative himself. Bush would have had no such cover and would most probably have been crushed politically.

Finally, Bush did not have the personal charm of Reagan. Gorbachev made no secret of the fact that, in their initial meetings, he was not impressed by Bush. He came to view the Bush administration as being of ancient vintage, even reporting to the Politburo: "These people were brought up in the years of the Cold War and still do not have any foreign policy alternative. . . . Big breakthroughs can hardly be expected."[19]

The relationship that played such an important role in allowing the Reagan-Gorbachev team to proceed based upon trust was unlikely to have developed with George Bush.

Without Ronald Reagan at the lead, the great drama known as the end of the Cold War, and the removal of the Soviet Union as a mortal threat to the United States and freedom and liberty worldwide, would not likely have taken place the way it did.

•   •   •

October 1970 had found Ronald Reagan approaching reelection as governor of California. On a Sunday afternoon in Sacramento, he was visited by his longtime friend Pat Boone and a handful of prominent religious leaders. As the men were leaving, someone suggested the group share a prayer together. As they joined hands, a Christian businessman named George Otis began to speak. Feeling inspired by the Holy Spirit, Otis pronounced a prayer within which he referred to the governor as "My son" and declared, "If you walk uprightly before Me, you will reside at 1600 Pennsylvania Avenue."

When Otis finished speaking, the group was silent for a long moment. The stillness was finally broken when Ronald Reagan simply uttered, "Well!"

Ten years later, after his defeat of Jimmy Carter, Boone called Reagan and asked him if he remembered the event. Reagan answered, "Of course I do."[20]

After his brush with death in March 1981, he wrote in his diary, "Whatever happens now I owe my life to God and will try to serve him in every way I can."[21]

In the early 1990s, Ronald Reagan and his friend Bill Clark were together when an admirer congratulated the former president for his success in ending the Cold War. Mr. Reagan smiled and replied, "No, not my success but a team effort by Divine Providence."[22]

Thanks to Ronald Reagan's vision and determination, the great darkness that had settled over America had lifted, bringing light and freedom to hundreds of millions of people throughout the world.

The Cold War was over.

The battle was won.

The Soviet Union was no longer a mortal threat to the United States. And in the entire fifty-year conflict, perhaps the most important shot that was fired was from the gun of a would-be assassin outside a Washington hotel, the bullet stopping less than an inch from the president's heart.

Notes

1. Gaddis, *Cold War*, 225.
2. For information about the economic, military, and foreign-affairs challenges facing Reagan, see Gaddis, *Cold War;* Johnson, *History of the American People*, 910–31; Kengor, *The Crusader;* Matlock, *Reagan and Gorbachev;* Reagan, *American Life;* Schweikart and Allen, *Patriot's History*, 739–62.
3. Speech delivered by Ralph Waldo Emerson, April 19, 1865, four days after Abraham Lincoln's assassination, at the Unitarian Church, Concord, Massachusetts, to be found at http://xroads.virginia.edu/~cap/LINCOLN/ emerson1.html.
4. Information about the success of Reagan's economic program comes from Johnson, *History of the American People*, 922–26; Reagan, *American Life*, 333–39; Schweikart and Allen, *Patriot's History*, 748–60.
5. Gaddis, *Cold War*, 223.
6. Ibid., 223–24.
7. Ibid., 225.
8. Kengor, *The Crusader*, 263–64.
9. Alan Ebenstein, "The Poverty of Samuelson's Economics," December 12, 2008, http://freedomkeys.com/samuelson.htm.
10. Kengor, *The Crusader*, 149.
11. Gaddis, *Cold War*, 228.
12. Matlock, *Reagan and Gorbachev*, 29.
13. Gaddis, *Cold War*, 231.
14. Matlock, *Reagan and Gorbachev*, 302.
15. Ibid., 302–3.
16. For information regarding the end of the Cold War, see Gaddis, *Cold War;* Johnson, *History of the American People*, 926–31; Kengor, *The Crusader;* Matlock, *Reagan and Gorbachev;* Reagan, *American Life;* Schweikart and Allen, *Patriot's History*, 757–62.
17. Gaddis, *Cold War*, 257.
18. Ibid., 239–40.
19. Ibid.
20. Meacham, *American Gospel*, 221.
21. Reagan, *American Life*, 263.
22. Kengor, *The Crusader*, 313.

Chapter 8

Why America Matters

We've discussed seven episodes in our nation's history in which miraculous fortunes preserved our nation from despair or saved us from destruction, including evidence that a Divine Hand:

- protected this nation from colonization by other kingdoms, holding it in reserve so that it might be settled by a Christian people. This in turn helped to free Europe from the doldrums of the Dark Ages while birthing a nation built upon the infant concepts of human rights and liberty.

- provided miracles in the creation and preservation of Jamestown, the last of which—the sighting of the resupply ships at the mouth of the Chesapeake Bay—took place just a few hours before it would have proven altogether too late. This assured the success of English colonization in North America.

- sent an August morning fog to protect a desperate and certain-to-be-defeated American army, allowing them to slip away to Valley Forge, then regroup with enough strength to defeat the greatest army on the earth.

- inspired men and circumstance in order to create the U.S. Constitution, the most important secular document ever written.

- prepared Abraham Lincoln for the incredible burdens he would carry throughout the Civil War, and then, when it appeared the fledgling democracy was actually going to fail, answered his desperate prayer to assure him of a victory at Gettysburg.

- provided for a series of incredibly unlikely events at Midway, a battle that proved to be one of the turning points in World War II.

- by a fraction of an inch preserved Ronald Reagan's life, allowing him the time he needed to help "tear down this wall," a feat that has had long-ranging and untold positive repercussions around the world.

But were those events truly miracles?

Did God really intervene to save us?

Much of the answer to this question lies in the reader's individual concepts of faith and fate and the role, or lack thereof, of miracles in our lives.

Many people are inclined to conclude that God—if there is a God—had nothing to do with the outcomes of these episodes. Exercising their best judgment, they ascribe these events to coincidence with a smattering of good luck. So although we believe that, even from a purely evidentiary point of view, there is ample proof to be convincing, we recognize that others will disagree. For those who draw different conclusions, there is little we could say that would likely change their minds.

But for many of us, when we read these experiences, something inside us seems to whisper, *These things are true.*

God did intervene to save us.

These were actually miracles.

Dew settles without the fanfare of thunder or the patter of falling rain, yet our wet feet in the morning still tell us *there is something there.* Sometimes miracles are like that. There is no overwhelming proof, but deep inside we know.

And to those who believe, it also seems clear that these events took place with a direction and a purpose. This country was too important to the future of mankind to let it fail. Despite our weaknesses, which are many, and our failings, which have existed since our inception, God has been willing to intervene so that this nation might survive.

If this is true, we ought to recognize it, for to do otherwise would reflect a self-serving arrogance and myopic view of human history that doesn't serve us well.

Why Does This Country Matter?

Consideration of these miraculous events (and there are many other instances we could have chronicled) reveals another observation that is worth bearing in mind: During each of these incredibly challenging episodes in our nation's history, *the outcome was not assured.* Many of those who suffered through these crises surely had reached the conclusion that their cause was doomed to fail. Indeed, there had to be times when not just a few but most of those involved in these struggles believed their effort was in vain.

But God did reveal His hand in His own due time—sometimes waiting until the final hour.

And if this is true, why did He do it?

What is it about this nation that would justify His intervention in the ways that have been presented in this book?

Could it be that America represents something important to God?

Though it's daunting to attempt to answer such questions, may we suggest two plausible explanations:

First, America is the wellspring of liberty and freedom on this earth.

Second, it has been the repository of—and an example of—certain virtues that, if emulated, would bring more happiness, prosperity, and well-being to all.

1. *The Wellspring of Liberty and Freedom.* God cares about liberty. He cares that men have free will and be allowed to exercise self-determination. And he desires this for all of His children, not just for those in this nation. It has always been so and will always be so.

But freedom requires that tyranny be defeated.

Prior to 1776, it is arguable that every government formed by man was devised to protect the power and wealth of a monarch or a ruling elite. America is the first place on earth where the freedom of its citizens was the first priority of its government. It is the first place where the entire framework of government was designed to maximize individual free will and to protect its citizens from tyranny by the government.

It remains the symbol for such priorities to the entire earth today.

Abraham Lincoln understood this as well as anyone in our nation's history. In his famous speech to the New Jersey senate, previously quoted, he acknowledged that the Founders were motivated by a desire not only to assure the blessing of liberty for Americans but to hold "out a great promise to all the people of the world to all time to come." Lincoln understood that America represented the "last, best hope of earth." He prayed in his Gettysburg Address that "government of the people, by the people, for the people" not perish from the earth.

A means of corroborating this conclusion about America can be found in the fact that America has been, and remains today, the prime target of the enemies of freedom and liberty and those who would exercise tyranny over mankind.

2. *A Symbol of Certain Public Virtues.* Beyond its role as the symbol of freedom and liberty, America has also been the repository of certain public virtues that have been responsible for its success. History teaches that for a nation to become great, it must possess a commitment to these public virtues. Any nation whose people do not adhere to these virtues cannot maintain freedom and liberty.

And what might those virtues be?

Over time, the following qualities have become commonly accepted as essential to maintain a free people and liberty.

- A commitment to a rule of law. The law, as reflected in the Constitution of the United States, is binding on all men. No man or woman is above the law or beyond the reach of the law—no matter what wealth they may possess or what office or station they may have attained.

- A commitment to justice for all. The structure of the government must assure that all are treated equally by the respective three branches. In particular, the judicial system must treat all equally. The oath of office taken by members of the United States Supreme Court from the beginning of our nation reads: "I do solemnly swear (or affirm) that I will administer justice without respect to persons, and do equal right to the poor and to the rich."[1] This reflects the Founders' understanding of the importance of this virtue. All citizens of the nation must have equal access to the protections of the law. Any distinctions under the law between groups or classes must meet constitutional scrutiny.

- Adherence to private morality. In 1978, Clare Boothe Luce, one of America's most perceptive thinkers, writers, and leaders of the twentieth century, made this observation:

> The question is a crucial one for the future of our country. All history bears witness to the fact that *there can be no public virtue without private morality.* There cannot be good government except in a good society. And there cannot be a good society unless the majority of individuals in it are at least *trying* to be good people. This is especially true in a democracy, where leaders and representatives are chosen from the people, by the people. The character of a democratic government will never be better than the character of the people it governs. A nation that is traveling the low road is a nation that is self-destructing. It is doomed, sooner or

later, to collapse from within, or to be destroyed from without. And not all its wealth, science and technology will be able to save it.[2]

Her argument seems unassailable. In a democracy, the government will never be better than the people who populate it. A government will never be better than what is expected or demanded of it by the people.

The Founders certainly understood that, in order for the government they were forming to be successful, a moral and virtuous people would be required. A sample of their thoughts on the subject includes:

John Adams: "We have no government armed with power capable of contending with human passions unbridled by morality and religion. Avarice, ambition, revenge or gallantry, would break the strongest cords of our Constitution as a whale goes through a net. Our Constitution was made only for a moral and religious people. It is wholly inadequate to the government of any other."[3]

James Madison: "Is there no virtue among us? If there be not, we are in a wretched situation. No theoretical checks—no form of government can render us secure. To suppose that any form of government will secure liberty or happiness without any virtue in the people, is a chimerical idea."[4]

Benjamin Franklin: "Only a virtuous people are capable of freedom. As nations become corrupt and vicious, they have more need of masters."[5]

Finally, George Washington, in his farewell address to the nation, stated: "Of all the dispositions and habits which lead to political prosperity, religion and morality are indispensable supports. . . . It is substantially true that virtue or morality is a necessary spring of popular government. The rule, indeed, extends with more or less force to every species of free government."[6]

In sum, a nation cannot live in freedom and liberty unless it is populated by a moral and virtuous people. That is true for any form of popular government, be it a republic, a democracy, or a mixture of the two. Government "of the people, by the people and for the people" demands a people possessed of private morality.

What does private morality consist of? Around that question there could be a lively debate; however, there are certain private virtues that seem to have been uniformly viewed as the marks of the moral person throughout history and in all civilizations. Ms. Luce's study and analysis of history revealed: "The 'universal morality' is based on these virtues—truthfulness, honesty, duty, responsibility, unselfishness, loyalty, honor, compassion and courage."

Ms. Luce also argued that these virtues have always been found in America's great men, its heroes, and its people. Of course, not all such virtues are to be found in all such men, but by and large America's leaders have been "exemplars of some, if not all, of these virtues."[7]

In addition to those virtues, we would suggest that America's greatness has also been tied to its citizens' hard work and industry, acceptance of personal responsibility, a sense of community, its free markets and the entrepreneurial spirit of its people, and its generosity to those in need both at home and abroad.

And though endangered—a glance at the surface of our culture may cause some to doubt—those virtues are still embraced by millions of Americans.

A person might ask, by what right do any people claim that God would select a particular people or country for special blessing? It is important to understand that He accomplishes this not by diminishing other nations, but by lifting a nation up. And if He raises up a nation, it is with the expectation that that nation will then lift up others.

The divine selection is not alone a prize, it is a duty imposed.

In the speech that President John F. Kennedy would have delivered had he not been assassinated on November 22, 1963, he boldly proclaimed, "We in this country, in this generation—by destiny rather than choice—are the watchmen on the wall of world freedom."[8]

We are the watchmen by God-appointed destiny—that is our privilege, our duty, and our responsibility.

Such an understanding raises a series of difficult questions:

Have we abandoned that which has made us great in order to seek that which can only make us rich?

Have we grown weary of supporting freedom, liberty, and public virtue?

And what is our personal responsibility to make certain that this land remains blessed?

Why We Should Have Hope

Putting those questions aside, but accepting that everything we have already discussed is true, we must ask a final and important question.

Is there any reason to have hope?

Some would suggest that things are different now. Even if God did respond to save our nation at times of crisis in the past, it has little to do with the challenges we face today, they say. So what if we were built upon a foundation of a public religion? Things are different now. This people, this culture, this nation are not like they used to be. And because so much has changed, some of us wonder: Has our moral corrosion weakened us to the point that we are no longer worthy of His intervention? Have we reached a point of no return?

Looking around us, it's easy to understand such an attitude of skepticism. Our nation is increasingly polarized. The lines between ideologies are broad and deep. It's too easy and far too common to ascribe the worst of intentions to those with whom we disagree. Policy differences are perceived as being criminal, or at least having criminal intent. Just a few years ago, Ronald Reagan, George H.W. Bush, and Bill Clinton entered their presidencies with fairly broad bipartisan support. Now it's assumed that a new presidency, regardless of the party, will enter office with very little support from the opposition.

Because of this, a new president is given only a few weeks to change deeply rooted and systemic problems within our economic, health, labor, and fiscal systems (to say nothing of foreign affairs) before his presidency is declared a failure. Indeed, the modern-day political honeymoon is very short.

Some people actually *hope* for U.S. failure at home or abroad, convinced that their causes are better served by such a failure. Anger and

bitterness are rising all around us. By any measure—liberal or conservative—the moral decay of our nation seems beyond dispute. Our
major institutions seem to be failing. Our financial establishments have
deceived us. Other nations decry our military interventions, ethics, policies, and postures. And all the while, our national leaders seem incapable of dealing with our problems in any substantive way, seeming
much more likely to make things worse as they pander to the lowest
common political denominator.

It's true: Enormous problems loom before us. Dangers that could
destroy our nation lie at every turn. Amidst it all, our faith in each other
seems to have fallen to a morale-sucking low.

Is it any surprise, then, that what used to be concern for our nation
has, in some circles, deepened into a pessimism that borders on despair?

Could it be that our moral corrosion has so weakened our confidence and spirit that we are no longer up to the task?

We don't think that is the case.

Despite our personal misgivings, this much is still true: God cares
about liberty.

He *still* cares about this country! He *loves* this nation. He *needs* this
nation. He is relying on this nation to be the light of freedom to the
world.

Some people don't believe that. Some claim we are too evil now,
too aggressive, too lazy, too greedy, too sensual, unaccountable, intoler-
ant, and judgmental. The list of bad things we might be is very long,
the perceived shortcomings coming from both sides of the political and
culture divide.

But while we may have our shortcomings and weaknesses, we are
still the greatest nation on this earth.

Why We Still Believe

Consider this: The United States makes up approximately 6 percent
of the world's land mass, and its population represents the same percentage of the world's population, yet it generates almost 30 percent of

the world's gross domestic product. By any measure of economic activity, the United States leads the way. In most every other significant measure, from the number of books published to the number of Nobel Prizes awarded, from the amount of aid given to needy nations to the number of service volunteers produced, from the number of world-class educational institutions to the amount of financial contributions made to the U.N., from the number of patents issued to the quality of medical care, from space travel to undersea exploration, from innovations in government to progress in elderly care, from advances in medicine, technology, transportation, education, science, music, media, to innovations in the law, the United States is the world's leader in them all.

We also remain an extraordinarily generous people. For example, charitable donations in the United States were estimated to be $307.65 billion in 2008, exceeding $300 billion for the second time in history. Almost $107 billion was given to religious organizations, $40.94 billion to educational institutions. And it wasn't just the rich who gave; 65 percent of all households with incomes less than $100,000 gave to charity as well, with more than 75 percent of the total charitable donations coming from individuals. The evidence clearly demonstrates that Americans are the most generous people on earth, giving more than *twice* as much to charities as the next most charitable country, Britain.[9]

In addition to this charitable giving, more than 61.8 million Americans regularly volunteer their time to serve in charitable community or religious organizations, providing more than three billion man-hours of service annually. The total value of this service is at least the equivalent of an additional $60 billion given to charity.[10]

The United States is also one of the most religious nations on earth. Sixty percent of adults in the United States attend church monthly. Almost half (44 percent) attend church at least once a week. A few nations—Nigeria, Ireland, and the Philippines, for example—exceed our church attendance, but most of the developed world shows little interest now in participating in religious services. For example, only 27 percent of the adult citizens in the United Kingdom attend church services regularly, along with 16 percent of Australians, 14 percent of South Koreans, 4 percent of Swedes, 3 percent of Japanese, and only 2 percent of Russians.[11]

The simple truth is, we are a nation still deeply rooted in a faith in God. Only 9 percent of the adults in the United States identify themselves as atheist, agnostic, or nonbelievers. Meanwhile, Europe has clearly become a post-Christian culture: 49 percent of the adults in Germany, 54 percent of the French, and 80 percent of the adults in Denmark identify themselves as atheist or agnostic, claiming no belief in God.[12]

And we don't have to consider just statistics to be reminded that America is still good. Look at the people you encounter in your everyday life. Most of them are honest. Most of them try to do their duty and live unselfish and responsible lives. Most Americans honor their commitments to their marriages, their families, their employers, their communities. Most Americans show compassion and courage to the needy. Most Americans still look at their children and see strength and optimism in their eyes.

Certainly we all fall short, but most of us still try.

And there are other reminders of the goodness of this nation that we ought to keep in mind as well.

No other nation is as willing as the United States to sacrifice blood and treasure in order to defend the peace and liberty of others. In World War I, 117,000 American soldiers were killed defending the democracies of Europe; 416,800 in World War II; and 55,200 on the Korean Peninsula. Untold billions were spent in the Cold War defeating communist oppression throughout the world. In addition, over the past fifty years, the United States has been the primary force in peacekeeping and defensive operations throughout the Baltics, Kosovo, Eastern Europe, eastern and central Africa, Vietnam, Laos, South America . . . the list goes on and on.

As an example of the kind of sacrifice we're talking about, we quote from a personal letter we recently received from the wife of a United States army officer:

On Jan. 7th 2007, I returned home to see a short message from my husband who was serving in Iraq. He said, "I need to talk. I lost my friend today."

When a soldier dies they put everyone on blackout so it was more than three days before I was able to talk to him. In the meantime, I was feeling this intense grief that had started long before I read the message. I could not place the feeling, but a manifestation was given to me to let me know what my husband was feeling, that it would not be the last time I would feel it and that I would need to share the feeling with others. I had no idea how I would do that. We all have stories that tear at our souls and mine was no different. It was just very personal.

My husband was finally able to share with me the circumstances of his friend's death. They had been riding together in an armored HUMVEE when a sniper shot rang out and hit his friend (who was the gunner) straight in the head. He instantly slumped forward and my husband knew something was wrong. After slicing through the straps that held him in place, he pulled him into his arms. As Eric lay in my husband's arms he exhaled one last time. My husband leaned forward and kissed him on his forehead and said, "I love you brother." He then treated his wounds as though he were yet alive and held him and prayed over him till they returned to the FOB where he carried him from the vehicle and placed him in the hands of others who took his body away.

This was a witness to me of the terrific love that develops between perfect strangers who, in almost any other circumstance, would not qualify for the depth of love they have for each other, a love that sometimes seems to be equal to or even greater than those who are blood relatives; that during the darkest time in someone's life, the ugliest things upon this earth, something so glorious as love can grow.

Thousands of letters such as this have been written over the past few years. Each of them stands as a testament to the greatness of the everyday people who make up this nation.

A Final Thought

There is an interesting story in the Bible that, we believe, gives a final reason to have hope.

The eighteenth chapter of Genesis tells the story of God appearing to Abraham and sharing His intentions to destroy the cities of Sodom and Gomorrah. Hearing this intent, Abraham asks God a rather pointed question. "Wilt thou also destroy the righteous with the wicked?" (v. 23).

Then he starts to bargain with the Lord. "Peradventure there be fifty righteous within the city: wilt thou also destroy and not spare the place for the fifty righteous that are therein?" (v. 24).

And God answers, "If I find in Sodom fifty righteous within the city, then I will spare all the place for their sakes" (v. 26).

Think about that. "I will spare all the place." The entire city. And why? *For their sakes.* For the sake of the good.

Then Abraham, apparently knowing that the people in Sodom and Gomorrah were really pretty bad, rethinks his proposition. Realizing there might not actually be fifty righteous within the cities, he makes a counteroffer, asking if God wouldn't spare the city for forty-five righteous (see v. 28).

And so they go, Abraham bargaining with God, essentially pleading on behalf of the righteous until they get down to ten. And God says, "I will not destroy it for ten's sake" (v. 32).

Surely there's a lesson for us here. Maybe we have reached the point where we, as an entire people, are no longer worthy of God's blessings. Are the good among us fewer than 60 percent of our population? Fewer than half? Fewer than 40 percent, or 30 percent? Is there any way to really know?

But, in a sense, it may not matter quite as much as we think, for

God has shown His willingness to save an entire people for the sake of the righteous, *even if they are but a few.*

If that is true, maybe we need not worry so much about our country and our people and whether our society has become too wicked, for surely there are a few wicked among us. Instead, maybe we need to concentrate on our own lives, our own goodness, our own families. Are we one of the fifty? One of the ten? Are we, those of us who still believe, living our lives in such a way that we could convince God to save our nation *if only for the few?*

No man is perfect. And neither is any nation. Yet, despite our weakness, we are still, as Abraham Lincoln said, the best nation ever given to man. Despite our faults, this nation is still the last, best hope of earth.

Though severe storms lie before us and around us, we do not struggle through the darkness by ourselves. As the early patriot John Page once wrote to Thomas Jefferson, "Do you not think an Angel rides in the whirlwind and directs this Storm?"[13]

Indeed, we do not walk alone.

Notes

1. See 28 United States Code Section 453; the original oath was contained in the Judiciary Act of 1789.

2. Luce, "Is the New Morality Destroying America?" 8. Clare Boothe Luce was one of the most acclaimed women of the twentieth century; her achievements included magazine editor, successful Broadway playwright, member of Congress, and ambassador to Italy.

3. Federer, *America's God and Country,* 10–11. Original source is an October 11, 1798, letter to military officers, in *The Works of John Adams—Second President of the United States,* 10 vols., edited by Charles Francis Adams (Boston: Little, Brown & Co., 1854), 9:228–29.

4. Virginia Ratifying Convention, *The Founders Constitution,* Vol. 1, Chapter 13, Document 36, available online at http://press-pubs.uchicago.edu/founders/print_documents/v1ch13s36.html.

5. Federer, *America's God and Country,* 247. Original source is an April 17, 1787, letter, in *The Writings of Benjamin Franklin,* 10 vols., edited by Albert Henry Smyth (New York: Haskell House Publishers, 1970), 9:569.

6. Ibid., 661. Several original sources are cited by Federer.

7. Luce, "Is the New Morality Destroying America?"
8. Bruce Loebs, "Kennedy, Vietnam, and Oliver Stone's big lie—John F. Kennedy," August 6, 2009, http://findarticles.com/p/articles/mi_m1272/is_n2576_ v121/ ai_13807584/.
9. See Gordon, *Empire of Wealth,* viii-xviii; Sharon Bond, "U.S. Charitable Giving Estimated to be $307.65 billion in 2008," August 8, 2009, http://www .givingusa.org/; Arthur C. Brooks, "Religious Faith and Charitable Giving," August 8, 2009, http://www.hoover.org/publications/policyreview/3447051.html; Arthur C. Brooks, "A Nation of Givers," August 8, 2009, http://www.american.com/ archive/2008/march-april-magazine-contents/a-nation-of-givers; Star Parker, "America's Generosity is Unmatched," August 8, 2009, http://www.realclear politics.com/articles/2008/06/americas_generosity_is_unmatch.html; Brett D. Schaefer, "American Generosity Is Underappreciated," August 8, 2009, http:// www.heritage.org/research/tradeandeconomicfreedom/wm630.cfm; "Volunteering in America Research Highlights," August 8, 2009, http://www.volunteeringin america.gov/.
10. United States Department of Labor, *Volunteering in the United States, 2008.*
11. "Studies on Agnostics and Atheists in Selected Countries," August 21, 2009, http://www.adherents.com/Na/Na_46.html; University of Michigan News Service, August 21, 2009, www.umich.edu.news/index.html?Releases/1997/Dec97/ chrl21097a.
12. "Studies on Agnostics and Atheists in Selected Countries," August 21, 2009, http://www.adherents.com/Na/Na_46.html.
13. Benson, *Angels in the Whirlwind,* 186.

Bibliography

Introduction

Bellah, Robert Neelly. "Civil Religion in America." *Journal of the American Academy of Arts and Sciences,* vol. 96, no. 1 (Winter 1967):1–21.

Bergen, Peter L. *The Osama bin Laden I Know.* New York: Free Press, 2006.

Bowman, Karlyn. "Understanding American Exceptionalism." *The Journal of the American Enterprise Institute,* April 28, 2008.

De Pauw, Cornelius. *Recherches philosophiques sur les Americains ou Memoires interessants pour servir a l'histoire de l'espece humaine.* London: n.p., 1768.

De Tocqueville, Alexis. *Democracy in America.* Chicago: University of Chicago Press, 2000.

Ellis, Joseph J. *His Excellency: George Washington.* New York: Alfred A. Knopf, 2004.

Flynn, Daniel J. *Intellectual Morons.* New York: Crown Forum, 2004.

Gelernter, David. *Americanism—The Fourth Great Western Religion.* New York: Doubleday, 2007.

Gordon, John Steele. *An Empire of Wealth.* New York: HarperCollins Publishers, 2004.

Hamilton, Alexander, John Jay, and James Madison, Jr. *The Federalist.* Washington, D.C.: Global Affairs Publishing Company, 1987.

Jacobs, Ron. "American Exceptionalism, A Disease of Conceit." *Counterpunch,* July 21, 2004.

Jefferson, Thomas. *Notes on the State of Virginia,* http://etext.virginia.edu/toc/modeng/public/JefVirg.html.

Larrain, Jorge. *Identity and Modernity in Latin America.* Boston, MA: Polity Books, 2001.

Meacham, Jon. *American Gospel.* New York: Random House, 2007.

Miller, John (ABC News), and Michael Stone; with Chris Mitchell. *The Cell.* New York: Hyperion, 2002.

Pethokoukis, James. "Al Qaeda's Failed War on the U.S. Economy." *U.S. News and World Report,* September 11, 2008.

Raynal, Abbé Guillaume-Thomas. *Histoire philosophique et politique des deux Indes: Amstredam,* 1770. "Democracy Project, Intellectual Cystitis," February 9, 2005, www.democracy-project.com/archives/001160.html.

Rubin, Barry, and Judith Colp Rubin. *Hating America: A History.* New York: Oxford University Press, 2004.

Rubin, Judy. *Five Stages of Anti-Americanism.* Foreign Policy Research Institute, 2004.

Schuck, Peter H., and James Q. Wilson, eds. *Understanding America: The Anatomy of an Exceptional Nation.* New York: PublicAffairs, 2008.

Van Doren, Carl. *Benjamin Franklin.* New York: The Viking Press, 1968.

Wright, Lawrence. *The Looming Tower.* New York: Alfred A. Knopf, 2006.

Zinn, Howard. "The Power and the Glory—Myths of American Exceptionalism." *Boston Review,* Summer 2005.

———. "The Greatest Generation." *The Progressive,* October 2001.

Chapter 1: The Miracle of Christopher Columbus and the Discovery of the New World

Clayre, Alasdair. *The Heart of the Dragon.* Boston: Houghton Mifflin Company, 1985.

Columbus, Christopher, editor. *The Book of Prophecies.* Volume III. Roberto

Rusconi, historical and textual editor. Eugene, Oregon: Wipf & Stock, 1997.

Columbus, Christopher. *The Journal of Christopher Columbus* (translated by Clements R. Markham). Elbron Classics, 2005.

Columbus, Christopher. *Select Letters of Christopher Columbus* (translated by R. H. Major). London: Hakluyt Society, 1847.

Fernandez-Armesto, Felipe. *Columbus.* Oxford, England: Oxford University Press, 1991.

Freedman, Russell. *Who Was First.* New York: Clarion Press, 2007.

Horwitz, Tony. *A Voyage Long and Strange.* Detroit: Thorndike Press, 2008.

Levathes, Louise. *When China Ruled the Seas.* New York: Oxford University Press, 1994.

Mann, Charles C. *1491—New Revelations of the Americas Before Columbus.* New York: Alfred A. Knopf, 2006.

Marrin, Alberi. *Dr. Jenner and the Speckled Monster, The Search for the Smallpox Vaccine.* New York: Penguin Young Readers Group, 2002.

Menzies, Gavin. *1421: The Year China Discovered America.* New York: William Morrow, 2002.

Morison, Samuel Eliot. *Admiral of the Ocean Sea.* New York: MJF Books, 1942.

Needham, Joseph, general editor. *Science and Civilisation in China.* Cambridge: Cambridge University Press, 2003.

Sale, Kirkpatrick. *The Conquest of Paradise.* New York: Penguin Press, 1990.

Schweikart, Larry, and Michael Allen. *A Patriot's History of the United States.* New York: Sentinel, 2004.

Stark, Rodney. *The Victory of Reason.* New York: Random House, 2005.

Stewart, Robert, Ph.D. *Mysteries of History.* Washington, D.C.: National Geographic Society, 2003.

Chapter 2: The Miracle at Jamestown

Egnal, Marc. *New World Economies: The Growth of the Thirteen Colonies and Early Canada.* Oxford University Press US, 1998.

Elliott, John H. *Empires of the Atlantic: Britain and Spain in America 1492–1830.* New Haven: Yale University Press, 2006.

Horn, James. *A Land As God Made It.* New York: Basic Books, 2005.

Horwitz, Tony. *A Voyage Long and Strange.* Detroit: Thorndike Press, 2008.

McCullough, David. *1776.* New York: Simon and Schuster, 2005.

Morison, Samuel Eliot, and Henry Steele Commager. *The Growth of the American Republic,* two vols. Volume One. New York: Oxford University Press, 1962.

Schweikart, Larry, and Michael Allen. *A Patriot's History of the United States.* New York: Sentinel, 2004.

Stark, Rodney. *The Victory of Reason.* New York: Random House, 2005.

Chapter 3: The Miracle of a Summer Fog

Brookhiser, Richard. *Founding Father.* New York: The Free Press, 1996.

Ellis, Joseph J. *His Excellency: George Washington.* New York: Alfred A. Knopf, 2004.

Ferling, John. *Almost a Miracle.* New York: Oxford University Press, 2007.

McCullough, David. *1776.* New York: Simon & Schuster, 2005.

———. *John Adams.* New York: Simon & Schuster, 2001.

Morison, Samuel Eliot, and Henry Steele Commager. *The Growth of the American Republic,* two vols. Volume One. New York: Oxford University Press, 1962.

Chapter 4: The Miracle of Our Constitution

Bailey, Sarah Loring. *Historical Sketches of Andover.* Cambridge: The Riverside Press, 1880.

Bowen, Catherine Drinker. *Miracle at Philadelphia.* Boston: Little, Brown and Company, 1966.

Ellis, Joseph J. *Founding Brothers.* New York: Vintage Books, 2000.

Hamilton, Alexander, John Jay, and James Madison. *The Federalist.* Washington, D.C.: Global Affairs Publishing Company, 1987.

Johnson, Paul. *A History of the American People.* New York: HarperCollins, 1997.

Kennedy, David M., Lizabeth Cohen, Thomas A. Bailey, and Mel Piehl. *The Brief American Pageant.* Boston: Houghton Mifflin Company, 2004.

Ketchum, Ralph, ed. *The Anti-Federalist Papers and the Constitutional Convention Debates.* New York: Signet Classic, 2003.

Madison, James. *Notes of Debates in the Federal Convention of 1787.* New York: W.W. Norton & Company, 1987.

McCullough, David. *John Adams.* New York: Simon & Schuster, 2001.

Morison, Samuel Eliot, and Henry Steele Commager. *The Growth of the American Republic,* two vols. Volume One. New York: Oxford University Press, 1962.

Schweikart, Larry, and Michael Allen. *A Patriot's History of the United States.* New York: Sentinel, 2004.

Chapter 5: The Miracle of Abraham Lincoln and the Battle of Gettysburg

Burlingame, Michael. *The Inner World of Abraham Lincoln.* University of Illinois Press, 1997.

Catton, Bruce. *Reflections on the Civil War.* New York: Berkley Books, 1982.

Donald, David Herbert. *Lincoln.* New York: Simon & Schuster, 1995.

Embassy of the United States of America. *Official Information Page,* Stockholm, Sweden, 2008.

Goodwin, Doris Kearns. *Team of Rivals.* New York: Simon & Schuster, 2005.

Herndon, H. William, and Jesse W. Weik. *Herndon's Lincoln: The True Story of a Great Life.* Springfield, Ill.: The Herndon's Lincoln Publishing Company, 1889.

Lind, Michael. *What Lincoln Believed.* New York: Doubleday, 2004.

Mason, Alpheus Thomas. *Free Government in the Making.* New York: Oxford University Press, 1965.

McCullough, David. *Truman.* New York: Touchstone, 1992.

Morison, Samuel Eliot, and Henry Steele Commager. *The Growth of the American Republic,* two vols. Volume One. New York: Oxford University Press, 1962.

Schweikart, Larry, and Michael Allen. *A Patriot's History of the United States.* New York: Sentinel, 2004.

Wilentz, Sean. *The Rise of American Democracy.* New York: W.W. Norton & Company, 2005.

Wilson, Rufus Rockwell. *Intimate Memories of Lincoln.* Elmira, New York: The Primavera Press, 1945.

Wolf, William J. *The Almost Chosen People.* Garden City, New York: Doubleday & Company, 1959.

Chapter 6: The Miracle at Midway

Dear, I.C.B., editor. *The Oxford Companion to World War II.* Oxford, England: Oxford University Press, 1995.

Department of the Navy, Naval Historical Center. *Battle of Midway: 4–7 June 1942: The Role of COMINT in the Battle of Midway (SRH-230).* Washington, D.C.: Washington Navy Yard, 2008.

Morison, Samuel Eliot, with Henry Steele Commager and William E. Leuchtenburg. *The Growth of the American Republic,* two vols. Volume Two. New York: Oxford University Press, 1969.

Prange, Gordon W., with Donald M. Goldstein and Katherine V. Dillon. *Miracle at Midway.* New York: Penguin, 1983.

Schweikart, Larry, and Michael Allen. *A Patriot's History of the United States.* New York: Sentinel, 2004.

Ward, Geoffrey C., and Ken Burns. *The War, An Intimate History.* New York: Alfred A. Knopf, 2007.

Chapter 7: The Miracle of a Fraction of an Inch

Gaddis, John Lewis. *The Cold War.* New York: Penguin Books, 2005.

Johnson, Paul. *A History of the American People.* New York: HarperCollins, 1998.

Kengor, Paul. *The Crusader.* New York: Harper Perennial, 2006.

Matlock, Jack F. *Reagan and Gorbachev.* New York: Random House, 2004.

Meacham, Jon. *American Gospel.* New York: Random House, 2007.

Reagan, Ronald. *An American Life.* New York: Simon & Schuster, 1990.

Schweikart, Larry, and Michael Allen. *A Patriot's History of the United States.* New York: Sentinel, 2004.

Chapter 8: Why America Matters

Benson, Brobrick. *Angels in the Whirlwind.* New York: Penguin Putnam Inc., 1997.

Federer, William J. *America's God and Country.* United States of America: Fame Publishing, Inc., 1996.

Giving USA 2008. Giving USA Foundation™.

Gordon, John Steele. *An Empire of Wealth.* New York: HarperCollins, 2004.

Guadiani, Claire. *The Greater Good: How Philanthropy Drives the American*

Economy and Can Save Capitalism. New York: Henry Holt and Company, 2003.

Luce, Clare Boothe. "Is the New Morality Destroying America?" *Human Life Review,* Summer 1978, reprinted in *Human Life Review,* Winter 1999.

United States Department of Labor. Bureau of Labor Statistics. *Volunteering in the United States, 2008.*

Index

About the Authors

CHRIS STEWART is a *New York Times* bestselling author who has published more than a dozen books, has been selected by the Book of the Month Club, and has released titles in multiple languages in seven countries. He has also been a guest editorialist for the *Detroit News*, among other publications, commenting on matters of military readiness and national security concerns. He is a world-record-setting Air Force pilot (fastest nonstop flight around the world) and president and CEO of The Shipley Group, a nationally recognized consulting and training company.

TED STEWART, also a *New York Times* bestselling author, was appointed as a United States District Court Judge in 1999 by President Bill Clinton. Prior to that, he served as chief of staff to Governor Michael O. Leavitt, as executive director of the State Department of Natural Resources, as a member and chairman of the Public Service Commission, and as chief of staff to Congressman Jim Hansen. He has been a visiting professor at two state universities, teaching courses in law and public policy.